Land of Pain
Land of Promise

Land of Pain
Land of Promise

First Person Accounts
by Ukrainian Pioneers 1891-1914

Research and Translation
by Harry Piniuta

Western Producer Prairie Books
Saskatoon, Saskatchewan

Jacket and book design by Warren Clark

Printed and bound in Canada by
Modern Press

Saskatoon, Saskatchewan

Western Producer Prairie Books publications are produced and
manufactured in the middle of western Canada by a unique publishing
venture owned by a group of prairie farmers who are members of
Saskatchewan Wheat Pool. Our first book in 1954 was a reprint of a
serial originally carried in *The Western Producer*, a weekly newspaper
serving western Canadian farmers since 1923. We continue the tradition
of providing enjoyable and informative reading for all Canadians.

CANADIAN CATALOGUING IN PUBLICATION DATA
     Piniuta, Harry, 1910-
          Land of pain, land of promise

          Includes bibliography and index.
          ISBN 0-88833-002-2

          1. Ukrainians in Western Canada - Biography.
     2. Ukrainians in Western Canada - History.
     1. Title.
     FC3230.U5P55   971.2'004'91791   C78-002081-2
     F1060.97.U5P55

To the memory
of the pioneers
nearest and dearest
to my heart -
my parents

Contents

Preface

When the Canadian government, in its desire to expedite the development of the vast prairie regions of this country, opened its doors to politically oppressed peasants from central Europe, was it taking a gamble? What guarantee had those responsible for Canada's immigration policy that their efforts would be rewarded? Would the immigrants prove equal to the tasks that lay ahead of them? And, above all, would they become good citizens of their adopted homeland?

Today, some eighty years later, the answers are clear for all Canadians to see. As we look back and survey the progress of these immigrants, among whom were between 100,000 and 200,000 Ukrainians who arrived before the First World War, we have no hesitation in stating that they did well beyond all expectations.

But at what cost to themselves? How did the immigrants feel about leaving their ancestral home for an unknown land? What difficulties and hardships did they experience in adjusting to the new social environment and in adapting themselves to their new status as citizens? For an appreciation of what the earliest Ukrainian immigrants thought, felt, and experienced, and how they related to their new and at first hostile environment, there can be no better source of information than their own personal accounts. Many of these have been committed to writing and are gathering dust in libraries, archives, or private homes across Canada. Others have been salvaged and printed as reminiscences in newspapers, almanacs, and a few books.

A number of these stories, translated into English, make up this volume. They tell of life on the homesteads and of work in mines, on railroad construction, in digging water mains and sewers, in helping to build our cities, and doing other menial jobs under incredibly harsh conditions. For the early Ukrainian settlers, it was a matter of life and death, do or die.

It would be gross injustice to overlook the pioneer woman. Not only did she devote her time to household duties and the care of children but, first and foremost, helped provide a home for the family. In this, she combined her efforts with her husband's. And, side by side with him, she toiled in the farmyard and in the field. When her husband had to leave home to earn a few much-needed dollars, she took his place and assumed his responsibilities. With her own hands (her children helped if they were old enough), she cleared the bush land, made hay, and harvested the crop. She was her husband's true partner "for better or worse," sharing with him all the woes of their pioneer life.

Besides being a faithful wife and a dedicated mother, she had at times to assume the roles of father, teacher, doctor, veterinarian, tailor, carpenter, and hunter. Yet in spite of all her time-consuming activities, so necessary for the survival of the family, she was able to bring up her children in the ancestral cultural traditions. In addition, many a pioneer woman found the time for Ukrainian folk arts and handicrafts or for writing. One notable example of such talent, among many who could be cited, was Maria Adamowska, whose reminiscences are included in this book. It is an under-statement to say that pioneer women were true heroines in the best sense of the word. The narratives of the four Ukrainian pioneer women in this volume testify to their courage.

While much has been said and written in recent years about the "two founding races" of Canada, one cannot afford to lose sight of the contributions made to the development of Canada by the so-called third force, including the Ukrainians. They have played an important part in the building of this country with their sweat and tears—and in defending it with their blood in two world wars—for it is now their country, the motherland of their children, their grandchildren, and today their great-grandchildren.

In translating the narratives in this volume, care was exercised to make each rendition as accurate in meaning as possible and to retain the style of the original. Changes were made only when they were unavoidable: some expressions peculiar to certain localities, and especially those born in a different culture, have no English equivalents. The Ukrainian language abounds in such colloquial and idiomatic expressions as well as in phraseology that defies exact interpretation. My aim was accuracy, if not in phrase, then in spirit. I have inserted footnotes to explain certain terms or elucidate references to Ukrainian customs or historical events with which the reader may be unfamiliar.

The transliteration of Ukrainian names is also troublesome. Ukrainians from different parts of the Austro-Hungarian Empire used different systems. In Canada, many eventually adopted English versions because of the difficulties encountered by English-speaking Canadians in spelling and pronouncing Ukrainian sur-names. Thus Bojko became Boyko, Czornyj became Chorny or Chorney, Klym became Klim or Clim, and so on. It is hoped that friends and relatives of the persons named in this volume will appreciate this difficulty and accept my spellings with a spirit of understanding.

I am most grateful to the staff of the Legislative Library of Manitoba for supplying me with microfilms and xeroxed copies of items from old Ukrainian newspapers, to authors Dokia Humenna of New York and Dr. M. I. Mandryka of Winnipeg and to editor Julian Serediak of Buenos Aires for permission to use their copyrighted materials, and to Olena Kobzey of Winnipeg for permission to use her late husband's copyrighted material and for her encouragement of my efforts.

The reminiscences in this book possess sufficient merit to be preserved for posterity, not only for the descendants of the pioneers but for all Canadians, regardless of their ethnic origin. Perhaps our generation, which enjoys the amenities of modern living, will gain a new appreciation of those whose toil, hardships, and privations have made our comfort possible. Although they are no longer in our midst, we nonetheless owe them a debt of gratitude. It is hoped that this book will in some small way honor their memory and be ·our way of saying thank you to them.

Introduction

A study of an immigrant people must necessarily include some account of the political, economic, and social conditions that compelled them to emigrate from their native land and establish new homes abroad.

The dawn of Ukrainian history was marked by the presence of several East Slavic tribes between the Carpathian Mountains and the Don River. By the ninth century, these people, ancestors of the present-day Ukrainians, were consolidated into a feudal state centering on Kiev—the Kievan Rus. Because of internal rivalries and persistent external attack, the Ukrainians eventually drifted into the control of Poland and Lithuania. The union of these two countries in 1386 doomed the hopes of Ukraine to recover its independence. Poland emerged as the dominant power, and every Ukrainian felt the iron hand of the autocratic, regimented Polish state.

Resistance to foreign rule persisted through the seventeenth century, under the leadership of the Cossacks, but the eighteenth and nineteenth centuries witnessed the destruction of political liberties in Ukraine. In 1795, as a result of the partitioning of Poland, Russia gained control of the larger part of the Ukrainian lands and Austria-Hungary annexed the Ukrainian provinces of Galicia and Bukovina.

In order to hold in subjection the various ethnic minorities that lived within the borders of the Austro-Hungarian Empire, its government followed the strategem of "divide and rule." The nationalist feelings of each ethnic group were encouraged, and the administrative units were so arranged that the two largest groups, the Poles and Ukrainians, were arrayed against each other. The Poles continued to oppress the Ukrainians, since there was no change in the dependence of Ukrainians on the great Polish landlords. The Ukrainians had few political liberties and were deprived of educational opportunities. The electoral process was weighed in favor of the Polish landlords, who usually became the heads of county councils. The Ukrainians had no effective majority in any governing body; consequently, the laws always favored the

Poles. The schools were controlled by Poles, and the language of instruction was Polish.

Throughout this period, Ukrainians worked politically to regain their national rights. When constitutional reforms were undertaken in 1848, the Ukrainians proposed to the Austrian Parliament that Galicia be divided into two parts — Western or Polish Galicia and Eastern or Ukrainian Galicia, but they got nowhere. In 1860, a new Austrian constitution gave local legislative assemblies the right to send elected representatives to the Reichsrat in Vienna. But the Poles invariably had a majority of seats, and Ukrainian proposals were routinely rejected. These conditions persisted until the downfall of the Austrian monarchy in World War 1. During this period, the political struggle of Ukrainians for their national freedom continued. They resisted the Poles, and with the support of the Ukrainians under Russian rule, they built up and strengthened the Ukrainian national movement.

The political situation of Ukrainians under Russian rule was even worse than for those ruled by Austria-Hungary. The Russians treated Ukraine as their colony and Ukrainians as subjects with few rights. Even their national identity was to be obliterated. The Ukrainians were referred to as "Little Russians" and their language as a dialect of the Great Russian language. Their culture was repressed, and to extinguish the independence of the Ukrainian spirit, the Russians adopted a policy of Russification.

Despite the prohibitions and repressions, the national revival among the Ukrainians continued to flourish. It was stimulated by the works of several outstanding Ukrainian writers of the nineteenth century—Shevchenko, Kulish, Shashkevich, Franko, and others. Their literary works brought about an awakening of national consciousness in both the Austrian-dominated West Ukraine and the Russian dominated East. This was one expression of the democratic and nationalistic enthusiasm that swept Europe after the Napoleonic era. Among the Ukrainians, these feelings lasted into the twentieth century and grew ever more intense.

As Ukrainian literature became political in character, the Russians attempted to suppress it. In 1863 the tsarist minister of the interior, Valuyev, issued an infamous decree stating that the Ukrainian language never existed, does not exist, and never can exist. The use of the Ukrainian language was banned, and the printing and importation of books in Ukrainian was prohibited.

The Ukrainian national movement, however, continued to develop, and in a further effort to suppress it, Tsar Alexander II signed a secret *ukase* (order) in Ems in 1876 prohibiting the printing and circulation of Ukrainian books, periodicals, and music, the production of Ukrainian theater, and the singing of Ukrainian songs in public. Several Ukrainian writers and cultural activists were compelled to seek refuge abroad where they continued to publish Ukrainian books and newspapers and defend Ukrainian interests.

While Ukrainian political thought found free (if futile) expression in Galicia, where the Austro-Hungarians held sway, it was forced underground in the lands under Russian rule. Secret societies were formed there, and clandestine congresses were regularly held. Contacts were maintained with Galician Ukrainians; revolutionary pamphlets printed in Galicia were smuggled into Russia, and a political party, the National Ukrainian Party, was formed. Its goal was political independence for Ukraine. Socialist and radical programs were put forward. Russian absolutism, weakened by its own internal deterioration, made some concessions to the pressure of public opinion. These nineteenth century attempts to free the people from Russian despotism culminated in the Revolution of 1905, which led to the creation of a Russian Imperial Parliament, or Duma, in which Ukrainians were represented.

Religion in Ukraine. Throughout their history the Ukrainians regarded their religion as closely related to their nationality. Oppression of one usually implied oppression of the other. Because the Ukrainians had been subjected to various powers in the course of their history, they were divided into different religious groups. The chief of these were the Greek Orthodox Church in Eastern Ukraine and the Greek Catholic Church—the Uniate Church—in Western Ukraine. The designation "Greek" as applied to churches among the Ukrainians refers to the country from which Christianity was introduced into Ukraine in the year 988. "Greek" was used to distinguish the Eastern form of Christianity, with its headquarters in Constantinople, from the Western or Roman form centered in Rome.

The Orthodox Church in Eastern Ukraine was nominally dependent on the Patriarch of Constantinople until the seventeenth century. After the fall of Constantinople to the Turks in 1453, Moscow had assumed the role of a "Third Rome," and Russia had been trying to bring all the Orthodox Churches under the jurisdiction of the Russian Orthodox Church. So, when Ukraine was absorbed by Muscovy, the Muscovite government compelled the Patriarch to surrender his jurisdiction over the Orthodox Church in Ukraine. Thus, in 1685 the Ukrainian Orthodox Church was made dependent on the Patriarch of Moscow. Although the Ukrainians resented the administration of their church by the Russians, there was little practical possibility of overthrowing this administration. The independence of the Ukrainian Orthodox Church did not come until 1918 when the tsarist empire collapsed and Ukraine emerged as a separate state. The Ukrainian Orthodox Church was then revived and proclaimed autocephalous, and Orthodox Ukrainians once again regained their religious freedom.

Much worse was the situation of the second largest religious group in Ukraine, the Baptists. Together with other evangelical groups and sectarians, they were ruthlessly persecuted for their faith not only by the government but also by the Russian Orthodox Church.

That was the situation in the east; the west had a different experience. When the Ukrainian province of Galicia came under Polish rule, the first step taken by the Polish rulers to break the national consciousness of the Ukrainians was to abolish their traditional church, the Orthodox Church, and substitute for it the faith of the Poles—Roman Catholicism. A plan was formulated during the reign of Sigismund III whereby the Ukrainians were allowed to retain the Eastern, or Orthodox, ceremonies but were to recognize the supreme authority of the Pope. This was adopted in 1596. Through the Union of Brest, the Orthodox Church in Poland was united with the Roman Catholic Church, and thus the Greek Catholic, or Uniate, Church came into being.

Only the nobles co-operated wholeheartedly with the Poles in this regard. The masses clung tenaciously to their Eastern rite and refused to embrace Roman Catholicism. The Uniate Church formed a separate religious organization, different from both Eastern Orthodoxy and Roman Catholicism. Its Basilian Order of monks took care of schools and education in general, and used the Ukrainian language in teaching and in their publications.

The Greek Catholic Church was accepted by Ukrainians in Galicia as their national church and was known by them as the Ukrainian Greek Catholic Church. (In Canada it is now officially the Ukrainian Catholic Church.) It was the only institution that helped to save the Ukrainian population from being absorbed by the Poles. The retention of the Eastern rite formed an important link with Ukrainians of the Orthodox religion under Russian rule.

As might be expected, many of their religious problems followed the Ukrainian immigrants into Canada. In the early years of their settlement here, the Ukrainian priests and parishes had to struggle constantly to preserve the Greek Catholic Church from the influence of Roman Catholic bishops. Similarly, both the Orthodox and Greek Catholic Ukrainians had to struggle against the encroachments of the Russian Orthodox missionaries.

Social and economic conditions. Hand in hand with the political oppression of the Ukrainian people by the Poles and the Russians went their social and economic oppression. Before serfdom was abolished in Austria in 1848 and in Russia in 1861, the condition of the Ukrainian peasant serf was pitiable and degrading. Extreme inequality existed between the landlord and his serf. A serf approaching the lord's mansion was required to take off his hat when he was still 100 meters away. He could not marry without his lord's permission. His child could not be sent to school without the lord's permission. The lord could have his serf beaten; he could enlist the serf's twelve-year-old son in the army. The serf could not be admitted before the lord to present his grievances.

The serf and his family lived in a hut on a small plot of land which he worked, though it belonged neither to him nor to the lord. He had to pay tithes and taxes on it but could not sell it, make any improvements on it, or divide it among his heirs without the lord's permission. He worked on the lord's lands a certain number of days a week without pay, and he had to give the lord a share of the produce from his own land. He paid taxes on the salt he used and the fruit he grew. He was forced to buy a specified quantity of whiskey from the lord's distillery and pay for it by extra work on the lord's lands. The lord was master, tax collector, lawmaker, and judge; and the serf was the lord's chattel in every sense of the word.

Even after the abolition of serfdom there was complete disregard for the interests of the peasant class. The peasants continued their dependence on the big landowners and lacked the means to improve their material conditions. The nobility still retained some ninety percent of the forest lands. In the provinces, the great landowners exercised control of the liquor industry and reaped huge profits from it. As late as 1892, the great landowners still owned forty-three percent of all the tilled lands. Eighty-three percent of the large estates (those over 1,000 morgs, or about 1,400 acres) were actually latifundia, the predominant form of ownership of land in Eastern Galicia. Of the 2,300,000 people who lived on these estates, only some 50,000 derived direct benefits as landlords. The others either had no land at all or so little that it could not provide the means of livelihood. In Galicia, half of the land that belonged to the peasants consisted of plots of not more than two hectares (approximately five acres), and in Bukovina, forty-two percent of peasant properties did not exceed three hectares. As there were no major industries to absorb the rapidly growing population, the peasant's son was forced to remain on a small subdivision of the few hectares owned by his father.

In addition to the hardships caused by the scarcity of land, the peasants bore a load of burdensome taxes imposed by the landlords, the state, and the church. The prices on peasants' produce were low, but prices on manufactured goods that peasants had to buy were disproportionately high. Interest on loans varied from six to twenty percent, depending on the district. Peasants who were unable to pay their debts lost their property. It was estimated that in the decade 1873-83, 23,237 peasants had their property seized for nonpayment of debts and taxes. In order to prevent the loss of their land in this way and to insure that they could provide for their families, small landowners were compelled to seek other sources of income. Unfortunately there were not enough industries, capital, and markets in either Galicia or Bukovina; hence it was difficult for wage earners to find jobs.

No less tyrannical was the rule of the Russian overlords. The episcopal and monastic estates that were confiscated from the Ukrainian Orthodox Church were given to new landlords whose power over the peasants exceeded any which had existed in the past. In 1847 the position of the peasants improved somewhat when "The Inventory Regulations" abolished the landlord's powers of taxation and introduced certain limitations on their other rights. In 1852, however, these regulations were nullified, and the serfs were oppressed more ruthlessly than ever before. Sporadic revolts by the peasants were cruelly suppressed. As a last resort, the peasants refused to do any work at all for the landlords, who called in police and military force to punish them. In 1855 the peasants once again went on strike, and police and military detachments were again dispatched to restore order. The peasants fought back, but more military force was sent, and the resistance was broken. Cruel reprisals were taken against the peasants, including exile to Siberia.

The Peasant Reform of 1861 brought emancipation to the serfs. In Ukraine, the peasants received allotments of land for which they had to pay by installments over a period of twenty years. Though they received personal freedom, the peasants felt the reform had not gone far enough, and they were not satisfied. Their political rights had been ignored. In several places the authorities had to use force to keep the peasants down.

In their search for ways and means to improve their lot, the Ukrainian peasants in the eastern parts of Ukraine resettled in the Kuban area, in Siberia, and in the area known as *Zelenyi Klyn* (The Green Wedge) in the basin of the Amur and Assur Rivers. Ukrainians from Galicia and Bukovina sought to escape from their hardships by taking seasonal employment in Hungary, Germany, and France. But increased earnings alone did not solve the political problems of the peasants, nor did they satisfy their thirst for freedom. The only solution was to be found in emigration.

Emigration. When the United States, Canada, and Brazil opened their doors to immigrants from central Europe, hundreds of thousands of Ukrainian peasants left their homes and their relatives in the hopes of bettering their lot. Settlement in Brazil brought the emigrants much grief, material loss, and sacrifice. Ukrainian colonists in Brazil suffer from poverty to this day. Emigration to Canada and the United States proved more successful in many respects. The first immigrants to the United States were job seekers who usually returned home after earning enough money, though many remained permanently in the new land. Estimates of the number of Ukrainian immigrants from Western Ukraine to arrive in Canada between 1890 and 1914 vary from 100,000 to 200,000. The exact figure is difficult to arrive at because Ukrainians were registered under several nationalities.

In this first wave of Ukrainian emigration to Canada, the vast majority were peasants with little if any formal education and with little or no capital. Some fifty percent of them were illiterate; only a comparatively small number belonged to the intellectual class. A few were skilled tradesmen. Although conservative to the core, they had the courage to face the unknown and start life all over again in a new country. While the majority settled on farmland, others took whatever jobs were available and hoped to earn enough money to return to their native villages and live there in comfort. Work was available on railway construction, in mines and factories, and in the construction industry in the towns and cities. Many also found seasonal employment in the lumber camps or on farms.

Economic conditions in Canada towards the end of the nineteenth century favored a program of mass immigration into this country. Millions of acres of Canadian prairies were ready to be converted from grassy pastures for the buffalo into a rich agricultural area. For this, settlers were needed. The population of eastern Canada was growing rapidly, concentrated in cities, and demand for agricultural products was increasing proportionately. The completion of the Canadian Pacific Railway in 1885, crossing the prairies and joining east to west in one country from sea to sea, encouraged the development of agriculture as well as other industries. Improvements in ocean transportation helped to link the newly settled areas of the world (of which Canada was one) with the established industrial and commercial centers. After 1896, the price of grain rose steadily while costs of transporting farm products to Europe dropped. The invention in 1870 of the chilled-steel plow permitted the breaking of the prairie sod; the development of a roller mill in 1878 made it possible to grind hard spring wheat into flour. In 1880, the introduction of a twine binder for cutting grain speeded up harvesting. The construction of the mechanical grain elevator and the development of dry-farming techniques that made farming possible in semi-arid areas were also accomplished before the turn of the century. Together, these and other factors led to an acceleration of prairie settlement.

Another necessary preparatory step was the development of early-maturing varieties of wheat. The first attempts to settle the west had failed in part because the crop was not adapted to prairie weather conditions; it froze before it matured. Then, in 1843, George Essen chanced to bring a sample of wheat which he had obtained from a cargo in Glasgow, Scotland, for his friend, David Fife, an Ontario farmer. This wheat matured ten days earlier than local wheat. Fife named it "Red Fife." In 1876 the wheat was introduced into western Canada. From it was bred Marquis wheat, which became the staple of western Canada's wheat production. The well-known agricultural scientist W. S. Saunders at Rosthern, Saskatchewan, announced that the three grains of "Red Fife" had arrived in Canada from Galicia. Thus, wheat from Western Ukraine preceded the arrival of Ukrainian settlers from that same area.

Ukrainian immigrants began to arrive in Canada in groups in the period 1890-96. Thomas Daly, the minister of the interior in the Conservative administrations of John Thompson and Mackenzie Bowell, in collaboration with Dr. Osyp Oleskiw, formulated a plan for the settlement of Ukrainians in the prairies of western Canada. During the lifetime of this administration, several Ukrainian colonies were established, mainly in Manitoba.

The federal government's program of western settlement, railway expansion, and industrial development called for new sources of manpower. Recognizing this need, the Liberal government of Wilfrid Laurier, which came to power in 1896, set vigorously to work to promote mass immigration. Clifford Sifton, the new minister of the interior, saw to it that the Canadian West was widely advertised in several European countries. Steamship companies were encouraged to bring over immigrants by government bonuses of five dollars for each head of a family and two dollars for anyone else that they brought. Some 5,000 to 6,000 agents scoured Galicia and Bukovina outlining the government's offer of 160 acres of free land per farmer and the prospect of jobs with good pay for workers.

The Ukrainian peasants were attracted by these offers, by the promise of political and religious liberty, and by the freedom from compulsory military service that existed in Canada. In addition to the government's intensive propaganda, the Ukrainian peasants were impressed by glowing accounts of Canada from Ivan Pylypiw, an emigrant who returned temporarily to Galicia. A further inducement to prospective emigrants came from pamphlets published by Dr. Oleskiw, who had personally investigated conditions in Canada.

An intellectual with a progressive outlook, Oleskiw was deeply concerned about the desperate economic straits of the Ukrainian peasantry. He was especially perturbed by the exploitation of the peasants by unscrupulous agents working for steamship companies and plantation owners in Brazil. In that country, serfdom was abolished in 1888, and the Brazilian plantation owners wanted the Galician peasants to take the place of their emancipated black serfs.

Oleskiw felt strongly that the peasants should be advised to go to some other country, more suitable for settlement. He had Canada in mind. He wrote a booklet entitled *About Free Lands* in which he argued convincingly against Brazil and in favor of Canada. The booklet was distributed to 351 village reading halls across Galicia and was widely read.

In 1895 Oleskiw and a colleague toured Canada as official representatives of the Galician Ukrainians, conferring with politicians and civil servants across Canada. All were impressed with Oleskiw's businesslike approach to the problems of mass immigration. Once back in Galicia, Oleskiw wrote another booklet, *About Immigration*, in which he described his impressions of Canada and foretold a happy future for emigrants. The booklet offered guidance to those who intended to settle in Canada and cured many of their misguided interest in Brazil.

With the assistance of a committee representing people from all parts of Galicia, Oleskiw worked out the details of the move. He was able to obtain financial assistance from the Canadian government between 1898 and 1900, the period during which he acted as an official representative of the Canadian immigration department in Austrian Galicia. With his help, the vanguard of the mass movement of Ukrainians to Canada arrived at Quebec on 30 April 1896. The party, which was led by Oleskiw's brother Volodymyr, numbered 107 persons.

Besides the free homestead of 160 acres which the government offered to the head of every household, the prospective settler had the right to purchase an adjoining quarter section of land. The Ukrainians preferred bush land, which would provide them with wood for building and for fuel, to treeless prairie, which was so unlike their old home. On some of the homesteads the land was rocky or marshy or covered with thick bush, unfit for agriculture. Whether or not they actively encouraged Ukrainian settlers to colonize outlying areas, government officials must at least have been aware of the unsuitability of these marginal lands.

A significant feature of the early Ukrainian settlement in the three prairie provinces was its homogeneity. Block settlements of Ukrainians run in a continuous line from southeastern Manitoba to northern Alberta. In some cases whole villages migrated and settled together. Dotting the map of Canada are some 180 Ukrainian place

21

names. As strangers in a foreign country, immigrants wanted to be among their own kind, to have someone to turn to. They visited and comforted each other, and helped one another to build their first homes and work on the land.

There were those among the English-speaking Canadians who criticized the government for permitting these block settlements and thus retarding the process of assimilation. Others inside and outside the Dominion Parliament condemned the Liberals for doing nothing to help the Ukrainian immigrants. The government was accused of dumping "Galicians" in the West, ignorant of the conditions, laws, and methods of farming, and leaving them to survive as best they could. The settlers lived in abject poverty, some in huts, some even in holes in the ground.

Education. Ukrainian immigrant parents were anxious to see their children enjoy a better life than they had themselves. Deprived of the benefits of education in their homeland, they wanted to give their children a good education and to have them learn English. But they also wished to take advantage of the freedoms that Canada offered them to preserve their national identity and to develop their culture which had been suppressed by the foreign rulers of their native land. They desired their children to learn Ukrainian as well as English.

Manitoba was the first of the three prairie provinces to organize schools in the Ukrainian settlements within its borders. This was accomplished with the aid of Ukrainian organizers engaged for that purpose. These schools, however, could not obtain qualified teachers, as it was impossible to get English-speaking teachers to teach in "backward," "foreign" districts. On the other hand, Ukrainians in all three provinces looked upon the English-speaking teachers with distrust as instruments of the government to assimilate the Ukrainians. And "assimilation" was a frightful word to the Ukrainians. It brought up memories of the Poles and the Russians who had ruled over them. As Dr. Hunter pointed out in his book *A Friendly Adventure,* "the Ukrainian understands that the lion assimilates the lamb when he eats him, and is resolved that his people shall not be assimilated in that way." Now that they were free, they would not be assimilated by the English in Canada.

It was not without cause that Ukrainians expressed this concern. Alarmed by the "foreign peril," educators, the press, the churches, and various other organizations brought pressure to bear on the government of Manitoba to see to it that the language, customs, and traditions of the central European immigrants were not perpetuated on Canadian soil.

At the same time, a more positive approach to the problem of integrating and/or assimilating the immigrant was being tried throughout Canada. To bridge the gulf between the Anglo-Saxon Canadians and the immigrant, Protestant missions took a direct interest in integrating the immigrant into the "Canadian" way of life. Although much good work was done by these Protestant organizations, they did not capture the fancy of Ukrainians who, justifiably or unjustifiably, suspected these missionary efforts as the thin edge of the wedge of assimilation.

The All People's Mission of the Methodist Church in Winnipeg and several institutions operated by the Presbyterian Church in Canada—the Robertson Institute in Winnipeg, Saint Christopher House in Toronto, Chalmers House in Montreal—did creditable work in ministering to the physical, social, moral, and religious needs of immigrants from several nations and in this way exerted an influence over them. To this list one might add the YMCA. The Presbyterians were the first to provide schools for children of immigrant settlers. In 1900 three schools were built in Ukrainian settlements. Dr. A. J. Hunter, one of the missionaries, who worked among the Ukrainians in the district of Teulon, Manitoba, established a residential school for boys in 1912 and, later, one for girls. Many of its students went to university and took up medicine, education, the law, and other professions.

It was apparent to many people that the most effective instrument of assimilation was the public school. While they willingly sent their children to public schools, the Ukrainians also insisted that their children be taught by Ukrainian teachers. In at least two of the prairie provinces, they were within their rights in doing so. In Manitoba the Laurier-Greenway agreement of 1897, known as Section 258 of the Public Schools Act, made provision for bilingual education in the province: "Where ten of the pupils speak the French language or any other language other than English as their native language, the teaching for such pupils shall be conducted in French or such other language and English upon the bilingual system." This meant that in the Ukrainian districts the Ukrainian language could be taught and used as a medium for teaching English.

The province of Saskatchewan had also made provisions for bilingual instruction in its public schools. Section 177 of The School Act read: "The board of any district may, subject to the regulation of the department, employ one or more competent persons to give instruction in any language other than English in the school to all pupils whose parents or guardians have signified a willingness that they should receive the same. . . ." Thus, the teaching of the foreign language could be done by any "competent person," instead of by the teacher in charge of the school as in Manitoba.

To supply the demand for Ukrainian teachers, the Conservative government of Manitoba in 1905 established a special school in

Winnipeg, the Ruthenian Training School, with teachers of Ukrainian on its staff. In 1907 the school was transferred to Brandon. Some 150 teachers were trained by the school before it was closed in 1916. One of them, Michael Stechishin, prepared the first and second bilingual readers with the English text on one page paralleled by its translation in Ukrainian on the other.

In Saskatchewan a similar school for the training of Ukrainian teachers was established in Regina in 1909. It was officially called the English School for Foreigners, since it enrolled students other than Ukrainians. It was operated on the same principles as the school in Brandon, except that there was no Ukrainian teacher on its staff. The Ukrainian public felt that teachers-in-training should receive full instruction in the Ukrainian language, literature, and history if they were to teach Ukrainian children.

The Alberta government tried a different approach with its English School for Foreigners, which was established in Vegreville in 1913. This was not a teacher-training school *per se*. It enrolled students who had attained any level from grade one to eleven. The purpose of the school was to prepare the students for departmental examinations and thus for entrance into normal school. The would-be teachers were disappointed with the school. It was also unpopular with other students, and many left. Only five of its students became qualified teachers.

The province of Alberta never accepted the concept of bilingualism in its schools. The Ukrainians there championed the idea, and one of them, Peter Svarich, even translated the first reader from English into Ukrainian. The minister of education exerted all his power to prevent the teaching of Ukrainian in Ukrainian school districts. He went so far as to dismiss Ukrainian teachers who held Manitoba teaching certificates, ostensibly because they were not qualified to teach in Alberta without Alberta certificates. Their jobs were then filled by English-speaking teachers. (Today, sixty years later, the ministers of education and of advanced education and manpower for the province of Alberta are both Ukrainian-Canadians.)

The bilingual system became a controversial issue in Manitoba, and in 1916 it was abolished by the Liberal government. In 1916 the teacher-training schools for Ukrainian teachers were closed in all three provinces. Some 200 Ukrainian teachers had been trained in these schools. In that year there were approximately 400 public schools across the prairies in which Ukrainian was taught. After 1916 it could be studied only in those districts where Ukrainian teachers were hired and only after school hours.

To lessen the danger of assimilation for Ukrainian students who continued their education in the cities, student hostels known as *bursas* were established near university campuses. In addition to lodging and board, the *bursas* provided classes in Ukrainian language, literature, and history, and an appreciation of Ukrainian cultural and religious traditions. In addition to *bursas,* separate, church-related schools came into being. Besides the official course of studies they provided instruction in Ukrainian subjects. Several of these *bursas* and private schools still operate today.

Wartime restrictions. The racial tensions between the English-speaking majority and the minority groups which climaxed in the bitter controversy over bilingual schools were only just beginning to mount when the First World War broke out. As often happens in the paranoic atmosphere of wartime, Canadians were encouraged in their racial prejudice. The victims were those who had come to Canada from enemy states—Germany or the Austro-Hungarian Empire. Of these the Ukrainians suffered the greatest hostility. Having lived in the Austro-Hungarian Empire before they emigrated to Canada, the Ukranians were regarded as enemy aliens. And they were treated as such, though actually they had not even enjoyed the full privileges of citizenship under Austro-Hungarian rule. Their insistence on teaching Ukrainian in their schools and on retaining their customs and traditions was construed by some as proof of disloyalty to Canada and to British institutions.

The situation was further aggravated by an injudicious pastoral letter issued by the Ukrainian Bishop Budka of the Greek Catholic Church in Canada. The church had its headquarters in Galicia, still under the jurisdiction of Austria, and the rulers of Austria regarded the "Ruthenians" as Austrian nationals. In his letter the bishop called on the faithful of his church to go back and fight on the side of Austria. However, as soon as Canada declared war on Austria and the Central Powers, Bishop Budka issued another statement. In it he renounced his former appeal to the Ukrainians and appealed for their enlistment in the Canadian army. Despite this reversal, the bishop was held to be pro-Austrian and his coreligionists of doubtful loyalty. When he was arrested for his utterances, his followers harbored bitter feelings against the English-speaking Canadians.

Repressive measures against the Ukrainians followed. Their naturalization was suspended, and the right to vote was taken away from them. Their newspapers were first suppressed and later reinstated on condition that they be printed in parallel columns, English and Ukrainian. When the call came for reinforcements for the Canadian forces overseas, police were sent through the Ukrainian settlements to round up those who had come to Canada before a certain date, so they could be forced into the army. Others who came after that arbitrary date were not allowed to enlist. Despite this restriction they found a way to demonstrate their loyalty to Canada: they simply told the recruiting officer that they were Poles, Russians, or some other nationality. More than 10,000 Ukrainians volunteered in this way. One of them, Philip Konoval, even won the Victoria Cross. Of two battalions recruited in northern Alberta for service overseas, one was eighty percent Ukrainian and the other sixty-five percent. All of these soldiers had been born in Galicia or were sons of men who had. The battalions were popularly known as "Irish Guards."

In Manitoba a delegation of English-speaking citizens petitioned their government to intern and deport all Ukrainians in the province. Thousands of Ukrainians in all parts of Canada were dismissed from their jobs, and thousands were rounded up by the police and herded into concentration camps. About 500 landed in a camp at Kapuskasing, Ontario. They were all kept behind barbed wire and under armed guard. Inmates who protested against the inhuman treatment, bad food, and hard labor in the bush in subzero weather, were straightaway locked up in solitary confinement cells. Many died during the 1918 flu epidemic.

Another group of over 100 "enemy aliens" of Ukrainian origin was rounded up in Montreal and sent to the concentration camp at Spirit Lake in northwestern Ontario. This group was also forced to do hard labor in the bush. Within a short time the Spirit Lake area had six concentration camps filled with about 800 Ukrainian internees. Other concentration camps in which Ukrainians were imprisoned were located in Vermilion and Lethbridge, Alberta, and Brandon, Manitoba. The total number of Ukrainian internees in all these concentration camps is unknown. Their only crime was their former Austrian citizenship. Other Ukrainian "Austrians," who were fortunate enough to escape internment, were regularly required to report their whereabouts to the police.

Some hold the view that the sufferings of immigrants in a new country is the price they have to pay for their admission to the status of full citizenship in that country. This certainly held true for the Ukrainians in Canada.

1 IVAN PYLYPIW
How We Came to Canada

Until recently, it was generally believed that the first Ukrainian settlers in this country were Ivan Pylypiw and Wasyl Eleniak, both of whom immigrated in 1891. More extensive research, however, has revealed evidence of the presence of Ukrainian settlers long before then. There were apparently a few Ukrainian soldiers in the Des Meurons and De Wateville regiments which arrived at Lord Selkirk's Red River colony in 1813 and 1817 respectively. At least one of them, a young man from Ternopil named Andrew Yankowskyi, is said to have settled on 100 acres of land he received in return for his services.

Researchers have also come across names of a few Ukrainians who arrived between 1860 and 1890, emigrating either directly from Europe or after settling briefly in the United States. Little is known about any of them; no personal accounts from this period have turned up.

The earliest available reminiscences date to 1931, when Professor Bobersky of Winnipeg interviewed Ivan Pylypiw of Lamont, Alberta. What follows is his story, as reported by Professor Bobersky and published in the Almanac of the Canadian Farmer for the Year 1937 *under the title* "Yak pershykh dwokh ukrayinstiw zayikhalo do Kanady" *(How the First Two Ukrainians Came to Canada).*

[Wasyl Eleniak and myself] . . . were the first ones in Nebyliw to go to Canada. It is a village near Kalush. I went to school and learned to read and write. The teacher used to talk about the United States and Canada, and later we heard about these places from some German people who had relatives there. Some men from our village worked on rafts at Lymnytsa, and they heard about Canada there, for at that time people everywhere were talking about this country.

One day I asked one of the Germans, "Do you have the address of your relatives?"

"I have."

"Write it down for me."

"Very well."

Harvey wrote the address of his son and daughter, and I wrote them a letter. They answered, "Leave the hills and the valleys behind and move here."

I wrote back, "Good, I will go."

I was seized by a strong urge to go. I would leave immediately. I reasoned, "There I will have bread, and I can read and write a little in German; in our village, none of my companions can read."

But my wife did not want to go. She had a fear of the oceans and foreign countries. Every day she would repeat to me, "I will not go; I will not go; I will not go."

"Very well, then stay here."

I lived at her place; she was my neighbor's daughter.[1]

I sold a team of horses and my oxen to get enough money to pay for the passage. I also sold some land.

My father said to my wife, "Do not go with him at this time. Let him go alone first to see what the land is like over there; then we shall see what to do next."

I applied for a passport for myself and my wife. I obtained it with considerable difficulty at the *starostvo*. . . .[2]

I was born in the year 1859. I had three children. Wasyl was eight, Yurko was three, and Nykola was also three. But although I obtained a passport for the whole family, I went alone. The wife wasn't brave enough to go; she stayed home with the children. This was in the fall of 1891.

Three of us set out: Wasyl Eleniak, Yurko Panischak, and myself. I advised them how to get passports. The other two were also from Nebyliw. Both were married, but they went without their wives, like myself. Yurko Panischak is my brother-in-law, my wife's brother. Fortunately, I had gone to the village school for four years and received my education there, for the teacher taught well. But the other two had not gone to school and did not know how to read. They listened to my advice and set out for Canada with me.

We arrived at Stryi, and then went to Peremyshl,[3] and from there to Oswienci [Auschwitz]. Here our papers were checked.

"Show me your money," one official demanded.

I had 600 *rynsky,* Eleniak had 190 *rynsky,* and Panischak had 120 *rynsky.*[4] The officials ordered Panischak to go back home to his village. He took the train back to Kalush. Only two of us reached Hamburg. There, an agent put us on a big ship which took us across the ocean.

We traveled for twenty-two days. It was a pretty fair voyage. The ship crossed the ocean and sailed up a river to a big city. It was Montreal.

We disembarked in the morning, and in the afternoon we boarded a train and were on our way across Canada. The trip was quite long; time dragged for two and a half days as we traversed

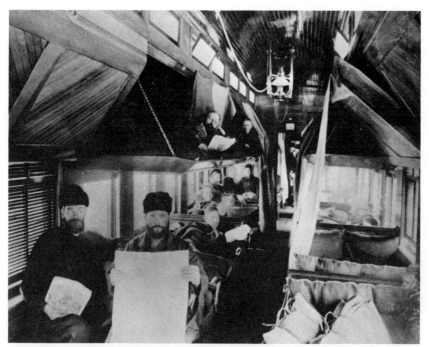

Interior of a CPR colonist car, about 1908

Ukrainian immigrants arriving at Quebec City, around 1911

rocks, forests, lakes, and open spaces where no one lived. It was quite clear that we were traversing a wilderness.

We came to some fair-sized town with wooden frame buildings. At the station, the officials told us to get off. They could speak our language but they did not seem to be our people;[5] apparently they were German. This was Winnipeg.

What day it was when we left Hamburg, what day when we arrived in Montreal, or when we got to Winnipeg, I honestly cannot recall. It was in the fall of 1891. My passport is gone; it was destroyed in a house fire on the farm at Bruderheim.

At the station in Winnipeg, an agent who spoke German and our language, Ukrainian, was assigned to our group. He was to show us the farmlands, and we could go wherever we wished, as travel by rail was free for us. This agent took us to Langenburg, to a farmer's home there — I forget his name. We both stayed at this farmer's place for a whole week. We were taken around and shown the lands so that we could pick a farm for ourselves. Here I met some German acquaintances who used to work under my supervision in the forest at Lymnitsa.

The lands were to our liking. I jotted down the number of one farm for myself and another number for Eleniak since he did not know how to write. We returned to Winnipeg and paid ten dollars apiece for the land that we claimed as our homesteads.

One German fellow, a shoemaker from Winnipeg who also came from Kalush, said to me, "In Alberta, it is warmer; go there and see for yourself."

I went to the office and said, "I want to go to Alberta to see the lands there."

"Very well" came their answer. "You will get free tickets. Go and pick a good farm for yourself. We have plenty of land."

We took the train to Calgary, for as yet there was no railway to Edmonton. We went as far as Greenfeld. Lands everywhere, lands whichever way you turned, all vacant! Get hold of a plow and start plowing. Quite unlike the old country where people live on narrow strips of land and do not have even a small plot for a garden. But we did not see any trees. After that we returned from Calgary to Winnipeg.

Here we met some Jews from Russia. They said to us, "Go to Gretna in Manitoba, not far from here. There you will find good land."

We bought tickets to Gretna and went there to see for ourselves.[6] At the station, we met some Germans who spoke Ukrainian. One of them hired us for threshing. There was plenty to eat and drink. We talked with the older ones in our language, but their young ones already knew English. They told us stories of their hard beginnings. They had suffered want for three or four years, but by hard work, they had become well-to-do.

I made up my mind to return to the old country for my wife and children. Eleniak asked me to bring his wife along with mine, as he himself would stay behind at his job at Gretna. I figured that it might be a good idea to bring other families from our village back with me as well. They would all be able to get land in a block, and thus they would not feel lonely in a foreign country. It occurred to me that it might even be possible to acquire a whole township. Do you know what a township is? It is thirty-six sections; one section contains four farms; the whole township contains 144 farms of 160 acres or, as we say, 113 morgs. This way 144 families could live side by side.

I left Gretna on 1 December. On 15 December, I traveled from Winnipeg to Montreal and then on to Boston. Here I had to wait five days for my ship. The voyage across the ocean to London took twenty-two days. I waited two days there before crossing to Hamburg. From there I went through Berlin, Auschwitz, Cracow, and Krekhowychi. At the station, I hired a carriage to Nebyliw, and on the fourth day after Christmas, I arrived at the village. This was in the year 1892.

People asked me all kinds of questions: where I had been and what I had seen. I told them many stories about Canada and urged them, "Flee, flee this place, for here you have nothing, and there you will have free land and be your own boss."

But the villagers were simple folk. "It is so far beyond the ocean," they said. Here was a mother shedding tears; although she had ten children, she had no desire to leave even should all her children starve to death with her. People came to my house — a houseful of curious men and women, every one asking me the same question, "Where have you been?"

The peasants did not understand that across the ocean free lands were available, without landlords, which could actually be acquired for little or no money. They listened to my stories and wondered.

The news spread around that a man had arrived from God only knew where and wanted to lead the people out to some sort of place called America. One day the magistrate of the village, the priest, the clerk, and a trustee of the church paid me a call. They began to quiz me to see whether or not I was telling the truth. They spread a map on the table and told me to stand aside.

The clerk asked me, "Where were you?"

I answered, "In America."

Very few knew where this country was, and even today it is difficult to tell someone who has no knowledge about the world.

"Which way did you go?" the magistrate asked.

I answered, "I went to Cracow, from there to Berlin, then to Hamburg. Then I traveled across the ocean to Montreal and from there by train to Winnipeg. I went by rail and by ship."

I stood aloof, talking, while they were searching the map.

"Where exactly have you been?" asked the priest.

I answered, "The country is called Canada. I was in Winnipeg, in Calgary, in Gretna. Wasyl Eleniak stayed behind in Gretna, at a farmer's place."

There was nothing they could do about it; they just had to believe me. The magistrate's only remark to me was "Watch yourself."

One day, I took a walk to Perehinska. A gendarme met me there and warned me, "Pylypiw, look out for yourself, or I'll lock you up one of these days."

"What for?" I asked.

"You'll see. Watch what you're saying."

It did not bother me a bit. I sat in the tavern and drank beer, either buying it myself or letting others pay for it. The curious ones would stand around me. I would tell them all they wanted to know. I would say, "Flee, flee, for here you have no land, and there you will have plenty of land. Here you are drudges; there you will be masters."

Altogether, twelve families got set for departure. . . .[7] They sold their fields and obtained their passports. To help them, I went with them to Kalush and interceded for them. They paid me a little for my assistance. It is no use concerning oneself about others for nothing, spending your time and effort so others might have everything in order. I struck a bargain with an agent in Hamburg whereby I would direct emigrants to his bureau to book passage on his ships and he would pay me five dollars for each family. Such an arrangement would be a common thing in Canada because a person must spend his time running around here and there, and he must live. Remuneration for work is a requirement, but our people were not wise to it. Raised in the village, they were simple in their ways. They found out that my work and my trouble would fetch me some cash, and they began to gossip.

One morning, a gendarme came to my house. I forget his name. He ordered me, "Come with me to the magistrate."

I did as I was told. The magistrate's name was Ivan Hrynkiw. The clerk was there, too. My brother-in-law was also summoned because he was helping me to recruit people to go to Canada, although he had never been there himself.

The magistrate defended us. He argued that there was nothing wrong with what we were doing, but the gendarme marched us to Kalush and took us to the police station. Here we were both interrogated and taken into custody.

The next day, the gendarme took us to court. He showed us a report and some letters from the agent in Hamburg. These were used as evidence that I was to be paid for recruiting emigrants to Canada. I did not think that I had done anything wrong. The judge spoke in our language, but he could not acquit us. He ordered that we be taken to Stanislaviw. Another gendarme conducted us to the railway station and accompanied us on the trip. The gendarmes did not handcuff us but simply marched us at bayonet point.

Our train took two hours to reach Stanislaviw. Once there, we were taken into jail. As the saying goes, this was our Inquisition. We were each thrown into a cell. Then we were hauled before the court. I had a lawyer, but I forget his name now. I paid him, and he defended both of us. The court reviewed our case.

The judge asked me, "What do you need land for? Don't you have enough here?"

I replied, "We have too little land."

The judge said, "You are enticing people to leave."

I answered, "No, they want to go themselves."

The judge lashed out at me, "Why don't you hold your tongue? You should have gone alone without dragging others along with you. You sold out the people to the agent. Our most illustrious emperor once helped to bring our people back from Argentina, thirty families at his own expense; do you expect him to come to the rescue again should anything go wrong?"

The trial lasted about three hours. We were sentenced to one month in jail.

We both went to jail, and those people went to the new country because they had made up their mind to go. Those who went were Mikhailo Romaniuk, now living in Chipman; Mikhailo Eleniak, who settled in Chipman but died of flu; Yusko Paish, now living at Delph; Antin Paish, who lived at Myrnam but is now dead; Mykola Tychkowskyi, who died at Star; and Dmytro Wyzynowych, who died at Chipman. All of these settled in Alberta. Only Wasyl Yatsiv, whose son Ivan completed higher education, is farming in Manitoba, at Ladywood. The other families did not leave the country until later on.

When I finished serving my jail sentence, I made arrangements to leave for Canada with my whole family. To make our voyage possible, I had to earn some money first. I agreed to act as agent for a wood buyer in Odessa, at a commission of five cents a cubic [meter]. I had people working for me, and I paid them so much per day. I got some horses, and we hauled the wood for shipment to Lymnitsa and then down the Dniester to Odessa. I worked in the bush until winter and then spent the winter at home.

In spring of 1893, on the third day after Easter, I set out. With me were my wife and four children.[8] The youngest, Anna, was six

Foreign quarter of Winnipeg, early 1900s

months old. We were joined by Yurko Panischak with his wife and two children, and Stefan Chichak with his wife and four children. We made the journey together through Lawoczne, Budapest, Vienna, Paris, and Rotterdam. From there, we went by ship across the ocean and up the river to Quebec. From Quebec, we took the train to Winnipeg.

I left my family there in a rented house, and went to work in North Dakota. In December, when I had earned some money, I returned with some German people who were going to Athabasca. In Winnipeg, I bought a yoke of oxen, a cow, a plow, a wagon, a sack of flour, salt, and sugar. I took all these commodities to the railway and loaded them into a boxcar. The freight charges for the shipment were forty dollars, and the shipper could travel free of charge.

Thus I journeyed to Edmonton and from there to Bruderheim where I took a homestead. I stayed there about six months and then moved to the Star district. It was then called Edna but now both the station and the post office are called Star. I have lived here since 1903. I acquired a farm the location of which is described thus: township fifty-six, range nineteen, section twenty-two, southwest quarter, 160 acres, west of the fourth meridian in Alberta. In the course of all those long years, I have acquired four more quarters, so that now I have five, all paid for and registered in my name. . . .

The years fly quickly. I am now seventy-three years old. I enjoy talking with people and getting together over a glass of beer. I am still keeping well, but my wife is rather sickly. She stays at home and takes care of her health. We keep hired help to look after the farm, for it is hard for just the two of us to attend to all the chores.

Our people have made progress in Canada and have learned a great deal. Canada also has made progress. People used to work with oxen, then with horses, and now with machines. Transportation by means of horses is too slow now, so people are buying cars. Most of our farmers now have cars. In Alberta, the Ukrainians have elected three members of Parliament, two to Edmonton and one to Ottawa. . . . In Manitoba, our people have elected two members of Parliament. . . .

In the old country, things are not so good; they have gotten worse for our people. From letters and newspapers, we learn that people are still being flogged there as in the days of serfdom. There they want our people to remain illiterate, without any schooling. The young people born in Canada do not understand that, but anyone who came from the old country remembers what life was like there. We were despised by the Poles. And how long will this go on?

2 REV NESTOR DMYTRIW
'Canadian Ruthenia'

A Traveler's Memoirs

This is the earliest firsthand account by a competent observer of the lot of Ukrainian immigrants in Canada. The author, Rev. Nestor Dmytriw, recorded his impressions in 1897, after a tour of the principal Ukrainian settlements in Canada. His observations were published in 1898 as a series of articles in Svoboda, *the oldest Ukrainian daily in North America, which had been founded in the United States in 1893.*

Reverend Dmytriw focused his attention on the seamy side of the immigrant's social life, rather than on economic conditions. His assessment of the ability of the Ukrainian immigrant to adapt to conditions in Canada is interesting in light of subsequent developments. In the following article, as in his other writings, he uses the now obsolete term "Ruthenian" to refer to Ukrainians from the Austro-Hungarian Empire.

I came to Winnipeg on 15 April [1897].... At the railway station ... I met a few of our peasants in sheepskin coats, shook hands with them, and discovered that they had come via Berlin from the vicinity of Brodiw. One of them even subscribed to *Svoboda*. Soon, Mr. Genyk appeared and directed me to the immigration house.[1]

And now a few of my observations about conditions here. After the last election, changes took place in the government, and the party that took over the reins brought in its own order.[2] It removed all former government officials and replaced them with its own. Consequently changes took place in matters relating to immigration. The new administrative staff, with its very energetic chief [Clifford Sifton] deals with immigration matters promptly, efficiently, and with bureaucratic formality. It includes persons who speak different languages. Among them is a Swede, a Frenchman, a German, and our Ruthenian, Mr. Genyk. The building itself is kept very clean, and, for an immigration home, it is quite comfortable, especially for our people. They get free lodging which is clean and comfortable, a kitchen for common use, and fuel.

I came across several families of our people here, mainly from the Borschiw area, who bring only disgrace upon our nation. Although some of them have been here several months, they still

Dominion government immigration hall

Immigration hall, Edmonton, before 1912

appear dirty and look wretched, and they still wear their old-country clothes and their long hair. In no way can they be persuaded to switch fashions. If they did, they say, they would lose their faith. One wife threatened to drown or hang herself if her husband dared to get his hair cut. These people are looked down upon as being something worse than Indians, since Indians here are considered to be a civilized people. They have their own newspaper and scriptures in their own language. One official suggested to me, quite seriously, that a few of our people be sent among the Indians for instruction.

Try to visualize this situation. A family arrives from Galicia — husband, wife, and eight children. On the way here, they spend all their money. The agents along the way extort the man's last penny. Ill-clad, half-naked, barefoot, dirty, destitute, they come to the immigration home like beggars. The administrators of the home wring their hands and are at a loss to know how to begin coping with these wretched people. Now and then, some kindhearted person will give this family a few cents so that they can have food for the time being. Their children make a nuisance of themselves in the stairway, crawling up and down and relieving themselves on the steps or beside the door. In desperation, the administration curses and turns to the government for guidance in dealing with such people. But since the government has no other source of immigrants to bank on at this time, it tolerates our people as *malum necessarium* [a necessary evil]. One can well imagine what they think of our people.

But let us return to our hapless family. The husband is given a job. He chops wood every day and earns on the average of fifty cents per day. His cost of living is very low. No demands are made on him; he saves his money and thinks he lives like a lord. Having got used to this kind of life in the city, our man does not work hard, eats white bread like they do only at Easter in Galicia — and then only in a prosperous year — and does not even give a thought about farming. In Winnipeg, there are a great many of our people like this fellow. But this kind of senseless gambling on their part only means loss of time, for even if they do manage to save some money, in the end the city mayor (he is also chief of the immigration bureau) will run them out of the city and force them to take up farming. But by that time, there will not be any good farmland left.

There are about 200 of our people in Winnipeg. They can be grouped into three categories. First, there are those who stay in the immigration home temporarily and have some cash with which they speculate, especially in buying land (some have already lost up to $300). In the end, after losing half their money, they settle on farms. The second group are the penniless who live in Winnipeg and work at different jobs so they might have money to settle on

39

land. The third group are the proletarians who live in the city, cut wood, carry water, and light fires in the homes of Russian Jews. Barely making a living, they show no interest in farming, contending that they had enough of hard work in Galicia.

The sons of these immigrants go to work for farmers, the daughters work for English and Jewish people, and small children go to English schools. A young boy, barely fourteen years of age, gets $60 a year working for a farmer. I met girls who work in hotels for $10 a month, and they speak English fairly well. Quite often, a farmer will hire the whole family for the summer for $150. At harvest time, our men trek from Winnipeg all the way to Minnesota and North Dakota, find harvest jobs, and earn a handsome wage to take home.

It is not easy to persuade our man, no matter how destitute his family, to go to work and earn a few dollars during the summer. He believes it is beneath his dignity as head of a household to work for others. And it is difficult to keep the boys from running away from their jobs, homesick for their daddy and mamma. It is the girls who make out the best. They learn the language more quickly than anyone else and more readily absorb the culture of this country. What these girls are like now will determine what sort of wives and mothers they will make some day; like mothers like children, and that is going to determine our future in Canada. These considerations should prompt the parents to send their daughters to work for English-speaking and other cultured peoples.

Our individual with his Galician upbringing is at present not adapted for work in America. He is in no position to compete with workers of other nationalities. Lifelong bondage and oppression have made a slave out of him, slothful and unconcerned. Life on the fief in Galicia demoralized him, and his physical weakness makes him incompetent for the kind of work demanded in America. He lacks the necessities of life, but he also lacks the qualities possessed by American workers of other ethnic groups, which are essential for earning money to provide those necessities.

Let me cite two cases which illustrate what I mean. In Edmonton, our people suffered grievously. The government gave them $250 in relief and provided jobs. Our people quit the jobs and continued to go hungry. Another example: a farmer 130 miles from Winnipeg hired one of our men to cut wood for him and promised him good wages. Since he was not getting the results he expected from the worker, he was not prepared to put up with him. Without any fuss, he asked the man to come for a ride in a wagon with him. Several miles away from home, he just dumped the fellow out in the open field and left him there to God's mercy. It was a case of either work or perish. Fortunately, the fellow had some money. He found his way to a railway station and took a train to Winnipeg where he is now sawing wood for Jewish families.

In Winnipeg, I also came upon that cursed division of our Ruthenian people into religious denominations. Ruthenians of the Latin rite have been taken in by a few overzealous Poles and have become alienated from their brothers, their friends, and their neighbors. The Polish priest comes around once a year to hear confession and to administer communion to whoever attends the French church.[3] Considering the denominational, ethnic, and organizational realities, we must get a priest of our own rite to come to Winnipeg this year. As regards the question of who is going to support him, that will be decided by our church hierarchy and subsequently by all the Ruthenians themselves. If we neglect this matter at the beginning, we will not be able to rectify the situation in ten years. . . .[4]

In the Lake Dauphin District. From Portage la Prairie to Dauphin, travel by train is very slow and tedious. A person forgets that he is in America, and his mind automatically goes back to the days when he used to travel by the wretched Galician train from Lviv to Ruska Rava or to Zhowkva. The train is jampacked with passengers of different origins. Among the ordinary sinners wrapped in sheepskin coats with woolly linings, there sits a French *pater* with his black cloak tightly buttoned from toes to neck and wrapping its wearer as though it meant never to release him from its embrace. The smoking car is extremely filthy due to the foul smoke from the different sorts of tobacco and the disgusting spitting. It is enough to kill anyone who is not used to this kind of atmosphere.

In this suffocating cloud of smoke, I was surprised to find a woman, and I wondered how she had stumbled into this filth. Upon closer observation, I concluded that she was one of our females — showing her true colors. her head was bound with a band, a thick band that seemed to be made up of ten kerchiefs; she wore a short, black jacket and underneath the jacket an even blacker blouse; her bosom was uncovered and her yellowish flesh was showing; a couple of aprons took the place of a skirt; her soiled ankle-length petticoat was repulsive to the sight. Her waxy face reflected some secret sadness or longing, perhaps even uncertainty about her own present existence. Seated beside her was a tall, thin man with a pale, depressed, melancholy countenance.

"Where are you going?" I asked.

Startled, the man scratched his head and haltingly replied, "Your pardon, sir, we are supposed to be going to our homestead."

"What do you mean, 'supposed to be going'?"

"That's the way it is, gracious sir, because we don't have a single penny to our name and can't afford a bite to eat, let alone to pay for the farm."

"But why are you sitting here in this smoke when there is room in the next coach?"

"We are not allowed there, sir; it's only for gentlemen. We were in that coach, but the conductor chased us out into this coach."

I looked up the conductor and found out that he had moved the couple into the smoking car at the request of other passengers who were offended by the dirty clothes of the Galician woman. With great difficulty, I persuaded the conductor to move them out of that smoke.

From further conversation, I learned that this destitute couple hailed from the district of Borschiw. Thanks to Missler,[5] they had emigrated to the state of Georgia along with a few other couples. Having suffered extreme penury there, they had managed almost miraculously to get to Philadelphia. There the unscrupulous Missler, with the assistance of the Austrian consul, disposed of them by packing them off to Winnipeg. During the winter, they had huddled together with others in the immigration home, and now, penniless, they were setting out for Dauphin to settle on land, in order, as the saying goes, to provide bread for the children. "Your pardon, sir," said the peasant, "we know that we will never become rich, but at least our children will not be beggars like us."

We arrived at Dauphin late in the evening. The train was only four hours late. Along the way, it made several stops while the railroad was being repaired where the grade had been washed out. In any case, being late in that part of the country does not create any serious hardship. I stayed overnight in the immigration home together with that wretched couple.

The immigration hostel in this small Canadian town is a two-story building held together by millions of nails large and small. The ground floor is one large room. In the middle of the room stands a large, English, iron kitchen stove on which each family cooks its own meals. Along the walls are wooden fixtures serving as bunks. Upstairs, the furnishing is identical. When a man comes to claim his homestead, he has the privilege of staying in this shack for ten days and of availing himself of the kitchen stove and a bunk. Wood for fuel is supplied, but each person must provide his own food. People fill up the place like a swarm of flies. Darkness and commotion engulf all. A very dim light from a small lamp barely illuminates one corner. Everyone chatters at the same time, and their voices blend into one loud confusion. Here one can find Frenchmen, Swedes, Germans, Russian Jews, Scotsmen, Ruthenians, Poles, and others. Some are undressing and getting ready for bed. One is whistling; one is gabbing away and laughing lustily. In a corner, a religious Frenchman is crossing himself, and right in the middle of the floor is our *muzhik* making himself at home as he

Ivan Lupul's home at Wostok, Alberta, 1902

repeatedly prostrates himself, forehead to floor, till the room resounds with thuds.[6] Not understanding the meaning of this ritual, the spectators watch his gymnastics, shake with laughter, and assume that perhaps this is the proper thing to do before retiring for the night.

I was favored with a separate bed, and being weary after the journey and the scenes I had witnessed, I fell sound asleep. My snoring was cut short by a poke in the ribs. I rubbed my eyes and saw a man standing over me and beginning to undress for bed. I moved right up against the wall. The stranger lay down beside me without saying a word and began to snore as soon as he hit the pillow. In the morning, as soon as he got up, he left without uttering a single word to me. I met him again in the hotel at the breakfast table, but he never spoke a word to me nor I to him. To the Europeans, such conduct may seem strange, but here it is common. Obviously, the man did not want to have anything to do with me. Nor I with him, for that matter.

In the afternoon, I hired a team of horses and set out for the colony which lies along the Drifting River and is named Terebowla by the settlers. It is sixteen miles from the Valley River railway station. The plain spread all around me. Groves of poplar trees dotted the wide-open spaces. In the distance, little white houses

Ukrainian settlement, Saint Julien, Saskatchewan, around 1910

could be seen about a mile apart from one another, or even farther. Near the houses were stables built of poplar logs, which looked like potato bins. The cattle and horses waded in the snow and pools of water and scratched for dry grass like the reindeer of the far north. Spread out before our eyes in every direction were vast spaces of wheat lands begging to be tilled. Mother Earth herself would be glad to feed her children who have been wronged, impoverished, humiliated by the dole of the landlords in Galicia, who are fainting from hunger. Here and there, the tall stubble of last year's wheat crop could be seen, with stems as thick as those of the wild prairie grass.

Absorbed in thought, I finally reached Valley River. To proceed farther by wagon was impossible. The river, which during the summertime is merely a trickle, could not be crossed by wagon. In the end, there was no other alternative but to continue the journey to the colony, a distance of some six miles, on foot, the way the apostles used to travel. Along the way, I crossed the river and came to the farmyard of an Englishman from whom I hired a wagon and a team of horses. For three hours, the wagon bounced through bush and across prairies, over stumps, and over logs, some of them half a meter across. Thus I got as far as the homestead of a young English farmer who lived alone in a small shack. Beyond this shack there was no track. It was impossible to penetrate the bush with a wagon. Again there was no choice but to proceed on foot.*

The sun was beginning to set, and its cold rays glistened on the larger patches of snow and reflected in the deep streams which made their way through a thick tangle of willow branches and everlasting grasses. For over an hour I wandered through the forest; for over an hour I trudged through snow and water; for over an hour I wandered astray in a land where only an Indian hunter had set foot before. It was getting dark. I was seized with fear. The fear experienced by a human being who feels as helpless as a tiny worm, surrounded by invincible yet silent nature. The fear experienced by one engulfed by a pitch-dark night in the heart of a primeval steppe or forest. I summoned my last spurt of energy and pushed on through the forest. Fortunately, I saw or, rather, came upon a road and joyfully followed it regardless of where it might lead me. After a half-hour tramp, I came upon a farm owned by a couple of young Scotsmen who lived here with their horses and cattle like a couple of hermits. One of the young men willingly hitched up a team of horses, and we slowly proceeded toward our colony.

A bright moon lit the sky; a veil of mist hung over the forests; a stream murmured softly. The horses sauntered unhurriedly, and my merry host talked in his peculiar English about his life experiences. Finally, we came to a cabin. The horses stopped, and I was glad to reach my destination.

The exterior of the cabin caught my attention. The walls were solidly constructed of roughly squared poplar logs, with neatly mitered corners. The roof was made of poplar boards covered with earth and manure. The cabin was low, and a small iron chimney protruded from the roof. From the chimney, smoke rose incessantly as there was an abundance of fuel.

Inside the cabin, it was quite warm. The heat came from the iron kitchen stove, which was red hot. On the stove, some gruel was cooking. It was made from white flour and water, without fat and without milk, as these people had no cow yet. Standing by the stove was our hostess in her Galician clothes, and around the stove squatted her children waiting for the gruel, as needless to say they were hungry. A bed, a table, a bench on which the host was seated—this was the sum total of the acquisitions of our peasant who had come to seek his fortune in Canada. And yet this was not his entire fortune. Under the bed, his chickens and pigeons were raising a hubbub, and a little pup hustled about the room. Outside, beside the cabin, was a stable and, in the stable, two oxen which were actually owned jointly by three farmers. Near the cabin stood a big wagon costing seventy dollars, which was also a joint possession of the three.

I did not stay very long at this place. The man I wished to visit lived farther up — a farm and a half away, they told me here. I set out toward his place, tramping through the bush for a long time before I came upon the man's house. That "farm and a half" was some size!

Team of oxen on a Ukrainian farm near Teulon, Manitoba

The setting was beautiful, especially in the moonlight. A stream meandered between wooded banks. Beside the stream stood a house, larger than the last one I was in; in front of the house stood a wagon which also served as a temporary pantry; under the wagon, kitchen utensils were stored, and one of the pots was covered with *Svoboda*. The stable was fairly large. In it, two cows, two calves, and two oxen.

In the yard stood two plows — the beginnings of husbandry.

In the house, the same kind of order prevailed as elsewhere. Making myself at home, I took off my soaking-wet shoes and dried my feet. After a hearty chat with my hosts, I went to bed and was soon fast asleep. On Sunday morning, I was awakened by the persistent crowing of a rooster under my bed.

In front of the house, a crowd of people was assembling. Most of the colony of fifteen families, or seventy-eight peersons, showed up and filled the yard. The errand boys had not yet returned from Valley River with my belongings.[7] It was believed they would not be back until evening. In the meantime, I went out for a walk to have a look at the farm.

Holy God! Could our peasant ever have dreamed that such a fortune would await his children? One hundred thirteen morgs of forest! Poplars, hazel shrubs, a shabby oak tree here and there, scarcely any pines. Excellent soil, and all of it belonged to the homesteader complete with the vetch, wild rye, and wild oats. Black soil, elbow-deep, for wheat growing, fertilized from time immemorial by rotted leaves. Grubbing the bush is quite easy as the roots are quite close to the surface. Lush meadows for pasturing cattle.

Pure water and such salubrious fresh air! True, the winter lasts from November until the end of April; it is bitterly cold, and the frosts are severe, very severe. But our settler says, "Let winter be really wintry, not like those foul winters in Galicia." Our man is afraid of hot weather, not of winter.

And what vast spaces! One hundred sixty acres — why, that's 113 Galician morgs of good, free land! All this calls for money and brains; anyone who comes here penniless and brainless will perish in these forests. Let no one set out for Canada without a cent; let him remain in Galicia, for it is easier to be a beggar there than here. There, a beggar will always be given a piece of black bread, but here no one gives anything away free.

Although one gets paid for his work here, there is no farm work to be found anywhere except, of course, on his own farm. But one cannot work on land without oxen and a plough; hence he is just doomed to starvation; there is no alternative. For a start in homesteading and for living expenses until such time as one is able to live off his land, he needs at least $300. Without that small capital, one either perishes or is doomed to a life of penury.

It was a big mistake on the part of our people to come to Canada just before winter. Needless to say, in winter one cannot obtain bread from under the snow. Whatever money one has will be spent on living during the winter, and by spring he is left penniless, knocking his head against the wall.

Those of our people who settled in the colony of Terebowla arrived here in winter, around Christmastime. The majority of them hailed from the districts of Borschiw, Chortkiw, Buchach, and Terebowla. I found that fifteen families owned five oxen, two cows, two calves, and of this number two oxen, two cows, and two calves belonged to one family. And what remained for the other families? One wagon and three oxen.

One observation that must be made about our peasant is that he readily resigns himself to the will of God. He is likely to lean his lazy body against his small hut all day long, maintaining that whatever will be will be as God wills. A profound philosophy, but God will not drop things from heaven if man will not apply his hands to help himself.

Late in the evening, the errand boys returned with my effects, and I began to hear confessions. The next morning it was snowing, and it was impossible to celebrate Mass outdoors; hence, it was necessary to improvise an altar in the house. The small home was jammed with worshippers. On hearing the first words of the liturgy—"Blessed is the kingdom . . ."—they gave way to their tears like little children. Neither was I myself able to restrain my tears during the sermon as I recalled those causes, those hardships, which drove us overseas into the snows and forests in search of a better

47

future for our children.

Following the liturgy, I baptized a small Canadian-Ruthenian and after that performed the ceremony of consecrating the "cross of freedom." On a knoll overlooking a river, our colonists erected a cross of poplar wood to commemorate the freedom which they attained in the year 1896. In a few words appropriate to the occasion, I mentioned the freedom gained in the year 1848 and reviewed briefly the history of our socio-economic development up to the year 1896.[8] I stressed the latter date which, with our emigration to Canada, became the year of our real freedom, real emancipation from the bondage of our lords and government. This cross was the first Ruthenian cross in the Canadian forests, on Canadian soil.

I bade farewell to these people and hit the trail for Dauphin. Along the way, I tried to ascertain in my mind the cause of the dissension among our people in that small Ruthenian colony. Two of the families did not show up for confession because they claimed they were Poles.[9] One person even stated that the Polish priest, on his departure from the colony, had left a stiff warning against confession before a Ruthenian priest even if it meant going without confession for four years. What Polish chauvinism! And where is the papal decree which grants the freedom to confess and to accept the sacraments in any rite in the event of an emergency? Papal decrees then are meaningless when it comes to Polonization. The concern of the Polish priests for the salvation of their motherland takes procedence over their concern for the salvation of souls. Our people heard enough of those wild fantasies about the "motherland," not only in Galicia but also on the way to Canada. How is it that in Winnipeg last year a Polish priest heard confession from our people and administered communion to them, assuring them that there was no difference between the rites? No, my Polish friends, you are not going to reach your goal in this manner. Our people see through your arguments and are aware of the differences. Persons of the Latin rite from eastern Galicia are definitely not Poles! They speak Ruthenian; they pray in Ruthenian; they bow themselves low,[10] though in their prayers they may be using some words that sound Polish. Your rosaries, the scapulars with which you have covered our women, will definitely not make Poles out of them. The fact is that we are fed up with Latinization. It is quite obvious now that the Latin rite has contributed to the Polonization of our people. Fortunately, there is no danger of it here. In a few years, there will be no trace left of the Polish-Latin influence. However, constant vigil is necessary over our people on the part of our intelligentsia.

3 REV NESTOR DMYTRIW
Assimilation!

While Reverend Dmytriw was in Canada, he officiated at an unusual wedding ceremony — one of the "firsts" in the annals of Ukrainian-Canadians. It was the marriage of Frank Nex and Anna Zarowna on 18 October 1897 at Dauphin, Manitoba. This was the first English-Ukrainian marriage in Canada. Reverend Dmytriw's account of the event originally appeared in Svoboda *on 24 March 1898.*

It was love at first sight though they could not understand one another, since neither knew a word of the other's strange language. But then, does love really need a language? Various writers tell us that love has its own mystical language which is understood by both him and her. It was this kind of language which established a bond between two people, an Englishman and a Ruthenian girl, in one of the Ruthenian colonies in Canada. Frank was born in London; Anna, in Galicia. They met, fell in love, and, as seldom happens, married for love. It was an interesting and original kind of wedding, and I shall try to tell about it.

There was a great buzz in the Ruthenian colony of D —— like the buzz of a beehive. They even talked about it in the neighboring colonies. A rare and unheard of event—a pure-blooded Englishman, born in the heart of London, a printer, obviously well educated, marrying a Ruthenian girl, the daughter of a poor Galician peasant. The date for the wedding was set, and the marriage was to be solemnized by a Ruthenian priest. All were patiently awaiting this wonder.

The day finally arrived. The weather was superb. A gorgeous, pleasantly cool autumn day smiled upon the world. All around the tidily kept farmhouse, farmers' wagons and buggies were neatly parked. And bicycles rested against the walls of the house. A crowd of people in their Sunday best surrounded the house and chattered gaily amongst themselves. Now and then the hushed tones of English words could be heard amidst the louder Ruthenian talk. The latest styles of clothes mingled with costumes from Galicia. American ladies, those most curious folk in the world, and buxom

49

Mr. and Mrs. Fred Chaba of the Eastgate area, Alberta, on their wedding day, 1911

Country wedding, Samburg, Saskatchewan, 1917

Galician girls in the same crowd. All were awaiting the arrival of the priest who was to marry the young couple.

Finally, he did arrive, and the crowd gave him a loud welcome. Our greeting, *"Slawa Isusu Khrystu"* ["Glory be to Jesus Christ"] intermingled with the English "Good morning." In no time, the small house was jammed with people. Many stood outside looking in through the windows.

When the divine liturgy was over, the sacrament of matrimony was administered. The English guests followed our lengthy Eastern ritual with interest. They were anxious to hear the marriage vows, but they could not understand the words. The groom could not understand the bride's vows in Ruthenian tongue. Neither could the bride understand the groom's vows in English. Nonetheless, it was done: vows were made by both parties. "What God hath joined together let no man put asunder," says the Holy Writ.

As is customary in all parts of the world, an important occasion such as this calls for celebration. The guests were seated at a long table. Gracing the head of the table were the priest and the bridal couple. Now the "Anglo-Ruthenian" conviviality got under way. I say "Anglo-Ruthenian" because, besides the English cakes, pies, and other such goodies set on the table were our generous-sized Ruthenian *pyrohy*. "Assimilation!" someone exclaimed, excited at the sight of such a variety of foods. Assimilation, indeed, in the full meaning of the term. The newlyweds nestled up to each other and from time to time exchanged loving glances which expressed their secret desires, feelings and hopes for their future. The guests — notwithstanding their different ethnic origins — mingled well in company, conversed with one another (if only in a few words) and shared the gifts of God which were set on the table. All this did not seem to make sense either in English or in Ruthenian.

After a meal, the English love to dally around the table and chat, and our people even more so, especially on an occasion such as a wedding. But this time it was different. They rose from the table, formed little groups, and joined in a lively chatter. From behind the door around the corner came the strains of a violin — a waltz tune. The newlyweds took to the floor; other couples joined them. Assimilation, I mused as I watched the mixed couples in their ebullience, swinging their partners.

The guests had a hilarious time and enjoyed themselves until daybreak the next morning. The lively English boys kept whirling the hefty Ruthenian girls until the lads were on the verge of collapsing from exhaustion. And the handsome, strapping, Ruthenian youths took a back seat to no one as they swung away with the delicate English girls on the dance floor.

"Assimilation!" trumpeted the Canadian newspapers. If only our culture could flourish at such a high level that the children of mixed marriages would retain the Ruthenian national characteristics, then a race of people would rise of whom we could be justly proud before the world. Otherwise, our women and the generations born of mixed marriages will be doomed in the sea of English civilization. But, on the other hand, they will not be beggars or slaves without a sense of human dignity, but they will be fully human. And that is all that matters. Or is it?

4 MARIA ADAMOWSKA
Beginnings in Canada

One of the most detailed and moving accounts of the life of the early Ukrainian settlers is that of the noted poet Maria Adamowska. In his History of Ukrainian Literature in Canada, *Dr. M. I. Mandryka explains that she was born Maria Oliynyk in 1890, in the village of Mykhalkove, Western Ukraine, and emigrated to Canada in 1899:*

> *Her love for self-education and reading stimulated her to express her thoughts and feelings in writing. She began in 1923, sending verses to the weekly* Ukrainian Voice, *in Winnipeg. Nostalgia possessed her all the time, although she came to Canada when only nine years old. . . .*
> *During the first years, she lived with her father, Dmytro Oliynyk, at Canora, Saskatchewan. Life was hard and painful. However, after several years of hardship, the conditions changed for the better. She joined local Ukrainian organizations and became one of the leading members. The last twenty years she lived at Melville, Saskatchewan, where she died in 1961, leaving many nostalgic verses on the pages of the* Ukrainian Voice.

> *Mrs. Adamowska actually wrote two articles about her pioneer experiences. The first appeared in the* Almanac *of the* Ukrainian Voice *for 1937 as "Pochatky w Kanadi" (Beginnings in Canada). The second published under the title "Pionirski harazdy w Kanadi" (The Lot of Pioneers in Canada), appeared in the* Almanac *for 1939. These two essays have been combined for inclusion in this book; passages from the 1939 article are here enclosed in square brackets.*

[It is now forty years since my parents and I left our native village of Mykhalkove, the familiar thatched cottage, the beautiful orchard, and all those lovely scenes of my early, carefree childhood. Inexpressible grief seized my young heart when all our relatives and everyone from the village met in our yard to wish us Godspeed into the faraway, unknown world. The parting and the mournful keening were heartbreaking. Old and young wept as they bade us farewell, perhaps forever. And little girls, my schoolmates and girlfriends, wept with me.

The mere mention of school broke my heart. It was as if my soul presaged the loss of the most valuable treasure in my life, one which I would never recover. I loved school and learning as I loved my dear mother. But cruel fate had decreed against me.

Amidst tears and despair, we seated ourselves in the wagon and set out for Cherniwtsi. When we reached the hill on the outskirts of the settlement, we paused for a last look at our dear native village, nestled proudly in the midst of its cherry orchards as if decked with garlands. Overcome by grief, none of us had the strength to utter a single word. Only the aching heart sang:

> Farewell my village, my native village,
> My native land,
> For God only knows whether
> I shall ever greet you again.

In Cherniwtsi, we boarded the train and proceeded on our way.

My father was a man of firm resolve. He was glad to tear himself away from the Polish yoke once and for all. Hence, having temporarily borne the pain of parting with his homeland, he began to take an interest in the beautiful scenery as it flashed past the windows of the train and began to weave golden visions of that fabulous land, Canada.

Mother, on the other hand, was tenderhearted. Of all the trials that had been her lot in life, this one was the most bitter. Whenever father had mentioned going to Canada, she had started to cry. And she cried all the way on the train and missed seeing the lovely sights in God's good world.

We arrived in Hamburg. Here we had to wait a few days for our ship. My childish fancy was captured by the sight of huge dogs hitched to carts full of large milk cans. The milk vendors shouted as they went about making their deliveries.

Finally, our ship arrived. It anchored some distance away from the shore, and we were transported to it in a small boat.

Aboard the ship, we met more of our countrymen from Galicia and Bukovina who were also on their way to Canada. We were assigned to cabins with bunks placed one above the other. The journey had its ill effects on a number of passengers. Many suffered from seasickness and had trouble holding food in their stomachs. Some ugly scenes took place, especially at night. If a person in the lower bunk forgot himself and stuck his head out, he ran the risk of being plastered with vomit from the bunk above him. When it happened, the sight was more deplorable than funny.

But there were others who were not affected by seasickness. They were characters for whom, as the proverb has it, "the sea was knee-deep."[1] Disregarding the dangers of voyage by water, they would deliberately offend others with off-color jokes. Two of them in particular, both from Bukovina, often got drunk, and then one of them would put on some rags to represent a priest's vestments and would impersonate a priest. He burlesqued a church service while others of his kind joined in with unearthly hoots. Another one gave strict orders to his wife to stand his pants up and hold them that way while he jumped into them from his bunk. People turned in disgust from such stupid antics.

On the other hand, there were those who commanded our respect. One man had a reed pipe. When he played it or sang a song, one could not help crying. His music and his songs were profoundly nostalgic, charged with keen longing for his Bukovina:

O, wild Bukovina, luxuriant, turbulent,
Why is there no longer any good in you?
Often have my feet crossed you
But nowhere could I find that good
Except on one riverbank —
Three leaves of myrtle.
I will pluck one and play a tune:
Somewhere in the world a father I have
I'll pluck another and play a tune:
Somewhere in the world a mother I have
A third I'll pluck and play a tune:
Somewhere in the world brothers I have.
O, falcon, dear falcon,
Do not let me pine away
For I'm weary and grief stricken,
From my kin separated;
From my kin, from my family—
Already half of me is wasted.[2]

Finally, we sailed into port at Halifax. On the shore, a crowd of people stared at us, some out of curiosity, some out of contempt. Our men, particularly those from Galicia, were dressed like gentlemen for the voyage, but the women and children traveled in their everyday peasant costumes. The older men from Bukovina attracted attention to themselves by their waist-length hair — greased with reeking lard — and by their smelly sheepskin coats. Perhaps that was the reason why the English people stopped their noses and glued their eyes upon us — a strange spectacle, indeed.

In Halifax, we boarded a train and continued on our journey. As we sped across Ontario with its rocks, hills, and tunnels, we were afraid we were coming to the end of the world. The heart of many a man sank to his heels, and the women and children raised such lamentation as defies description.

At last we arrived in Winnipeg. At that time, Winnipeg was very much like any other small farmers' town. From the train we were taken to the immigration home. Here one great source of consolation was Kyrylo Genyk.[3] He spoke with each one of us and offered his kind advice. And he inquired of those from his native village about his schoolmate Mykhailo Dorundiak.]

One must remember that times were different then. Nowadays when an immigrant arrives in Canada, he feels more or less at home. Here he can find his own people everywhere and hear his own language. But in those days you had to wander far and wide before you could meet one of your countrymen. No matter what direction you turned, all you could see was the prairie like a vast sea on which wild animals howled and red-skinned Indians roamed. It was not until after our arrival that the mass immigration of Ukrainians to Canada began. . . .

[From Winnipeg, we went to Yorkton, Saskatchewan. There we hired a rig which took us more than thirty miles farther north. At long last, after a miserable trip — we were nearly devoured alive by

Maria Adamowska, far right, about 1916, with her daughter, niece, infant nephew, and sister

mosquitoes — we managed to reach our destination, the home of our acquaintances.

Our host, who had emigrated to Canada a year or two before, had written us to boast of the prosperity he had attained in such a short time. He said that he had a home like a mansion, a large cultivated field, and that his wife was dressed like a lady. In short, he depicted Canada as a country of incredible abundance whose borders were braided with sausage like some fantastic land in a fairy tale.

How great was our disenchantment when we approached that mansion of his and an entirely different scene met our eyes! It was actually just a small log cabin, only partly plastered and roofed with sod. Beside the cabin was a garden plot which had been dug with a spade. The man's face was smeared with dirt from ear to ear, and he looked weird, like some unearthly creature. He was grubbing up stumps near the house, and his wife was poking away in the garden. She reminded us of Robinson Crusoe on an uninhabited island. She was suntanned like a gypsy and was dressed in old, torn overalls. A wide-brimmed hat covered her head.

When mother saw this scarecrow, she started crying again. Later on, father reprimanded the man for writing us such nonsense. But his only answer was, "Let someone else have a taste of our good life here."

Yes, indeed, we did have a taste of that good life, God only knows. First of all, we had a taste of fear. We were so frightened that our souls almost parted from us prematurely — and all over a trifle! One night a few days after our arrival, we were fast asleep, like a litter of pigs on a mattress of hay spread out on the floor, when a frightful racket, as though the end of the world was coming, awakened us. We all sprang to our feet. The first thought that flashed through our minds was that surely it was the Indians — there were so many of them around — laying siege to our fortress. There was no time to waste. Everyone grabbed a weapon. Father leaped for the peg on the wall and snatched down the gun that he brought over with him. Our host grabbed an ax from a nook in the oven;[4] his wife grasped an oven rake and a rolling pin; and we kids, sticks of wood.[5] With shouts of "Cut them down! Kill 'em! Shoot!" we rushed out to fall upon our foe. But did we ever get a surprise when, after chasing around the house several times, we found no one anywhere in sight! After consultation with one another we came to the conclusion that the enemy must have been scared by our war whoops and have taken shelter in the nearby woods, only to fall upon us later with redoubled ferocity. We decided to get back into the house again and wait, weapons poised, for the second attack. Then quietly, without a rustle, we would rush upon the enemy and force him to retreat! But when we reentered the house, we were greeted by such a horrible stench that the only sensible response would have been to stop our noses and run.

Instead, we all began, very cautiously, to search every little nook and cranny. For suppose there was another bomb! To our great astonishment, all we found was a huge glass jug shattered to pieces under the bed; from it flowed a stream of some awful stinking mess.

Later the mystery was solved: our hostess had picked a batch of wild berries, dumped them into the jug, added some sugar, corked it up tightly, and set it under the bed. What was to become of the mixture I do not know. But this I do know: it was that damned juice which caused the explosion and drove such profound fear into our hearts that I shall never forget it.]

Our troubles and worries were only just beginning. The house was small, and there were eighteen of us jammed within its four walls. What was one to do?

My father had brought some money with him, and with it he bought a cow and, later, a horse. Needless to say, I was the cowherd.

One day, as I was herding the cow some two miles away from home, I unexpectedly came upon a tent. In front of it was a bonfire, and in a circle around it, several elderly Indians were squatting. A couple of them were busy skinning some animals, and a squaw was stringing the flesh on a stick and roasting it over the fire. At this sight, I froze on the spot. I felt the urge to run, but my feet refused to obey me. What's more, I could tell that these strange people had spied me, though all they could see was my head, poked above the grass. To my bewilderment, the woman started to move towards me with a piece of her roast. Its appetizing aroma tickled my nose. She offered me the meat, gave me a pat on the back, and rejoined her group. How I enjoyed that meat—as though it were some rare delicacy! I discovered afterwards that it was roasted gopher.

But that was not the end of the story. I suddenly realized to my horror that my cow had vanished. There was not a trace of her. I burst into tears and reluctantly decided to go back home. The path I followed ran along a river. I happened to turn my eyes towards the stream, and lo and behold, there were the horns of my cow sticking out of the water! I could not help but cry all the harder now, and I ran home as fast as I could, yelling, "Help! Come quickly! Our cow has drowned!"

In an instant, we were all racing to the scene of the tragedy. When we got there, the cow was serenely cropping the tender green grass along the riverbank. She seemed happy to see us and greeted us with a moo that probably meant, "See, you foolish humans, how easily you can be scared?" For a long time afterwards, that incident was the subject of many jokes.

Winter was setting in. Dreading the idea of having to spend the season in such cramped quarters, my father dug a cave in a riverbank, covered it with turf, and there was our apartment, all ready to move into. Oh, how fortunate we felt! We would not have traded that root cellar for a royal palace. [To this spot, we carried hay in bed sheets on our backs and stacked it. We also dragged firewood on our backs and made other preparations.

Day by day, our provisions ran lower and lower. The older folk were able to put up with hunger, but the famished children howled pitifully, like wolves.

One day I sneaked into our hostess' garden and pulled a turnip. Then I slipped out of the patch and ran as fast as I could into a gorge where I planned to hide myself in the tall grass and enjoy a real treat. Unfortunately, our hostess spied me, grabbed a club, and chased after me with the speed of a demon. To escape, I hid in some tall grass, but this heartless woman searched until she found me. There she stood over me and, as she raised her club, hissed, "You detestable intruder! One blow with this, and you'll be dead like a dog."

Fear of death made me forget about the turnip. It did not matter now how hungry I was: life was still sweet. And the woman was so ferocious that one blow of that club would certainly have meant the end of my life.

With tears in my eyes I began to plead, "Auntie darling, forgive me. I'll never again set my foot in your garden as long as I live."[6]

Spitting at me with disgust the woman said, "Remember! Write that down on your forehead."

And so, for a piddling turnip, I almost paid with my life.]

Came winter. Our cow stopped giving milk. Aside from bread, there was nothing to eat at home. Was one to gnaw the walls? One time I happened to notice tears rolling down mother's cheeks as she sipped something from a small pot. We children began to weep with her. "Mother, why are you crying? Won't you let us taste what you're eating?"

Mother divided the gruel among us. She tried to say something, but all she could manage was "My chil —"; further words died on her lips. Only a moan of anguish escaped from her breast. We learned afterwards that, late in the fall, mother had visited the garden of our former host and painstakingly raked the ground for potatoes that had been too small to be worth picking at potato-digging time. She had found a few tiny ones, no larger than hazel nuts. From these potatoes, she had made a gruel that tasted like potato soup, and it was this gruel which we children shared, tears flooding our eyes. Who knows how we would have managed if father had not brought his gun from the old country. With it he went hunting, and we had game all winter.

Before spring arrived, father went to look for a farm. He found one some fifteen miles to the west of us, and we began to build a house. [We dug a round pit in the ground about five yards in diameter, just deep enough to scrape the black earth off the top and reach clay underneath. We mixed hay and water with the clay and kneaded it with our bare feet. With this clay, we plastered our house. In the spring, we moved into it. By that time, all our provisions had run out.]

And so it was that father left home one day, on foot, prepared to tramp hundreds of miles to find a job. He left us without a piece of bread, to the mercy of fate.

While father was away, mother dug a plot of ground and planted the wheat she had brought from the old country, tied up in a small bundle. Every day, she watered it with her tears.

That done, there was no time to waste; every moment was precious. Mother and I began to clear our land. But since I was hardly strong enough for the job, I helped by grabbing hold of the top of each bush and pulling on it while mother cut the roots with the ax. Next we dug the ground with spades. How well did I do? At best, I had barely enough strength to thrust half the depth of the blade into the ground, no deeper. But that did not excuse me from digging. Where the ground was hard, mother had to correct my work, and thus the two of us cleared and dug close to four acres of land.

We lived on milk. One meal would consist of sweet milk

Mr. and Mrs. Joe Wacha plastering their house, near Vita, Manitoba, 1916

followed by sour milk; the next meal would consist of sour milk followed by sweet milk. We looked like living corpses.

[In the beginning of our life in Canada, old and young alike had to work grievously hard, often in the cold and in hunger. The effects of this hard work can now be painfully felt in even the tiniest bones of our bodies.

Oftentimes, from the depths of some long-suffering breast and lonely heart, there rose a new but sad song:

> At the foot of a hill, by a river
> In my lovely country
> There nestles my beloved native village
> Thither my eyes turn longingly
>
> Beside a knoll, near an orchard
> There stands my little cottage
> In the cottage my father and mother
> And all our family dwell
>
> O, falcon, dear falcon,
> Your wings take you the world o'er
> Tell me what news you have
> Of my father and mother
>
> Are they well? and how are
> My brothers? the rest of my kin?
> Does my little native cottage
> Still look the same?
>
> Is the green maple tree
> Still standing by the gate?
> Has my young orchard
> Grown up more beautiful?
>
> O, to see once again
> My little native cottage!
> O, to make merry at home
> For yet another hour!
>
> For in this world there is no other
> Like one's father and mother;
> There's nothing more lovely
> Than one's little native cottage.
>
> O, cottage, my beloved cottage,
> How dear you are to me!
> Some irresistible strange force
> Always draws me to you.][7]

Our Rumanian neighbor, who lived a mile from our place, had made himself a small handmill for grinding wheat into flour. In the fall, when our wheat was ripe, mother reaped it very thoroughly, every last head of it, rubbed the kernels out, winnowed the grain, and poured it into a sack. Then she sent me with this grain — about eight pounds of it — to have it ground at our neighbor's mill.

It was the first time I had ever been to his place. As soon as I entered the vestibule of the house, I could see the hand mill in the corner. Now a new problem faced me: I had not the faintest idea how to operate the mill, and there was no one around to show me. I sat down and began to cry. After a while, the neighbor's wife showed up and spoke to me, but I could not understand her so I just kept on crying. I had the feeling that she was scolding me for sneaking into her house. I pointed to the bag of wheat. She understood what I wanted, pointed to the hand mill, and went inside the house, leaving the door open. She sat down at the table, picked up a piece of bread which was as dark as the ground we walked on, dipped it in salt, and munched away at it.

As I watched her, I almost choked with grief. Oh, how strong was my urge to throw myself at her feet and plead for at least one bite of that bread. But, as she obviously was not thinking of me, I got ahold of myself. That piece of bread might well have been the last she had in the house. That experience gave me the most profound shock of my entire life. No one can fully appreciate what I went through unless he has lived through something similar himself.

Continually swallowing my saliva, I kept grinding the wheat until I had finished. Then I ran home with that little bit of flour, joyfully looking forward to the moment when we, too, would have bread.

But my joy quickly evaporated. Mother pondered a moment and said, "This will make two or three loaves of bread, and the flour will be all gone. Not enough to eat and not enough to feast our eyes upon. I'm going to cook cornmeal for you; it will last longer." And so we teased ourselves with cornmeal for some time.[8]

On his way home from the other side of Brandon, where he'd been working, father stopped at Yorkton and bought a fifty-pound sack of flour. He carried it home on his back every inch of the twenty-eight miles. When we saw him coming home, we bounced with excitement and greeted him with joyous laughter mixed with tears. And all this excitement over the prospect of a piece of bread! Father had not earned much money, for he had lost a lot of time job-hunting. Then, at work, he had fallen from a stack onto the tines of a pitchfork and been laid up for a long time. But he had managed to earn something like twenty dollars, enough for flour to last us for a time.[9]

Outdoor bake oven, 1916

The coming of winter presented new problems. We had nothing to wear on our feet. Something had to be done about that. Mother had brought a couple of woolen sheets from the old country. From these she sewed us footwear that kept our feet warm all winter.

That winter our horse died. We were now left with only one horse and he was just a year-old colt, though he looked like a two-year old. Father made a harness from some ropes, and a sled, and began to break him in.

[...Even in winter we had no rest. We had settled in a low-lying area. In the summertime, water lay everywhere, and the croaking of frogs filled the air. And it never rained but poured in those days. Often the downpour continued for two or three weeks without a letup. In the winter, the water in the lakes froze up, the wells — always few in number — dried up, and there was nothing one could do about it. We were concerned not so much about ourselves as about our few head of livestock, which would have no water. We could not let them die; a way had to be found to obtain water for them.

Father found a piece of tin somewhere, shaped it into a trough, built an enclosure out of stones, placed the trough over it, built a fire in the enclosure under the trough, kept the trough filled with snow, and, as the snow melted, collected the water in a tub at the bottom end of the trough. But this was not the best way to water cattle. A cow could drink up a couple of tubs of water at a time and then look around and moo for more.

As a result, we messed around with snow all winter long, until at times the marrow in our bones was chilled. And talk about snow in those days! Mountains of it! Your cattle might be lowing pitifully in the stable, and you could not get to them because heaps of snow blocked your way. It might take a hard morning's work before a tunnel could be dug to the stable, and the cattle fed.]

During Lent, we ran out of flour. Although there were still a few cents in the house, it was not easy to get to Yorkton because of snowdrifts. One evening, father decided to call on our Rumanian neighbor and borrow some flour to tide us over until we could buy our own. He was gone a long time. We waited until midnight, but still no father. And so we went to bed thinking that perhaps the two men had had a lot to talk about, for the Rumanian spoke a little Ukrainian. Then, too, maybe father had decided to stay overnight.

In the morning, father dragged himself home, more dead than alive. Without suspecting anything wrong, mother asked, "Did you have to stay there overnight? Was it so far to come home?"

Then father began to explain. "What I lived through last night, I would hate to see happen even to my worst enemy. When I got to the neighbor's, I only stayed for about an hour. I explained why I had come, he let me have half a bag of flour, and I left for home. But the blizzard was so fierce that I strayed from my path and went God knows where. I tramped all night with with the bag of flour on my back. I was so exhausted that several times I felt like sitting down for a rest. However, I had enough presence of mind to realize that if I did, I would never get up again. So I summoned all my strength and trudged on.

"Came dawn, I looked about but in no way could I get my bearings. Not far off I saw a house. Worn down by exhaustion, I proceeded to crawl toward it. Even as I got closer to the house, I still could not recognize it. It was a strange house. I had never seen it before. I concluded that I must have wandered a long way during the night. But there I was. I knocked at the door. A man answered and came out. Horrified to see me in this plight, he clutched his hair and exclaimed, 'Oh, dear! You didn't get home last night, Mr. Oliynyk? Oh, you poor soul!'

"It was then that I got my bearings. I recognized the man — he was the same one I had visited last night. He took me in. I got warmed up and recounted my unfortunate experience. The man then dressed up, put the sack of flour on his back, took me to within sight of our house, and went back home.

"There's my whole story. And if you want proof of it, retrace my footsteps and you will see for yourselves under what sort of eiderdown cover I slept last night."

We put father to bed and, to satisfy our curiosity, went out to see what he was talking about. About a quarter of a mile from our Rumanian neighbor's home, there was a deep ravine. It was around this gully that father had tramped all night. The storm had abated by midnight, and by morning he had beaten a path solid enough to roll a ball on.

Father's mishap was not without its harmful effect on his health. He was confined to bed for over a month. His fingers were frozen, and all the skin on his feet peeled off. We barely escaped becoming orphans, and father barely escaped ending up as an invalid for the rest of his life.

[Ours was a life of hard work, misery, and destitution. Things got a little better only after we acquired a yoke of oxen to work with. But when we first got them, we experienced some unhappy and frustrating moments.

The first time that we harnessed the oxen, we hitched them to the plow. As soon as the plowshare dug into the ground, presto! our oxen balked and refused to budge. Then, as if acting on command, they both lay down. Try as we might to make them get up on their feet—pleading as best we knew how, then persuading them with the switch—the dumb beasts would only lie down again.

We had a spirited but hair-brained young horse which was causing us a lot of grief. Father turned to me: "As the last resort, let's have that confounded creature here."

We hitched the horse in front of the oxen and — "Giddap!" The horse tugged with all his might but the oxen would not budge. It was as if they were under a curse. The plow jerked forward just far enough to shear the heel piece of the ox on the right. Then the horse gave another tug, and the traces snapped. This time the horse whirled around in a flash, reared on his hind legs, and lunged at the horns of the oxen. One of them pierced his shoulder blade. It all happpened so suddenly — like the crack of a whip.

We were all in tears. Father cursed. We unhitched the injured creatures and went back to digging with our spades until the animals had licked at their wounds and regained strength.

Our cattle always grazed together with Paul Denys'. In the evening, we had to look for them and bring them home. One evening, it was my turn. I searched until nightfall but in vain. Then we all searched for two long days, but still no cattle. It was as if the earth had swallowed them up. "Wait," I said to Father, "I'm going to get on that horse, and I'm going to find the creatures — they're there somewhere."

I mounted the horse and set out. Beginning at Paul's farm, a

*Ukrainian farmers clearing and plowing with oxen near
Saint Julien, Saskatchewan, around 1908*

large lake stretched to the north. Though the ground was soft
between the lake and the fence, the cattle used to pass that way, and
they had beat a path which was now full of holes. In order to save
time, I decided to follow the path all the way instead of going
around the lake. But about half way down, my crippled horse got
stuck in the mud. Then, with an enormous surge of effort, he gave

one big leap and got himself out. But at the same time, he left the path and pressed against the fence. The barbed wire scraped off his skin, and the sharp barbs cut the flesh on my legs to the bone. With all my might, I tried to steer the horse back onto the path, but the harder I tried, the closer he pressed against the fence. There was no help for us. The whole flank of the horse was getting skinned. And bits of flesh dangled from my leg. I had no recourse but to dismount and return home. But what was the good of it when there was neither doctor nor medicine available?

My leg took a long time to heal. And the damned horse suffered, too, before his flank was better.

And the cattle? We looked for them for about a week, but in vain. Since our first cow had been bought at Yorkton, father and Paul decided to search for it there.

And, sure enough, there it was! After three years that cow had not forgotten its former home and had led our cattle all the way to Yorkton, a distance of twenty-eight miles. Since the cows had not been milked for such a long time, they all dried up. But it was good to find them anyway.

With each day of labor, our poor settlers could see some progress. They now lived in hastily built houses, as everyone was sick and tired of living in damp, smelly root cellars. Although these houses lacked in comfort, there was at least fresh air in them. By now, each settler had dug up a piece of land and owned a few head of cattle and other livestock.]

Letters from the old country brought news that several families from the neighboring village — the Stratychuks and some others — were leaving for Canada. Father wrote to grandpa (his father) in the old country and asked him to send a set of iron harrow-teeth with the emigrants.

In the spring, father was able to get some seed wheat. When he finished seeding our tiny, little field, he left home to look for a job again. At home, the family buckled down to clearing, digging, and haying. Mother mowed the hay with a scythe, and we children raked it, carried it home on our backs, and stacked it. We also brought a supply of wood for the winter.

In the meantime, the people from the old country had arrived. This added a touch of brightness to our social life. The newcomers, Mrs. D. F. Stratychuk and Mrs. P. Denys, even helped us to harvest our crop.

The crop yielded well. We had a few good-sized stacks of grain. But I shall never forget that harvest. As I was reaping with a sickle, I cut my finger. The gash was so deep that the finger dangled, just barely held on by the skin. Mother managed to splice it somehow, and the wound healed. But the scar still shows to this very day.

That autumn father's earnings were a little more substantial. He was able to buy another cow and another steer. And he bought me a pair of shoes and material for a skirt. Those shoes meant more to me than any ordinary ones. It seemed as though they came right out of Ivan Franko's tale about Abou-Kazem's slippers.[10] They were about the size of a medium-sized sled. They were made from leather that was no more pliable than tin, and for lacing each had six eyes as large as a cow's; you could not have missed them on the darkest of nights with an inch-and-a-half thickness of rope. They pinched and burned my feet badly enough to bring tears to my eyes.

As for their durability, suffice it to say that when one of us girls got married, she handed the shoes down to the younger sister, and the process was repeated until four of us had worn them, each for a few years. And who knows how many more generations those shoes would have survived if it had not been for mother. She got so disgusted with them that she threw them into the stove one day and burned them.

As for my skirt, it was made of the finest quality "silk," the kind used for making overalls. So one can imagine how I looked in that gorgeous costume. But, poor me, I was quite happy with it.

In the wintertime, father used to ask some of his neighbors to give him a hand in threshing his wheat with flails.[11] Once the threshing was done, he had other work to do, such as making a yoke for the oxen and repairing the harrow and the plow, so that everything would be ready for spring work.

I helped father with spring work. When we did the plowing, father guided the plow by walking behind it and clutching the handles while I drove the oxen. Then came harrowing. Father hitched the horse to the harrow and handed the reins over to me, saying, "Here, this will be your job."

I had scarcely made a couple of rounds when that crazy horse of ours tore himself away from me and took off. He chased around the field like mad until there was nothing left of the harrow but bits and pieces. Did he ever get it from father for smashing the harrow! And so did I for letting the horse get away from me. I bore my punishment stoically in the hope that father's turn for a jig with the horse would come soon, for I well knew the nature of that beast.

That summer, father returned home from work earlier than usual, as his help was needed during harvest. We continued to reap our wheat with sickles, but to cut oats, father used a scythe with a cradle.[12]

At this time, Yakiw Danylchuk (father of the poet John Danylchuk), a carpenter by trade, built himself a hand mill, a large one with a crank.[13] Did I ever have my share of cranking it! I would hitch the horse to our old gig, father would load it with bags of wheat, and I would haul it to Danylchuk's mill. I would stay there several days until I had ground all of the wheat into flour. Then, how glad I was to come home!

After harvest, when our plowing was done, father used to help the neighbors with their plowing until freeze-up.

[There lived in our neighborhood a Ukrainian from Bukovina, one Tanasko Dorosh. Aside from his humdrum everyday life, nothing in the world interested him. He continued to live in his beloved root cellar and never gave a thought to parting with it some day. In the summertime he loafed around and sunned himself, and in the winter, he spent his time on the hearth in his den. Now and then, he would visit us because of some need or just for a little chitchat. He did not like to listen to what others had to say, but it pleased him no end when others listened to him. And he talked mostly on Biblical themes, such as Jesus's sermon about feeding the hungry or taking strangers in. But those who had heard him before were soon tired of his blabbing, all the more so since his actions did not square with his words.

One winter night when our neighbor Paul dropped in to see us, he said to father, "Listen, Dmytro, we've had enough of Tanasko's sermons about living right with one's neighbors; they're coming out of our ears. It would be a good idea to test his sincerity."

"I've thought of it myself, more than once," my father replied, "but there was no real opportunity for it. However, today would be a good time, with the blizzard raging outside. Let's go to Tanasko's and beg for shelter overnight. If he takes us in, it will be a miracle. He will qualify to be counted among the saints in his lifetime. But he must not recognize us; we must change our voices and our speech. We'll try to talk like Doukhobors."[14]

To give the stunt a semblance of reality, my mother wrapped a sheet around her and joined the company.

As our fake travelers approached Tanasko's habitation, the light in his window shone until the crunching of snow under foot could be heard outside the door. Then, out went the light.

Paul knocked at the door first. "Hey, master, we are travelers; for Christ's sake let us in for a while to get warmed up — we are freezing."

But instead of Tanasko, it was his wife who answered the door. She came out with a long fork in her hand and, pointing it to the east, jabbered, "I can't let you in; my husband is not home. Go to the hamlet where you hear the dogs barking. Someone will put you up for the night there."

At this point, mother began to moan, "Oh, oh, oh, honest to God, I'm freezing. Oh, oh, oh!"

Father turned to her in a subdued voice, "Hush, woman. We'll report him to the police tomorrow."

"*Da, da,*" added Paul, "to the police! They'll execute him." And with these words, they set out toward Fedir Stratychuk's place.

After a while, they could hear something puffing behind them. Turning around, they saw Tanasko running after them for all he was worth. He yelled, "Hey, come back! You see, I was not at home. I just got back from the hamlet. Come back, I'll put you up for the night."

Chuckling to herself, mother now wailed even louder that she was freezing.

"*Nyet,*" answered father angrily. "When our old woman freezes to death, you'll answer for it in the court tomorrow."

And they ran as fast as they could until they got to Fedir's.

"You're out of breath," exclaimed Fedir. "A pack of wolves chasing you?"

"A pack? No," answered Paul, "only one wolf, a two-legged one, and he was right at our heels."

"How's that? Who was it?" asked Fedir's wife.

"Who else but Tanasko!" mother explained. "The snow is deep, I got left behind, and Tanasko was catching up to me. Gosh, I thought, if he catches me, he'll drag me into his den, and then how could I explain myself?"

Then all three took turns telling their versions of the story about Tanasko, and they roared with laughter. After a pause Fedir commented gravely, "Here we have an elderly man trying to teach others, but how remote are his words from his actions! He talks about a truly Christian sense of duty but would not let you into his home. He would rather hide himself. Fear of punishment drove him to chase after you almost a mile to call you back. We must be on guard against the likes of him."

One Sunday, mother and Mrs. Denys, dressed up in their Sunday best, took a notion to visit Fedir's wife. As they approached Tanasko's place, they noticed that he was working at something with his broadax. Surprised to see them, he asked, "And where are you two off to in your Sunday best?"

"We're going to visit Mrs. Stratychuk," answered Mrs. Denys. "It's Sunday today, you know."

"Sunday?" groaned Tanasko. "And I wasn't aware of it. Here am I, making an oven rake. God forgive me. I'm going to chop it up into splinters; it would be a sin to use it. But the bread my old woman is baking today is sacred. We have to eat it."

"Well," said mother to her companion as they continued on their way, "one would think that a man living among civilized people would learn civilized ways and not live like a savage who knows nothing."

These two episodes involving Tanasko lost him the respect of his neighbors. No one would stop to talk with him. People taunted him, "Hey, Tanasko, what was it that Christ taught?"

And poor Tanasko, bent in two, would turn away to find an escape. . . .

One day late in the fall, we were stripping the fiber off our hemp plants.[15] Father spun it on a spinning wheel to make rope for tying cattle in their stalls in the winter. While we were busy doing this, our neighbor Paul came with sad news. "Did you hear that Joseph Yakiwchuk has died?"

We were so stunned that we just sat there agape. We had never even heard that he was ill, let alone that he was dead.

"Well," began father, "he was a good man. May God receive him into His kingdom. We'll have to go and pay our last respects to the deceased as our Christian custom bids."

The sun was dipping toward the horizon. Mother and Paul's wife made two small candles from wax brought from the old country, for it was not proper to visit empty-handed on such an occasion. We wished father and Paul a good journey, then got down on our knees and piously offered our prayers before the throne of God for the soul of the deceased.

Our "pilgrims" had a long walk ahead of them, some fifteen miles. By the time they got there, it was late night. But did they ever get a surprise when, as they approached the house of the deceased, they could not detect the slightest stir in the yard. What was even stranger, there was no light in the house.

"It's just the same as usual," said father to Paul. "We'll knock at the door."

Inside, a light flashed on. Mrs. Yakiwchuk asked them in. Now came the surprise of their life — there was Joseph, alive and well! He greeted the two with "What the deuce brought you here at this unearthly hour?"

"Why ask?" answered Paul. "We came with these candles in our hands to offer prayers for your soul." And then they explained.

"It appears," concluded Joseph, "that some rascal has played a good joke on us. But since you are already here, be my guests. We seldom see one another because of the distance. Stay overnight, and tomorrow, God willing, you can go back."

The next day, our pilgrims returned home and told their story We all had a good laugh.

In our neighborhood, there were settlers of other nationalities, mainly Rumanian. One of them put on a wedding for his daughter and invited us to attend. We accepted first because there had not been such an event in the few years that we had been in Canada, and second, out of simple curiosity to see a Rumanian ceremony.

Well, we did see it, with all its comical features. We Ukrainians have more than a few ceremonies, but there is no end to theirs. On the other hand, they have only one kind of dance. They form couples and dance in a circle. When they finish the dance, they start

71

all over again. We did not hear any singing. Through all the dancing, they kept chanting over and over again to the tune of the music, "Hop-zop-zop, hop-zop-zop," and the women added in their high-pitched voices, "Dzyob-dzyob-dzyob, dzyob-dzyob-dzob." And the Ukrainians from Bukovina joined them but with a slightly different version, "Hop-zop-zop, hop-zop-zop," ending with "Hopai-zop!"

All that "dzyobing" stuck in our childish minds, and for a long time after the wedding, we repeated the chant incessantly wherever we went. We even "dzyobed" in our sleep.]

The town of Canora was founded five miles from our place. Our people were quite happy about that, and they were happy when its first store was opened by a Jewish merchant.[16] For one thing, we were fed up with traveling all that distance to Yorkton to do our shopping. Secondly, with a Jew we could always speak in our own language, for at that time how many of us immigrants could speak English? When we did try, it was only by means of sign language.

[One day a number of country folk who happened to be in town gathered at the railway station to meet the train. Suddenly, a Bukovinian fellow, Ivan Kobylka, appeared in their midst, apparently out of thin air. His sheepskin coat was spotlessly white. He wore his best shoes and his best pantaloons, neatly pleated as was customary when one went to town; and his long hair, generously greased, fairly gleamed in the sun.

When the train ground to a stop at the station, the conductor got off and immediately focused his attention on Kobylka. He ambled up to him, gave him a pat on the back, and, jabbering all the while, pulled the sleeve of the sheepskin coat off Kobylka's arm, slipped behind him and presto! the coat was now on the conductor's back. It was done so smoothly one would have thought it an act performed on a theater stage.

At that moment, the train started to move out of the station, and the conductor quickly boarded the coach on the tail end. Poor Mr. Kobylka! He began to run after the train, yelling, "Hey, listen here! Give me back my coat, or God will strike you!"

But the conductor only waved his hand and shouted back, "Good-bye, mister!"

The poor fellow chased the train for about a quarter of a mile, but realizing that he could not catch up, he came back cursing the day and hour when, for no reason at all, he had wandered onto the station platform. And so his curiosity ended in the loss of his sheepskin coat, unrecovered to this very day.]

Here again I recall a humorous but unfortunate incident which took place — it seems like only yesterday that it happened. Mother had saved up several dozen eggs for sale, so father hitched up that rambunctious horse of ours and settled himself into the seat of the buggy, all set to go to town. He looked so imposing, like some high-ranking dignitary. He clicked his tongue to the horse and drove off to Canora. But he had hardly gone half a mile from home when we heard a loud shout, a terrible crash, and a racket as though the world was coming to an end. We ran for all we were worth to see what had happened. And this was the scene that met our eyes: father, pitched out of the buggy, landed on a rock. Gripping his back, he was moaning and cursing in the same breath. There was no sign of the eggs except for broken shells. Strewn all around were pieces of what had been the buggy. That confounded brute of a horse, the cause of all the mess, was standing over father, holding father's hat in his teeth and fanning him with it as if to say, "Sorry I caused you pain; now I'll cool you off." It took a long time for father to recover from that mishap.

The troubles that horse brought upon us stemmed from our good care of him. But he had one good trait: he never ran too far away from his starting point. He would chase around until he realized that he was dragging something behind him. Then he would stop or run straight toward you for help.

Year by year the cultivated area of our farm grew in size. And when the field got too large to be harvested with sickles, father had to buy a binder. For the first couple of years we used it, we hitched our oxen to it. That was a miserable experience. Cutting grain of medium height posed no problem, but if it was heavy or lying flat and you had to give the binder a little more speed, you could not make the oxen move faster even by lighting a fire under them. They kept to the same slow pace no matter what. The only way to cope with this problem was to buy another horse. A team of horses made harvesting so much easier.

During the long winter evenings, I taught younger children to read in Ukrainian. Among my students were a girl or non-Ukrainian descent and an elderly gentleman. There were no schools anywhere around in those days. Children grew up like barbarians. . . .

[We had quite a few books at home. Father had brought a lot of them from the old country, all on serious subjects. Later on, when Ukrainian newspapers began to be published, none of them escaped father's attention. Even if he had to go without food and live on water for a whole week, he found the money for newspaper subscriptions. Since there were several literate people in our community, they used to get together at our home on the long winter evenings, to read the papers and discuss their contents. Many a sunrise found these men, though weary from the previous day's hard toil, going without a wink of sleep to forge a happier lot for themselves and their children.

Ukrainian family harvesting, 1918

Those sleepless nights were not spent in vain. In 1904-05, thanks
to the efforts of our pioneer fathers, a small but beautiful school
was built. Its first teacher was the scholarly and patriotic Ukrainian,
the late Joseph Bychynsky.]

[In regards to the young people of those days: they had little
education but a much better moral upbringing than the young
people of today. Parents were treated as parents ought to be.
Father's word was sacred law. Older people were always treated
with respect. Young people were industrious and thrifty because
they knew that every little thing and every cent came the hard
way.]

As for churches or Ukrainian priests, you could not have found
one if you'd searched the country with a fine-tooth comb.
Occasionally a priest would stray our way, but he was what we
called an "Indian priest," and we could not understand him, nor he
us. Our poor settlers consulted among themselves and decided to
meet every Sunday and sing at least those parts of the liturgy that
were meant to be sung by the cantor. Since our house was large
enough, that was where the meetings were held. On Sunday
morning, everyone hurried to our house the way one would to
church. The late Fedir Stratychuk . . . was an excellent cantor. Even
yet I can hear his voice in my mind. W. Gabora and my father
harmonized with him, and all the others followed them. And so it
was that we were able to gratify, at least partially, the longings of
our souls.

In due course, the Bukovinians built themselves a church in

which services were at first conducted by a visiting Russian priest. Often we were invited to attend but we could not understand their service, which was in Rumanian.

Later, other priests, the so-called *Serafymtsi,* made their appearance.[17] [One of them, Julian Bohonko, announced the first blessing of the *paska* at the home of Tserkowniak, ten miles away from our place.[18] What rejoicing! Mother began to bake *paska* and to decorate *pysanky,*[19] and tears of joy rolled down her emaciated cheeks.

That year Easter came very early. It was the Saturday before Easter, but only here and there was the snow beginning to melt. The day before, a severe blizzard had piled up banks of snow and drifted over all the roads. But there was no power on earth which could have stopped us from carrying out our plans.

Mother wrapped the Easter goodies in an immaculately white tablecloth, and in the afternoon father and I set out on foot toward Tserkowniak's. At first everything seemed to be going fine, and I managed to keep up with father, but as we got farther along—good Lord! I sank into snow up to my waist and did not have the strength to get out. Father had to help me, though not without a few harsh words. With great difficulty, we reached our destination.

Although we were dead tired, our souls were heartened early Sunday morning by the glad Easter hymn, "Christ is Risen from the Dead." Immediately after the service, we hastened to return home. It was already dark when we got back. We had fasted all day long, not only father and I, but also those at home, waiting with deep reverence for the gifts from God which had been blessed by the priest. . . .

Whatever the course of later events, it must be recognized that, in the beginning, the pioneer priests contributed a great deal to the cultural development of our people here, in what was then a foreign land to them. And for their efforts and troubles, they sought no favors from anyone. They suffered the same woes and miseries as did everyone else. In short, they proved themselves to be true sons of the Ukrainian people. And some of them, like the late Osyp Cherniawsky, even laid down their lives for the sacred ideals for which they toiled with such dedication.][20]

We were well pleased with Osyp Cherniawsky's work as a priest, all the more so because he was a true flesh-and-blood Ukrainian. He helped to open the eyes of many to the true nature of Catholicism, its aims, objectives, and so on. His witticisms and jokes brightened the lives of many, even in their gloomiest moments and most difficult circumstances, though he himself suffered incredible hardships and trials.

Let me give you one example. The community built him a small log cabin on W. Owchar's farm. It was chinked hastily with clay.

Into this "home," he brought his family from Alberta. One day, he paid us a visit and pleaded with father, "Let your Marusia come and whitewash the interior of our sty, at least after a fashion, so we will not have to prowl around in the shadowy candlelight and collide with one another, forehead to forehead. Maybe if the place were whitewashed, we could see one another better."

To this father replied, "Sorry, but it can't be done. We are so busy now there is no time to scratch one's head."

Cherniawsky responded, "Mr. Oliynyk, I would rather see a hundred traitors afflicted with sores than hear you denying me help."

This remark softened father, and he yielded to the appeal with a smile. In short, Cherniawsky was the sort of person who stood firmly on principles and did not waver, while there were those who betrayed their own and served others.

In those days, no one dreamed of such luxuries as paint or lime. For whitewashing jobs, people used a kind of ash-gray clay found under the surface of the ground cover in swampy areas. They dug this clay, pressed it into flat cakes, and dried it. Dissolved in water, it was used for whitewashing.

Bitter and unenviable were our beginnings, but by hard work and with God's help, we gradually got established. Not very far from our place a few neighbors pooled their resources and bought a steam threshing outfit in partnership. Father decided it was time, we, too, had our threshing done by a threshing machine.

It was at this time that I had another misadventure which almost cost me my life. Water for the steam engine was hauled in a wheeled water tank, but since we could not afford such a vehicle, water had to be brought in barrels. This was my job. I hitched the horses to the wagon and drove to a neighbor's place about two miles away to borrow a few more barrels. It was evening, and a beautiful moon shone brightly. The neighbor loaded the barrels onto the wagon, and I started out for home. After traveling only a short distance, the horses were frightened by something and took off like a whirlwind. I pulled on the reins with all my might to hold them back, but to no avail. The clatter of the barrels on the wagon only made them gallop all the faster. I began to scream in an odd voice. Neighbors who lived along the road heard the clamor, ran out, and tried to stop the runaways, but their efforts were in vain. The horses must have gone berserk. The wagon jerked and tossed me up and down and from side to side until I was afraid my soul would jump out of my body. But the horses continued to gallop. They came to our farm, went right through a barbed-wire fence, and kept on galloping. The folks at home heard the racket and my desperate cry for help. They dashed out of the house, grabbing bed sheets on their way. They ran into the path of the wagon and flung

Ukrainians threshing with their own outfit at Stuartburn, Manitoba, 1902

the sheets over the horses' heads as soon as they got close enough. To our amazement, the trick worked. The horses reared on their hind legs and came to a sudden halt. I owe my life to the double wagon box.[21] Without it, I would have been tossed out of the wagon and would have met my death.

In 1908, father traded farms with an Englishman, and our family moved thirty miles farther north, to the Hyas district. [The origin of the name "Hyas" goes back to the time when our people used oxen for driving and urged them on by shouting "*Heys, ta heys!*" That *heys* appealed so much to the English people that they named the district "Hyas." Before that, it was called "Ulric."

By moving to Hyas, we had to start all over again and suffer the same hardships as in the beginning. But hope of better times lifted our spirits and gave us courage and strength to face future labors.]

Such were the tremendous hardships our people had to endure in the early days of immigration. Since there were as yet no railways, they were compelled to travel hundreds of miles on foot. Toiling in cold and hunger, they cleared the forests, cleanded the land of rocks, and converted the inaccesible areas into fertile fields. Many of the pioneers who came here in the prime of their lives are no longer with us. Those who are still with us are stooped with age;

tomorrow it will be their turn to leave us for their eternal rest. Should all this be forgotten? No. The hardships, trials, and tribulations of our first settlers ought to be recorded for posterity.

5 YUREICHUK / KOTYK
Encounters with the Indians

The two stories that follow tell of the first meetings between the Ukrainian immigrants in Canada and the natives of this country, the Indians. In each case, the encounter proved beneficial to the Ukrainians and enabled them to discover for themselves some of the fine qualities of the Indian people, particularly their hospitality and willingness to help those in need.

In each case, the story is told by one woman and recorded by another, Dokia Humenna, in her book Vichni vohni Alberty (Eternal Flames of Alberta) *which was published in Edmonton in 1959. Maria Yureichuk's story appeared as "How We Traveled On a Raft from Edmonton to Our Homestead" and Mrs. Kotyk's as "My First Encounter with the Indians." Yureichuk is from Hamlin and Kotyk from Smoky Lake, both in Alberta.*

Maria Yureichuk: Our Trip by Raft

It was towards the end of September [1899] when our group of eight families, five from Bukovina and two from Galicia, arrived at Strathcona in Alberta.* The Bukovinians visited with their acquaintances here, and on the third day, they hired a wagon for fifteen dollars per family to take them to Ihlyky, now the district of Andrew, in Alberta. We could have gone with them, but we did not have enough money. All we had was $7.50, and we needed it to buy food.

Our husbands then decided to look for homesteads closer to Edmonton. They tramped all over the country for a whole week, famished and exhausted, trying to find a homestead in the woods, in the sandy areas, and in the muskegs, but they could not find any good land. All the good land had already been taken. One would have to go some hundreds of miles farther east or north. The man who accompanied my husband in search of a homestead at least had the good fortune to meet up with an old acquaintace who lived with his family in the sandy area.

*Strathcona — part of Edmonton (Dokia Humenna).

Woman and child, Sheho, Saskatchewan, around 1907. Under pioneer conditions, women were challenged to do things they had never attempted before.

I was left alone with my children, lodged in a livery barn in Strathcona. As long as there were other people around, I was not lonely, but as soon as my husband departed and I was left alone with the children, my heart broke with loneliness. I almost died of boredom. I wept, my children wept, and my despair almost drove me crazy. We could, of course, have gone to Victoria, but we could find no one who would transport us there, to Pasichny's place (we had his address), for less than twenty dollars.[1] We did not have that kind of money, but there was still no point in our staying at Strathcona with winter coming if we had no money to live on.

To solve the problem, my husband decided to build a raft which would take us the 120 miles east down the river to Pasichny's . . . on the bank of the North Saskatchewan. My husband was strong and healthy, but he was a clumsy *hutsul*.[2] We were called *hutsuls* because we had lived in the Carpathian Mountains of Galicia. My husband had worked there driving log booms down the Cheremosh River as far as Moldavia. In Bukovina, he had heard that people were leaving for Canada, and all of a sudden, without giving any thought to the problem of how to make a living there, he, too, had taken a notion to pull up stakes and go to Canada.

As soon as he had put a raft together on the river at Strathcona, we carried our luggage down and loaded it on. Everything went well until we started to move our chest, which contained all our most precious belongings and weighed around 400 pounds. Spectators began to congregate to watch our stupidity and have fun at our expense. My husband could not speak English and did not know how to ask someone to cart the chest to the raft. As our luck would have it, someone happened to come by with a wagon. Seeing us struggle as we rolled the chest along the street, he drove up to us and asked us to load the chest onto the wagon. My husband then walked ahead of the wagon to lead the way to the raft. When the wagon reached the river, the driver chuckled to himself, and the kids from town came running down to the river to watch us float away. Everyone had a good laugh, and we heard someone say, "Galician go homestead." The kind man who had helped us did not want to accept any pay for carting the chest; he only waved to us and said, "Bye-bye."

It was already afternoon when we launched our raft and shoved off from the shore. The water in the river was very shallow, and the raft drifted sluggishly. Toward evening of the next day we docked at Fort Saskatchewan, twenty-five miles east of Edmonton. We met some German people who could speak Russian, and we learned from them that Victoria was still a long distance away and that it would take us a whole week to reach it. We had just enough food to last us a couple of days, so my husband dashed to the store at the Fort and bought some potatoes, pork fat, and bread. On the raft, we had a pan in which we built a fire and baked potatoes. We smeared them with the pork fat, and that was our meal.

To shelter us from rain and storm, and to provide a place for the children to sleep at night, my husband built a hut on the raft. As the raft floated at night, one of us would nap while the other kept watch lest we founder on the shoals or smash up against the riverbank.

On the third night, heavy snow began to fall. We wrapped ourselves in blankets and huddled in the hut. We failed to notice that our raft had run aground on a sandy shoal and come to a dead stop. To free it, we had to get down into the water with our bare feet, but no matter how hard we pushed the raft and struggled with it, in no way could we dislodge it from the sandbar. Morning found us there, crouched at the entrance of our shelter. And the snow came down like an avalanche, as though it were trying to bury us alive. To pitch a tent was out of the question, for the snow that had fallen during the night was over twenty inches deep. The firewood that my husband had picked up in Edmonton got soaked and would not burn. We were so cold our teeth chattered, and we were afraid that by morning it would be the end of us. I wept bitterly over my fate and cursed my husband and his Canada.

It was already late morning when some Indians who lived near the river noticed a strange object sitting on top of the sandbank and came down to investigate. They took us into their home (an old shack), made some tea, gave us some dry biscuits to eat, and we gradually thawed out. Our children were not as cold as my husband and I. They had slept all through the night tucked in a featherbed that I had brought from the old country. But we had both caught severe colds as we waded in the icy water trying to free the raft from the sand.

I will not forget that incident as long as I live. Just picture what it was like to be out there on a river in the middle of nowhere, surrounded by water, wading in the mud, heavy snow beating down on you without a letup. You don't know where you are or how far from your destination, and no people around to help you push the raft back into the water. It was a great blessing from God that the Indians caught sight of our raft, for without their help we would have perished there.

The Indians who rescued us and our raft had been fording the river at this spot. They safely removed all our possessions from the raft, but when it came to our chest, they too had problems with it.

As soon as we had warmed ourselves, the Indians tried to tell us something, but we could not understand them at all. My husband had been advised in Edmonton that if we happened to meet someone on the way, we should say to him, "Me go homestead, Pasichny, Victoria." He repeated those words to the Indians. It seemed that they understood him, and they asked him, "You Galician?" My husband did not know what those words meant, but he nodded his head as if to say "yes." They then motioned to him to come outside and pointed to a path that led up the hill. They told him to follow the path all the way; it would take him to a Galician's place. That was where Steve Ratsoy lived. One Indian spreaded out all the fingers on his both hands to indicate that the distance was ten miles. My husband understood and set out.

He got as far as Pakan, and there some half-breeds directed him to Ratsoy's place. Ratsoy had been living there for two years already and had his own team of horses. In the meantime, the children and I stayed with the Indians. They had children, too, and their children wanted to talk with our children, but unfortunately they could not understand one another.

Toward evening, Steve Ratsoy came for us in a wagon and took us to his place at Pakan.

Mrs. M. Kotyk: Lost in the Wilds

I came to Canada when I was twelve years old. At the farm there was nothing to eat, so my parents took me to the immigration

*Students at the presbyterian mission, Teulon,
Manitoba. Life in the new world could be strange and
frightening for immigrant children.*

*"Galician" hay market in Edmonton, 1903; perhaps the place
to which Mrs. Kotyk was taken by the Indian man.*

building in Edmonton. I wanted to find a job as a housemaid. Some English-speaking women who came to hire me took one look and concluded, "She still needs someone to look after herself." No one hired me. I stayed there three days, and then I could no longer afford to buy any food. Besides, I had to pay for my overnight accommodation.

On the fourth day, I left Edmonton and headed for home on foot. But instead of setting out toward the east as I should have done, I set out toward the north where even an adult would have got lost, for it was total wilderness, and there was not a single settler there yet.

My route took me past a tepee, a rather fine-looking dwelling alongside the road. I began to hurry in order to get past it quickly, for I had been warned at home to be on guard against a tribe of black people in Canada who were called Indians and who killed and ate our people. Just as I was about to pass by the tepee, an old Indian with braided hair rushed out of it, grabbed me by the hand, and began to drag me inside. Although I struggled and resisted him with all my might, he had me inside the tepee in no time and made me sit on an animal skin which was spread out on the ground. I was seized by fear. "There is no question; he is going to kill me right here and now."

Meanwhile, his wife was busying herself by the fire. She poured some soup into a cup, handed it to me, and gave me a biscuit. I was terribly frightened and trembled like a leaf. In sign language, I tried to tell her that I was not hungry.

The old man opened some boxes and took out of them several pairs of moccassins. He sat down beside me and proceeded to take off my shoes. "This is it," I said to myself. "He is getting me ready for the knife." I had on my old-country shoes, and I wore the stockings that mother had knitted for me, with designs on them. He examined them, shook his head, and tried a pair of moccasins on my feet. That pair was too large. He searched and found another pair. They were just the right size for my feet. He put them on and laced them up tight. Then he rummaged through his boxes once again. He took some bread and meat out of one box, made up a package of food, handed it to me, took me by the hand, and gently led me out of the tepee.

Back to Edmonton! Once in the city, he led me to the market square. There were many Ukrainians there who had come from different places, and he released me right into their midst. "Here," he spoke, "these are your people."

Truly, that kindhearted old Indian saved me from a disastrous end in that northern wilderness.

⑥ ANNA FARION
Homestead Girlhood

Like Mrs. Kotyk, the young Anna Farion was expected to help support her family. Everyone old enough to earn a wage did so, except for mother who stayed on the homestead with the smaller children. Anna Farion's recollections of her own work and of her mother's death were first published in the Almanac of the Ukrainian Voice *in 1942, under the title* "Moyi spomyny" *(My Recollections).*

I came to Canada from the village of Zawale, district of Terebowla, Galicia, in the year 1897. I was seventeen years old.

A year earlier, my father's nephew, Wasyl Ksionzyk, together with another relative from Terebowla, had emigrated to Canada, and in their letters to father they boasted about their good fortunes here. They claimed they had all kinds of land, woods, and pastures. They never lacked meat, they said, as rabbits came hopping right into the house, and deer and moose roamed in herds. (They mentioned nothing about lack of bread and salt; we made that discovery for ourselves when we got to Canada.)

When we arrived in Winnipeg, we were besieged by all sorts of agents. Some of them advised us to buy land close to Winnipeg; others to go to the United States where there were more jobs. The immigration official, Kyrylo Genyk, advised us to go out in the country and see a colony for ourselves. The idea appealed to my father and to Ivan Yarosh from Terebowla, and we set out for the settlement at Dauphin, for it was here that our relative Wasyl Ksionzyk had taken a farm. As for the others, some remained in Winnipeg, and some, accompanied by agents, went to the state of Carolina in the United States. But they soon returned from there and settled near Bismarck in North Dakota. It seems to me that the ones who remained in Winnipeg made the wisest choice. They became prosperous and have enjoyed living there to this very day. Certainly they did not have to put up with the kind of hardships that we had on the farm.

When we arrived at Dauphin, my father had only fifty dollars left. We hired a rig to take us to the home of friends from Zawale

85

who now lived eighteen miles west of Dauphin. The farmer we hired loaded our luggage and the children onto the wagon, but the adults had to walk behind.

On our way we passed farms close to town which had been settled by English or Scottish farmers. Their homes were built of logs, and there were other buildings in the farmyard. We saw fields of grain, and cattle in the pastures. All of this looked odd to us, and we could not help making jokes about their houses. Father kept telling us that uncle's house would look better than these. For, after all, what sort of a house was it, that was built of logs with sand and lime in between?

We came to a river—Valley River. Our driver let his horses rest, and we waded across to relax in a thick, green grove.

As we continued our journey on the other side of the river, the road got progressively more and more horrible. It was full of holes and stumps, and on each side there was a wall of thick forest. The horses dragged their feet even more wearily than we did. Farther along the trail, we were surprised to hear the voices of children in the forest. We wondered how they could ever have got there. Shortly afterwards, we saw smoke rising above the trees, and a little later we came upon a hovel.

The man who lived in this hovel was the same J—— whom the steamship agent Moravets had had write letters to peasants in Galicia, urging them to come to Canada, the land he called paradise. Rumors circulated that Moravets paid him well for his aid, and immigrants cursed him.

We came to a riverbank. There were small garden plots, but we could not see a house. All of a sudden, from a cave in the bank, emerged—my auntie.[1] Wiping tears from her eyes, she kissed mother and invited us in. By this time, my brothers had run down the bank to look for fish in the river, but I stood there leaning against a big poplar tree, weeping. Auntie came out and called me in, but I only cried all the harder. For what kind of a house was it, dug in the ground? I would rather auntie had said she was inviting me into a cave, instead of calling it a house. I did not want to go inside this "house" and continued to cry under the tree. Finally, father came out and said to me, "Silly girl! Why are you crying? Do you see that forest? In one month we'll have a house."

Well, with father I did go in.

The root house measured about ten by twelve feet. In it there were two small beds and a small iron stove. In this hole there were now fourteen persons — four adults and ten children. And all of us ate and slept in this place, since eating and sleeping outdoors was out of the question because of the mosquitoes.

We stayed in this place until father built us a house. This came about not within a month, as father had promised, but in six weeks.

Ukrainian couple clearing land near Hadashville,
Manitoba, 1917

By trade, father was a carpenter. He felled the trees and squared the logs. Mother and we kids carried those logs and piled them in one place. We placed a thick stick under each end of a log, and by means of these levers, we raised it and carried it to the designated spot on top of the hill. Of course, it was the adults who handled the thick end of the log, and we kids the thin one. In this manner we brought all the logs that were needed to build the house. The palms of our hands were covered with calluses.

When the house was finished (and it was quite spacious), it was time to make hay. Father and uncle mowed the hay, and mother and we kids raked it and carried it home on our backs. We needed the hay to feed the two cows that father bought with the fifty dollars he had brought with him from the old country. Uncle did not have any cattle; he had had a yoke of oxen and a cow, but they had died of starvation during the winter. He had come to Canada too late in the fall to make hay. In winter, he had had to dig through the snow to find old, dry grass to feed his stock. But the animals could not survive on such fodder.

When father finished haying, he and uncle left home to look for jobs. They hoofed it all the way to Brandon where farmers were quite well-to-do and able to pay good wages. In two months, father earned forty dollars and thought he had done very well. So that he could bring this money home without spending any of it, he chose to walk all the way back.

While passing through Neepawa, he struck up an acquaintance with a Hungarian by the name of Kolessar who had been a shoe-maker in that town for many years.[2] Father learned from him that there was a demand for working girls in town. When he got home, he discussed this matter with us, and as a result, I decided to go to work in Neepawa. Maria Baschak agreed to join me.

At Gladstone, we missed the train to Neepawa and had to wait a day and a half for the next one. We spent all that time sitting on the bench at the station without so much as a wink of sleep, for fear of missing the next passenger train. The station agent recognized our plight and arranged for our passage to Neepawa on a freight train.

We both huddled in the corner of the coach, frightened, like birds in a cage. The brakemen spoke to us, but we both turned our faces away from them and sat there, scarcely daring to breathe.

It was late at night. The brakemen had their lunch and offered us some dry crackers, but my companion cautioned me in a whisper not to accept the offer, as the biscuits could be poisoned. I took her advice because I looked upon her as more knowledgeable in such matters, having already lived in Canada for a whole year. She claimed that such things had happened to her. She also claimed she could speak English, but when the brakemen spoke to her she only nodded her head. Perhaps she was too shy to talk.

We finally arrived in some town or other, and our caboose was spotted on a side track. Since it was nightime, we did not get off but waited for daybreak. My companion did not know the name of the town, and we were afraid to leave the caboose to find out. When dawn began to break, we ventured out and headed toward the station. As we approached the building, we could see the sign in big letters: "Neepawa." We were very happy to know that we had arrived at our destination.

We walked up the street until we came upon a building with the sign "Gregor Kolessar, Shoemaker." He was the same shoemaker who had spoken to my father about the demand for girls to do housework in Neepawa. We tried the door; it was locked. It was late November; the weather was quite chilly, and we were dressed lightly. Not knowing where to turn, we just parked ourselves and our luggage there in front of the building.

A man on the other side of the street saw us and beckoned us to come over. At first we hesitated to go, but he persisted in calling us. His gestures were so polite that we no longer hesitated but went across, though we were not sure where we were going or why. As soon as we reached him, he took us into a blacksmith shop, right up to the forge, to get warmed up. We stayed there, warming ourselves, until we saw smoke from Kolessar's chimney.

We went over to his shop. He greeted us with "Good morning, young ladies from Lake Dauphin." His dark eyes, glowing like live coals, drove fear into our hearts.

Just then, my companion's brother appeared on the scene, and we were happy to meet someone who spoke our language. But how terribly depressed I felt when he took his sister away from me to some home where a job had been found for her and left me behind! There I was, not because it was my will, but because the Magyar had something to do with things. Turning to me he said, "You will go to Sam Faryna's." Strange as it may seem, I never again saw my companion [Maria] Baschak, after we parted that day.

Accompanied by the Magyar Kolessar, I arrived at the home of Sam Faryna, who lived about half a mile out of town. I could not figure out why Faryna needed a girl to work, when his house only consisted of one small room. I asked Kolessar what my duties would be. He laughed and replied, "She will ask you to dance." Then he said a few words to my prospective mistress and walked out without even telling me what my wages were.

On my arrival at Faryna's, his wife was washing clothes. She immediately showed me how she wanted me to rinse them. I was surprised that the rinsing was done in the house and not in the river the way we had done it in the old country. I was used to washing clothes by beating them with a paddle in the Seret River and rinsing them there, too. But I said nothing about it to my mistress since I could not speak her language.

When I was finished with the clothes, my mistress gave me orders to scrub the floor. Never before in my life had I scrubbed floors, but when I finished, she said my job was "good." But it evidently was not all that good, because, after a while, a thin sheet of ice formed in front of the door where I had not wiped the floor well enough.

As bad luck would have it, my mistress then sent me to fetch a couple of pails of water. While I was crossing the threshold with the water, I slipped on this ice and fell, spilling the water all over the floor. I got to my feet as fast as I could and, overcome by fear, did not know whether to cry or run away. I was sure that my mistress would give me a severe tongue-lashing.

But she was not that kind of a woman. Not only did she not scold me, she split her sides with laughter. I grabbed a broom and began to sweep the water toward the door. Just at that moment her husband entered. After taking note of what had happened, he spoke to her, and in the course of their conversation, they both cast glances at my shoes.

Those shoes were extraordinary. Father had bought them for me for eighty cents. They were men's work shoes, made of coarse leather, size eight. They were too large and too heavy for me, but I presumed that was what shoes were supposed to be.

That same evening, Mr. Faryna brought me a new pair from the store. They were ladies' shoes, size seven, still about two sizes too large.

A young Ukrainian settler, Sophie Hrynchuk,
at Redwater, Alberta, 1912

A few days later, the Farynas started to pack and to haul their baggage away somewhere in a sleigh. I went to the shoemaker's to tell him that the Farynas were moving away, and I was anxious to know what they were going to do with me now. He replied that they had a sawmill in the bush. They were moving there, and they were taking me with them. When I asked the shoemaker if he knew what my wages would be, he replied that first they wanted to see how much I was worth.

With that answer, I returned to my job, and a few days later, I left with my employers for the bush. The site of the sawmill was about twenty miles north of Neepawa. The buildings, or "camps" as they were called, were built of logs chinked with mud. When the frosts came, the mud fell away and we stuffed rags in its place. The camp was cold, and most of the time, I was cold in it.

As to my wages, I was paid one dollar for the month, and I sent home every cent of my earnings, for in their letter, my parents complained to me about their poverty. All they had to eat was rabbit meat, and without bread at that. I wept until my head ached every time I read that letter. For how could I keep from crying when there was more food at my employer's table than there was room for it? And yet my parents had no bread. Often, as I sat at the table, I could not help thinking about conditions at home. A lump would form in my throat, and I would leave the table to have a good cry. My bosses presumed that I was homesick. And they were not wrong. I wanted to go home so badly that if I had known the way I would have taken off despite the severe cold. I would rather eat rabbit meat with my parents than live with strangers in a camp.

Now that I knew enough English, I asked my mistress how much she was paying me per month. She replied that for the first two months the pay was $1.50 a month; for the second two months, $2.50 a month; and after that I would be paid $4.00 a month. I protested against such low pay for such hard work. I pointed out to her that looking after twenty to twenty-five men was, indeed, hard work, but she brushed me off with the rejoinder that she had trained me for the job and, besides, she had paid Kolessar $5.00 for me.

Her words hurt me deeply. Evidently, I had been sold by Kolessar for five dollars, and I was now the slave of my employers. But what could I do about it? Where could I go for advice? The people around me were all strangers. There I was, saddled with a job at which I was forced to do hard labor.

The long, severe winter came to an end, and I returned with my taskmasters to Neepawa. Every time I visited the Kolessars, I complained about the low wages, and each time Kolessar had only one answer: "She is paying you well, girl."

Convinced that I could not get any help from Kolessar, I took matters into my own hands and kept pestering Mrs. Faryna for a raise. Reluctantly, she raised me two dollars a month so that now my monthly pay went up to six dollars. My duties were to milk three cows and to look after three children and two hired men.

For the next two months I worked at the new, higher wages. One day I met a neighbor from back home, and in the course of our conversation, I happened to mention that I worked for six dollars a month. He told me that he knew a farmer who was looking for a girl to work at eight dollars a month. I begged him to come to Neepawa in a week's time when my month had ended to pick me up and take me to this farmer's place.

He did so, and now I worked for eight dollars a month. About two months later, my father came to work for my boss's father; my fourteen-year old brother Bill had been working there since spring. My life was happier now, and I did not feel so homesick. When harvesting was over and father was ready to go home, he took me and brother Bill with him. He explained that if he returned home alone, mother would be very unhappy, and there would be no end to her tears.

And so we went home together. From Neepawa to Glenella we walked—about thirty miles. From there we took the train to Dauphin, and from Dauphin we walked home eighteen miles. My feet were swollen from that long walk, but we had no other choice as there was no one in town who was going our way in a wagon.

When we got home, mother wept with joy to see us back. She called uncle over—he had arrived from the old country in the spring and lived nearby—and we all wept with joy.

We stayed home all winter. When spring arrived, we had to look for jobs again as we needed the money. This time I did not go alone. I was joined by my brother Bill, my cousin Anna Gayowski (now Mrs. Luciuk) and two English boys (our neighbors) who owned their own sleigh and horses. We set out for Neepawa before the snow melted, and it took us two days to get there.

As soon as we drove into Neepawa, my cousin got hired by a farmer. My brother set out on foot for Franklin where he had worked the year before. Then his farmer came to Neepawa and hired me, too, for housework. We were paid eight dollars a month. At that time, it was considered to be a good wage. We each resolved to send our parents five dollars every month. We kept it up as long as our employment lasted, and the neighbors at home used to say, "Chickens in Neepawa lay golden eggs for the Perchaluks."

My work was harder than the year before as there were four children, and four or five hired men to look after. But I stuck it out, as I wanted to help my parents as much as I could. I worked all summer and then stayed on for the winter. My brother did likewise, all the more willingly because the farmer was fond of him. Having no children of his own, the farmer was like a father to my brother. He bought him a copy of the first English reader and taught him how to read and write in English. He tried to persuade my brother to work for him as long as he lived and offered to sign his property over to my brother. But neither my brother nor I believed him, because we did not think that Protestants were as trustworthy as we were.

Next spring, about the time of the festival of the Pentecost, I received a letter from dad saying that he wanted me to come home because mother was not feeling well. He also wrote that once I came home he would not let me go back to work again, since he could earn as much in two months as I could in a year.

But I had no wish to leave my mistress, chiefly because I had agreed to work for her all year. But neither could I disobey father. I had to tell my mistress that he wanted me to come home. She began to cry and begged me to stay on. When she finally offered me $100 per year, I decided to remain with her.

But now that she had raised my wages, the woman made me work harder than ever. I did the work of two — myself and a man — from early morning until late night. It was killing me. When I complained about it to my brother, he answered, "Don't worry; I'll think of something."

And he did. When we got our next letter from home, my brother went with it to our boss and explained that mother was seriously ill and wished to see us, her children. He let us go, and without wasting much time, we both hastened to the railway station and took the train home.

When we got home, we were surprised to find mother up and around doing her usual work. We asked what had made her write that she was ill, and she replied, "Just because you don't see me in bed, don't be fooled. I am going to die soon, and I wanted to see you before my death."

There was a ring of sincerity in mother's words, but we could not bring ourselves to believe her. Father even joked about it: "Yeh, sure, the pigs have started to dig her grave."

This remark brought tears to mother's eyes, and she walked away without saying a word. Then she took me outside to show me her lovely garden. She told me how she had helped to grub out trees for this garden, to clear the land and dig it with a spade, to pull out roots with her bare hands until the skin on the palms cracked. Even yet she had a hard time kneeding bread dough with her hands. Pointing to the garden she added, "Beautiful garden, but I have a feeling that I shall not reap it."

And she was right. When father left home to look for a harvest job, he left orders with us to keep an eye on mother. And he said that if mother should die, he would not return home.

Hearing these words, mother sorrowfully put this question to him: "Will it be my fault when death comes for me?"

The next day, mother went to bed with a bad leg. It was all swollen and tender. We children could not hold back our tears, and we asked her why she had not spoken to father about her condition.

"I didn't want to say anything that would alarm him; besides, there was still no swelling yesterday," she justified herself.

In the afternoon of the same day, mother summoned us to her bedside for what turned out to be her last parting with us. We were both dismayed and in tears. She talked and then suddenly, she stopped. We could see that she was feverish.

The next day, mother fell unconscious. Outdoors, the rain came down in torrents. The sod-covered roof of our hut began to leak, and the floor soon flooded. We covered mother with whatever we could and placed an umbrella over her head. Then the sodden clay on the roof began to splash down piece by piece, and the water from the roof came pouring in as though from a bucket. We moved the bed with mother on it to another corner of the hut where the soggy sod from the roof had already come down to the floor. Now the two of us stood in the middle of the floor wondering what was coming next. We were so drenched there wasn't a dry thread on our bodies.

When the rain abated and the water ceased pouring into our hut, we wrote to father, urging him to come home as soon as possible because mother was dying. Later, father told us that he received the letter one afternoon, and as soon as he read it, he put

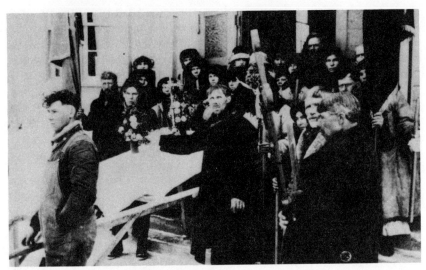

The funeral of Mary Sopiwnyk

Dwelling and grave marker

his hat on and started to run toward the railway station. But his farmer called him back and gave him money for the train ticket. Unfortunately, father missed the train and had to hoof it home. He said he ran more than he walked. But he got home too late. Mother was already dead.

She died without confession and without the sacrament of Communion, and we buried her body without a priest. The day after the funeral, an uncanny and incredible thing happened. As I was preparing breakfast, tears flooding my eyes, I heard mother's voice calling me. My small four-year-old brother, who was close to me at the time, also heard the voice. I couldn't believe my ears so I walked out and searched around the house but found no one. But I was convinced that mother had really called me, since two of us had heard her voice.

Sometime after the burial, my brother went back to his job near Franklin, but father never did go back to his job. As time passed, he remarried, and I went to work again, this time in Brandon. Dauphin was too small, and jobs were hard to come by there.

It was as if fate had decreed that I should move to Brandon, for it was there that I got married to a young man and made my home with his parents on a five-acre farm by the river. After suffering so many hardships in the country, I got to like city life and hoped that my new life would be much happier.

True, there were those who tried to advise me against living with a mother-in-law, but I rejected their advice. I stuck to my belief that I could live in peace with anyone. However, I discovered later that they were right, and I was wrong. My husband and I were not able to get along with his parents. We built ourselves a home just across the road from them and enjoyed it. But not for very long.

My husband did not like bosses, and as a result, he was unable to hold a job for long. Finally, he decided to take up farming so that no one could order him around. I had no objections, since there was no other choice for us. The only obstacle was our lack of money to buy a farm; consequently, we had to look for a homestead. And there were not many good ones left. However, we ended up by finding one close to my father's farm. There were more rocks on it than on my father's homestead, but my husband consoled himself by saying, "For ten dollars, it's good enough."

After only a few years of farming, it became clear to us that, in spite of all our hard work, we could not make ends meet. We therefore decided to sell all our personal belongings and move to town. We chose to make our home in Sifton. There, in partnership with another man, we bought the old gristmill in which Serafym in his day had ordained his deacons and some of his semiliterate priests.[3]

Business was good, and although we did not make much profit, we earned enough for a living. It appeared as though we would stay in the business permanently. But, as the proverb has it, "Man proposes, God disposes." The partners could not get along and were compelled to dissolve the partnership. The terms of the settlement gave our partner the land and the building, and my husband got the machines and other equipment. But the mill was no longer of any benefit to either one.

We lost all we had, and now, in our old age, we live in a rented house. Where we will end our life we don't know. True, we have children, seven of them, scattered across Canada—some in Saskatchewan and others in Ontario. They remember us and from time to time send us help. Their help, together with my husband's earnings, keep us going. We have no complaints whatsoever, neither against God nor against people. . . .

7 DMYTRO ROMANCHYCH
The Dauphin District

Up to this point, most of the accounts have followed the progress of particular individuals or families. In his reminiscences, Dmytro Romanchych surveys the development of a number of Ukrainian settlements around Dauphin, Manitoba. He takes us back to the beginning again — to the decision to emigrate, the choice of a homestead, and the first difficult years on the land. From there, he goes on to describe the evolution of stable community life, complete with libraries, schools, churches, and political institutions. His memoirs were recorded by Ivan Bodrug and published as "Ukrayinski koloniyi w okruzi Dawfyn" *in* Propamyatna knyha ukrayinskoho narodnoho domu w Wynypegu *("Ukrainian Colonies in the Dauphin District," The Memorial Book of the Ukrainian National Home in Winnipeg) in 1949.*

Who am I? I am a descendant of an old family of petty gentry from Bereziw. My ancestors were not serfs, and thus our family were not accustomed to blind obedience to foreign masters. We were able to be indepedent in our thoughts and actions. . . .

In the eighteenth century, when Oleksa Dowbush of Pechenizhyn tried to bring about a just social order in the Carpathians, one of my ancestors in the Pokutia, Mykhailo Romanchych, was Dowbush's right-hand man. When Dowbush died of a bullet in Kosmach, the Austrian *landsdragoons* soon struck the trail of his band, which was now left without a leader.[1] They were at the heels of my ancestor as he fled during the night and on horseback from Bereziw to Kimpolung in Bukovina. There, he settled in the mountains, became rich, and lived to the ripe old age of 110 years. My grandfather, Ivan Romanchych, often used to visit him and bring back valuable gifts.

In Canada, I have survived with dignity half a century of the vicissitudes common to all immigrants. In our colony, I was always among the first, if not the first, to help with my efforts and money in every community cause. I was an avid reader, and it was here in Canada that I learned "who we are, and whose children."[2] I have always tried to respect all that is worthy and that is historically near and dear to us—our language, religion, national traditions, and customs—and to accept what is best in foreign cultures. And I have always advised others to do likewise.

In the fifty years of my life in Canada, I grubbed up with my own hands thousands of oak, poplar, birch and other tree stumps on my three forest-covered quarter sections and brought the land under cultivation as rich fields of grain. That is why now my hand does not lend itself to legible writing. Consequently, for all that is accurately recorded here, I am grateful to the good friend of my boyhood years with whom I used to tend cattle and sheep in the pastures along the Carpathians in Bereziw Vizhnyi. It is my desire to pass on to posterity what has been preserved in the memory of a few, for someday many will seek this information.

Although the first Ukrainian immigrants began to arrive in Canada in small groups after 1891, mass immigration did not begin until the year 1896 or 1897. I recall that we first learned about Canada from a booklet written by Dr. Oleskiw of Lviv, which made its appearance in Galicia and Bukovina.[3] In it, Dr. Oleskiw relates observations and impressions from his Canadian tour. He describes central Canada as a boundless expanse in North America, settled only here and there, and the rest of the country as primeval, virgin land awaiting landless peasants from other countries of the wide world.

In order to settle these vast Canadian spaces with agriculturalists, [Oleskiw reported,] the Canadian government had decided to divide the southern steppes and forests, which extended for a thousand miles, into six-mile squares, known as "townships." Every

Breaking land with a walking plow, Treherne, Manitoba, about 1914

township was divided into thirty-six squares, each a mile in area and called a "section." Each section in turn was divided into four quarters of 160 acres (113 morgs); these were the "homesteads" for the settlers. Every immigrant eighteen years of age and over was eligible for one such homestead upon payment of a small fee of ten dollars. In each township, two sections were reserved to fund future schools, and two sections were given to the Hudson's Bay Company for its pioneering in trade with the Indians. A strip six-miles wide on each side of the railway track was granted to the CPR, which built the first railway across Canada from sea to sea. This area was not divided into homesteads. That was the gist of the information passed on by Dr. Oleskiw in his booklet, to the landless peasants in Galicia and Bukovina. . . .[4]

Our first impressions of the new land. On 1 May, we sailed into the port of Quebec. The sun had just reached its noonday position. It was a beautiful day, so calm and sunny. Behind us spread the still waters of the Saint Lawrence River whose banks were covered with scrub and charred trees. Between the hills, dirty, gray snow that lingered after the long Canadian winter streaked across the ravines. The entire landscape—wild, sad, uninviting—at once made it obvious to us that Canada was a sparsely settled and inhospitable country. Only three weeks before, we had seen green meadows, willows, and shrubs in Europe, and here we had only the first signs of spring. The sight of the landscape depressed us.

In the port of Quebec, we were met by our Kyrylo Genyk, dressed in his official uniform with yellow buttons and wearing a cap with the words "Immigration Interpreter" just above the peak.[5] He welcomed us cheerfully but could not enter into a conversation with us because we were in a hurry to pick up our luggage and catch the train that was waiting for us nearby. The immigrants from our ship filled twelve trains, each twelve coaches long. Some trains were designated to take us to Winnipeg, others to Yorkton, Prince Albert, and Edmonton. We passed through Montreal at night, so we were not able to see that city.

In the morning we got a good view of the capital of Canada, Ottawa. At that time it was only a small town, spread out along the wide river of the same name. Along the river, sawmills surrounded by piles of lumber, slabs, and sawdust were in operation. And the river was covered with large booms of peeled logs ready for the sawmills and the paper mills. We were very pleasantly impressed by the massive stone buildings of the Canadian Parliament, built on a hill overlooking the river. Across the river to the west, the landscape was wild through and through. The low, bare, rocky banks and sickly trees made an unpleasant impression upon us.

As our train carried us farther west, we had our first glimpse of the Ontario farmers working in their farmyards or fields. The farms were enclosed by rail fences built without posts at the corners. In some places, fences were built of piled stones. Here and there in the fields stood a stately, solitary maple, elm, or oak whose spreading branches reminded one of an umbrella. The sight of crows and other birds unfamiliar to us convinced us that this land bore little resemblance to Europe with its natural grandeur.

Our train sped on farther and farther west. After a few hours, we left behind the cultivated Ontario farmland and entered that desolate country of granite rocks and cliffs, burned-out forests, and lakes in which we could see no living thing except for the occasional wild duck. Only here and there did we see human habitations—pointed wigwams, blackened by smoke, usually nestled in a valley beside a lake. These were the homes of the true Canadians, the Indians. Beside their smoke-darkened wigwams stood groups of Indians watching the train. They were wrapped in odd-looking coarse garb, and their eyes seemed to draw us away into the depths of the Ontario wilderness.

Railway stations were few and far between. The train stopped only at the larger ones, spaced about 200 miles apart, in order to replenish its supply of coal and water. We were beginning to wonder if we would ever leave behind those cursed rocks and emerge into a land suitable for human habitation. After a day and a half of that depressing ride, we arrived at Fort William. There things seemed to look a lot more encouraging. For one thing, the mountains were fewer and much smaller. Genyk assured us that during the night we would leave the rocky terrain behind and emerge into the seemingly boundless plains of fertile black soil. It was in that direction which we were headed.

In Manitoba. Finally, our train ground to a halt in Winnipeg, and we were asked to get off. After a rest stop, other trains continued their journey westward into the North West Territories. (At that time, there were as yet no organized provinces of Saskatchewan and Alberta to the west of Manitoba.) The city of Winnipeg, the capital of Manitoba, had a population of 36,000 . . . spread far and wide over the plain. The railway station, built of wood, was not a large building, but beside it was a large immigration home, also a wooden structure. Next to it was a small building, the immigration office. In this office, we were met by a Ukrainian priest, Rev. Nestor Dmytriw who had come from the United States at the invitation of the immigration authorities to help us in his capacity as pastor and interpreter. We were also met by our countrymen who had arrived here with Genyk the previous fall and settled southeast of Winnipeg in the district of Stuartburn (they pronounced it

"Shtombur"). These people were apparently happy, although we noticed a big change in their appearance. During the winter their faces had turned swarthy, like the Indians', from the severe Canadian weather.

After a two-day rest in Winnipeg, we organized ourselves into groups and, escorted by our agents, departed by train for the vacant lands surrounding Winnipeg. In the vicinity of Stuartburn, the land was very fertile but too rocky. The area around Teulon, north of Winnipeg, was all bush and muskeg, and east of Winnipeg, it was swampy and sandy. Some of the folks from Bereziw chose to settle in those areas, but the majority of us decided to look for better lands farther to the northwest of Winnipeg, around Dauphin, at the end of the railway.

How "Ukraina" came into being in Canada. The distance from Winnipeg to Dauphin is only 200 miles, but it took us first Ukrainian immigrants almost a whole day to get there by train. The new railroad was not as yet properly leveled; hence it was not ready for fast travel. Often the train had to be stopped to chase away cattle that were lying on the track sunning themselves. (At that time, cattle were cheap in Manitoba. The best cow sold for five to ten dollars, and a good yoke of oxen cost from thirty to forty dollars. Horses, however, were much higher in price as they required feed and a barn, while oxen could graze in the summertime and spend the winter under a straw stack in the field.)

We arrived in Dauphin on 6 May 1897. The village of Dauphin was then just in the early stages of its development. We camped in tents beside the railway station. The next morning, we left our wives and children in the camp and set out on foot into the wide-open spaces to the north and west to look for land suitable for settlement, as the best lands in the immediate vicinity of Dauphin had already been taken up by the English and Scottish settlers who had got there before us. Our guide was Paul Wood, an immigration agent who was thoroughly familiar with that area. He was Swiss and spoke German fluently. Thanks to [Ivan] Bodrug and Yurko Syrotiuk of Balyntsi, who joined us as interpreters, we learned a great deal from Wood about the various things that aroused our curiosity along the way.

To me, a twenty-year-old youth, was assigned the task of carrying bags packed with provisions for our band of prospectors on this expedition. Equipped with spades and axes, they forged ahead, testing the quality of the soil here and there. During the first day, we covered about thirty miles as we tramped to the northwest, inspecting an area of dense brush interspersed with thick forests. We went beyond the projected terminus of the railway line, a place named Sifton after Clifford Sifton who was then minister of the interior in Ottawa.

Some ten miles west of Sifton, we put up for the night in the woods. After setting up our tent, we spent a good part of the night sitting around a bonfire, which served as a smudge to keep the mosquitoes away, and talking about the different things we had seen on our trek that day. This part of the country appealed to us, and we had a feeling that before long it would be settled by Ukrainian immigrants. In the course of our conversation, someone raised the question of a suitable name for that future colony. Among the various names that were suggested, the one proposed by Bodrug was "Ukraina." Paul Wood jotted down our resolution in his notebook and promised to submit it to the Department of Immigration at Ottawa. . . . When the railway was eventually built through this area in 1898, the station did receive the name "Ukraina."

The next day, our party headed farther to the northwest to take a look at the lands along the Fork River. Finding the land there too rocky and sandy, we pushed on and, by nightfall, we reached a small grove of trees at the site of the present Ukrainian village of Ethelbert. There we found some fine chernozem, and for the next few days, we wandered about investigating this area. . . . Those who picked their homesteads here remained on them a few days to erect temporary shelters for their families, who were still waiting at Dauphin. A small group of us who had not yet made our choices tried farther to the north. . . .[6]

On 22 May 1897, another group of immigrants arrived, most of them from the district of Borschiw. They, too, settled in the neighborhood of Sifton. Among them were Yakiw Standryk and his son Wasyl. Wasyl was very active. He was the first one in Dauphin to acquire his citizenship papers. . . .[7]

There were still fifteen families from Bereziw who had not as yet found homesteads for ourselves, so we decided to search the area to the southwest of Dauphin, close to the . . . [Riding Mountains] which reminded us so much of our Carpathians. Although P. Wood had cautioned us not to apply for land there because it was designated as a timber reserve and was not open for homesteading, we insisted on having our own way and investigated it. We trudged through the bush as far as the foothills and found the land to be chernozem of the highest quality, with the forest burnt out as far as the Vermilion River. Here we selected our homesteads and, thanks to Genyk's assistance, we were allowed to keep them. At first, we were promised only half a farm each, but later, again thanks to Genyk's efforts, we were allowed to claim a whole quarter section. Beyond the Vermilion River, the entire area was heavy bush and rocks, unsuitable for cultivation. . . .[8] In May, a sizeable group of immigrants from Hleschova in the Terebowla district arrived. They all settled in our neighborhood.

This then is the story of the founding of the first Ukrainian settlements in the Dauphin area of Manitoba. They grew and expanded across a large area which, after a few years, extended to Swan River and the Saskatchewan border, some 100 miles to the northwest of Dauphin.

Schools. During the first few years of our life as immigrants, one thing perturbed us constantly: our children were growing up illiterate. The new province was unable to provide either schools or teachers for all the colonies of the various European nationalities which rapidly filled its open spaces. Even if we could have afforded to build a school in our district by our own efforts, would any English-speaking teacher have wanted to live with us and share our misery?

In our predicament, we received assistance from Mr. Bodrug. After completing his theology course at Manitoba College, he visited our colony as a student in the fall of 1900 and called a meeting of the farmers. Speaking with candor and conviction, he told them, "You will soon do well on these good lands, and in time you will become prosperous. But your children will grow up in this wilderness without education and will live in degradation among the cultured people of Canada. No one will have anything to do with you in social or political matters. It is essential that you build a school for your children without delay. True, you are all poor and

Pioneer Ukrainian teachers, Vegreville, Alberta, 1917

at present have no money for a school or to hire a teacher, but I have some advice for you. If you don't heed it, God help you! Listen carefully."

We were curious to hear what he had to say and listened willingly.

"Here it is," said Mr. Bodrug. "Cut some logs in the forest, haul them to a site you think suitable for a school, and start building. I will do my part to obtain a loan for you to pay for the building and to buy school equipment. The executive of the home mission of the Presbyterian Church assured me that it will loan from its mission fund whatever amount is necessary for the erection of schools in our immigrant communities. It will also pay the teachers' salaries until such time as the province is ready to convert these schools into public schools and assist in paying the teachers. If you get to work immediately and erect a school building, I will get you the money for the shingles, floor, windows, doors, and all the equipment and supplies for the school. Your school should be ready before winter sets in, and I, a teacher by profession, shall teach your children."

The community readily accepted Mr. Bodrug's proposition, and in two months, we opened our school, probably the first school among the Ukrainians in Canada. Under similar arrangements, a school was built seven miles south of Ethelbert. Its first teacher was John Negrych, Bodrug's schoolmate (he died in Winnipeg in 1946).

Plum Ridge School, among the first schools for Ukrainians in Manitoba, 1908

At our settlement in the foothills, there were seventy children of school age. Bodrug was our teacher. He lived near the school with the Petro Pidodworny family. They alone sent four children to school. In the winter, we managed to build a lean-to on the school as a sort of living quarters for the teacher. We filled the cracks and crannies of the lean-to with lime mixed with sand, but the lime in the chinks froze instantly. Bodrug brought his young wife and a small son from Ethelbert to live with him in this shack. The winter was very severe. As soon as a fire was lit in the heater, the lime in the chinks thawed and fell away. The wind blew right through the dwelling, and during a snowstorm, the floor was covered with snow. The Bodrugs stopped the chinks with rags and somehow managed to survive the winter in this "palace."

After the summer holidays, Bodrug contracted to teach in a new public school near Sifton. To take his place as teacher in our school, he recommended Ivan Danylchuk, a student at Manitoba College. Danylchuk taught in our school until the summer of 1902. He was followed by McLean, a Scotsman by nationality, during whose teaching term our school was converted from a mission school into a public school.

We paid our Presbyterian benefactors part of the money they loaned us to build our school. They never asked for the balance, and it was never paid back. . . .

During Danylchuk's teaching term, we began to subscribe to *Svoboda* from the United States, and when [Wasyl] Smuk came to be our teacher, we founded the reading society *Prosvita* and built a hall for it.[9] Besides myself and Smuk, seven others signed up as members: Bihun, Leskiw, Pidodworny, Chorny, Koshowsky, Sklepovich, and Ficych. We then ordered a batch of books for the reading-society library.

In the interests of fairness, it must be mentioned that our reading society showed very gratifying progress with the coming of J. Arsenych, a law student from Winnipeg, as our teacher. In the year 1910, our library in the literary society's hall at Kosiw was worth about $1,000. It was second only to the Ukrainian library at the *Prosvita* literary-society hall in Winnipeg. . . .

One year, a fierce election campaign was raging, and the candidates sought my advice as to what would be an appropriate treat for the voters at their rallies. In those days, it was customary during an election campaign for a candidate to bring gallons of whiskey and cases of cigars to his rally as a treat for the voters. My advice to them was that our people did not want any part of it since they had escaped from that kind of political bribery at elections in the old country. As his treat, the Liberal candidate donated twenty-five dollars to our reading society.

The harsh beginnings of our colony, Kosiw. Not only our colony but also all the other Ukrainian colonies in the Dauphin area passed through woeful times in their beginnings. However, the group of immigrants who had settled at the foot of the Riding Mountains south of Dauphin was confident that in time the colony would develop into one of the finest Ukrainian communities in Canada. Although the landscape of this entire area was marred by charred trees and young brush covering the land, the soil here was everywhere first-class chernozem. Many years of hard work awaited us, but we were confident that in time our labors would transform those spaces of wilderness into open fields.

It took many years of painful toil on our farms before we could reap the rewards of bountiful harvests. During those years, we experienced extreme hardships. The majority of us came almost empty-handed and some even burdened with debts. In our first year here, many of us had to trek long distances from home to earn what little cash we could to buy the bare essentials of life for the family. One of these necessities was a cow for the children, who were crying for milk.

In those days, one was fortunate to earn four dollars a week. In my own case, I earned only fifteen dollars during the entire harvest season. But the farmer who hired me had no money to pay my wages, so he gave me a rifle and two bucketsful of milk instead. To test the rifle, Ivan Bodrug fired a shot at a barn door 200 paces away, then at 100 paces, then at 50 paces, but still he could not hit the target. The bullet managed to fly out of the rifle barrel but dropped to the ground no farther than ten paces away. For our survival, we continued to rely on flour and the rabbits we snared. The only person in our district who had a good gun was Dmytro Malkowich. For tobacco, smokers used to scrape the bark off the red willow and console themselves with the delusion that the smokes were, in fact, quite delightful.

During the first few days after we got settled, the women and children were busy digging a garden. Even though summer is short here, we had our garden plots and grew enough potatoes and other vegetables for the winter. Those who as yet had no oxen or horses relied on their feet for transportation. The wives and children walked to town carrying pails of wild berries on their backs— raspberries and saskatoons and, in the fall, cranberries — to trade for flour, salt, and sugar. The next day, they would return home from their shopping expedition carrying sacks full of provisions on their backs. For some, the distance to town was fifteen or twenty miles.

In the summer, the women and children plastered and whitewashed their log cabins inside and out. In these humble dwellings, they could now enjoy life as much as they knew how,

Ukrainian woman returning from the store at Kreuzburg
(Fraserwood), Manitoba, 1915

while awaiting the return of their menfolk from their summer jobs.
In those days, our women were true heroines in their encounters
with extreme poverty, insect pests, and the bears which were
frequent uninvited guests in our immigrant settlements. In the event
of a misfortune, it was futile to expect any help, as there were no
neighbors close by.

Thus passed the first years of our life in Canada. The
immigrants were beginning to see the gradual fulfilment of their

hopes. They did not dream of getting rich quickly, but the hope of a better tomorrow gave them courage, strength, and patience. As time marched on, barns and other buildings besides our houses, as well as increasing numbers of cattle and poultry, began to enrich our farmyards. And simple corrals kept our fine horses enclosed. Gone was our fear of famine as our garden plots grew into large gardens and our tiny patches of grain into large, golden fields.

It took some ten years from the time we got settled until we became full-fledged farmers. In the sixth year, my partner and I built a gristmill on the Vermilion River, and in the tenth year, I bought a steam threshing outfit, also in partnership.

In due course, our district got its post office, Kosiw. But while we were considering the choice of a suitable site, the postmaster, Ilko Skakun, had the name changed to "Keld" for some reason. (Some say he acted on the advice of the Belgian Catholic missionary, Father Sabourin.) However, it is highly unlikely that the original name given our colony will ever die in the memories of our people. That name is being kept alive by our school and our People's Home. . . .[10]

General economic progress. Since that time, the community of Kosiw has been transformed beyond recognition. Today one sees wide-open, carefully cultivated areas that proudly display their beautiful fields of grain. Our well-kept farmyards are sheltered from the north winds by thick groves. Between the farms, wide roads run perpendicular to each other. Along the roads, in front of each home, sits a mailbox, and almost every home can boast a telephone. The sons and grandsons of our first settlers have become well-to-do. Through our efforts, schools, beautiful churches, and People's Homes sprang up. Everywhere in our community one hears the Ukrainian language and Ukrainian songs.

Around Dauphin, our people are buying up land—and in town, businesses—from our English-speaking neighbors, so that half the town has become Ukrainian. Thirty miles to the north of Dauphin, the village of Ethelbert has only two English-speaking families, and the rest of its population is all Ukrainian . . . .

Our social and religious life. We Ukrainians were the only people who came to Canada without spiritual leaders and intelligentsia. Among the first immigrants, there were neither priests nor laymen with higher education. Both groups looked upon us as lost forever to Ukraine and the church. But the fact is that we simple immigrants of Ukrainian descent wished to live our lives among the non-Ukrainians in our distinctly Ukrainian way.

In the beginning, our religious life in Canada was very confusing. The first missionaries to rove around among our people were Polish and Belgian Roman Catholics. The Protestants had one preacher serving as a missionary among us, a Baptist, Ivan Burgdorf. He was a Russian German who preached and sang psalms in Russian.[11] In some of our colonies, Russian Orthodox priests made their appearance, but their stay was brief. They were sent to the United States and Canada by the holy synod. The Ukrainians here flatly refused to convert to the Russian Orthodox teachings. Neither did they have any desire to become Roman Catholics, nor to be rebaptized into the Baptist Church, for they had been taught to believe in one baptism.[12]

We met our religious needs as best we could. Some of our neighbors raised unbaptized children for several years while awaiting the arrival of the shepherds of souls. Our young people were married either by Roman Catholic missionaries or in Anglican and Presbyterian Churches. The lack of spiritual leaders continued until the spring of 1903 when a bishop of the Orthodox Church, Serafym, arrived in Canada from a monastery on the holy Mount Athos. That year, he visited all the Ukrainian settlements in Canada, consecrated a number of cantors and ordained into the ministry a number of Ukrainians with higher education. Among them was our former teacher, Ivan Bodrug. Serafym was a very staunch Moscovite for whom "Mother Russia, single and indivisible" was the be-all and end-all. Bodrug and Serafym did not see eye to eye, for Bodrug was a sincere and dedicated Ukrainian.

In the spring of 1904, Serafym went to Russia to solicit subsidies for his mission in Canada. In the meantime, Bodrug, knowing that the Ukrainians could not go along with Serafym, summoned a church council of Serafym's leading priests and delegates from each parish served by the Orthodox mission or Church. At this council, held in Winnipeg, the Ukrainian (then "Ruthenian") Independent Orthodox Church was founded.[13] A constitution was drawn up on democratic principles; a consistory was elected by an equal number of priests and lay delegates as the governing body of the church. The council decided to change auricular confession to general confession, and this change was gladly accepted by the people. As organizer of the church, the council elected Ivan Bodrug himself.

After a few months, Serafym returned from Russia but without a subsidy because the newspapers in Russia had spread the news of Bodrug's "heresy." In public appearances and statements in the press after his return to Canada, Serafym cast an anathema on Bodrug and his fellow priests, some twenty of them in all. However, they ignored Serafym's denunciation and, under the direction of their consistory, applied themselves zealously to missionary work among the Ukrainians in Canada. Among other activities, they began to publish the newspaper *Ranok,* which fought the inroads

Saint Michael's Church, Gardenton, Manitoba, the first Ukrainian Orthodox Church in Canada

Interior of a Ukrainian church, Manitoba, about 1910

of tsarist Orthodoxy and Roman Catholicism among the Ukrainians.[14]

In 1902, we got some logs and built a church at Kosiw. We named it Saint Michael's. For all intents and purposes, it was a Greek Catholic church. However, when the Independent Ruthenian Orthodox Church came into being under Bodrug's leadership, we switched to it and renamed our church the Independent Church. The first minister of this Independent Church was an elderly priest, Hryhory Pryhrodsky. For a long time after Pryhrodsky left, our spiritual needs were taken care of by the ministers Semen Kachkowsky and Dowhun from Sifton. . . .

Incidentally, the Greek Catholic priest Rev. P. Bozyk wrote a book in which he made the statement that the minister S[emen] Kachkowsky, out of remorse for giving up the Catholic faith, committed suicide by throwing himself under the wheels of an express train. But this is a falsehood invented by bigots, because the late minister Semen Kachkowsky died a natural death caused by pleurisy, a fact which can be verified by his highly esteemed relatives and close friends.

The priests of the Independent Church served our spiritual needs for nine years. They found it difficult to conduct their mission throughout the whole of western Canada, for our people were still very poor and could not lend the necessary material support to the mission. The Presbyterian mission helped them through its colporteurs, but the assistance, given in dribs and drabs, was far from adequate for the priests alone, much less their families.[15] In the spring of 1913, therefore, the priests decided to take the examination in theology at Manitoba College and to affiliate with the Presbyterian Church of Canada. They would thus qualify for support from the mission fund of that church. This they did that very spring and, in June of the same year, the General Council of the Presbyterian Church in Toronto accepted them as its ministers.

As Protestant ministers, they could no longer adhere to Orthodox rituals but accepted the simple Presbyterian service of worship. However, the Ukrainian immigrants could not reconcile themselves to such denominational changes. In their disaffection, they eventually renounced these ministers. Only a few Ukrainian families here and there remained in the reformed church.

The majority of the ministers abandoned the mission completely. Two of them joined the Russian Orthodox Church, and a few remained with the Presbyterians to the ends of their lives. Bodrug withdrew from the Presbyterian ministry in 1914 and resumed secular life, establishing his residence in Toronto. Here he enjoyed general respect among Ukrainians and other Canadians as a prominent leader of the Ukrainian community in its national cultural activities.

The idea of a distinctly Ukrainian church among our people did not die out. During the First World War, our farmers in Canada suddenly came into wealth. In due time, our leaders, most of whom were associated with newspapers or politics, organized the Ukrainian Greek Orthodox Autocephalous Church (independent of other churches) in Canada, to which all of the more progressive Ukrainians throughout Canada declared their allegiance. This church has an illustrious history from its beginning to the present time, but it is not my intention to talk about it here.

Following the liquidation of the Ruthenian Independent Church in Canada, our parish was in the charge of a Russian Orthodox priest, Rev. P. Bozyk. When, on one occasion, he expressed the opinion that "there is no Ukraine," we parted company with him without even bidding him Godspeed. . . .

At Sifton, too, there . . . was no end to the religious disputes, for both the Russian Orthodox and the Catholics vied for control of the wealth of the church, but the people wanted to be independent of both and opposed them. To satisfy their spiritual needs, the people went to the Presbyterians more often than to their own clergy. There was strong opposition to the Belgian and French priests, who could not speak Ukrainian properly. The Presbyterians at that time had established schools for Ukrainian students and hospitals for the sick, and donated clothes to poor immigrants. At Sifton, the Presbyterians paved the way for the education of the Potocki brothers and of Ogryzlo, Hrushowy, Halinsky, and others. The Belgian priest, Father Delaere, spared no effort to maintain his [Roman Catholic] church at Sifton, but Ogryzlo and other Ukrainians prevented him from carrying out his designs. The old man Yakiw Standryk of Sifton once heard from his priest in the old country that there was no room for a Greek Catholic Church in Canada, since the Roman Catholics were in control, and they would not accept Greek Catholic priests. It was a warning to the Ukrainian emigrants that in Canada they must gradually and against their own will become Roman Caholics and lose their national identity in favor of the Poles or the French.

When Reverend Krochmalny, a married Greek Catholic priest, arrived in Sifton, he was warmly received by the people as their minister. At one of his services, he asked the congregation to remain in church for an important announcement immediately after the service. He announced that he was forced to leave the congregation without delay and return to Europe; the church authorities had recalled him to Galicia because he was married. He advised the people that, if they wished to retain their national identity in Canada, they must renounce the protection of the Roman Catholics and join the Orthodox Church. But the Orthodox missionaries, because of their Russian leanings, failed to sway our people at Sifton towards their church, and after much effort and numerous attempts, they gave up and left the Ukrainian communities. In the course of time, the Basilian fathers became dominant in Sifton's religious life. However, several highly respected families remained Protestant, and they were served by Pastor H. Tymchuk and other Ukrainian Protestant ministers.

Our farmers were eager to satisfy their educational needs. They organized literary societies everywhere, and in this effort they were aided at first by Serafym's and Bodrug's priests, and later by teachers and Ukrainian Orthodox ministers. Pawlo Potocki ... of Dauphin likes to tell how the Presbyterian colporteurs distributed Bibles among the Ukrainian immigrants during their earliest days in Canada and called upon them to read the Holy Word. To counteract this Protestant influence, the Catholic missionaries sounded an alarm and forbade our people to read anything without priestly blessing. They scared people with hell and cast anathemas upon the "guilty," removing them from church membership. These threats only served to whet the enthusiasm of our people for the Bible, and from that time on many Ukrainians trusted more in the Word of God than in the various church missions.

Throughout Canada, there were several major court cases to settle disputes over church matters among the Ukrainians. Many who were involved in these actions lost their farms.[16] In the name of religion, murders were even committed, like that of one of Serafym's priests, Osyp Cherniawsky, at Goodeve, Saskatchewan. He was killed by a Catholic fanatic who regularly went to the Belgian priests for confession. All over Canada, quarrels, hostilities, and hatred in the name of religion were common among our people. Only after a couple of decades of life in this country did they learn to tolerate one another's religious convictions.

The Ukrainian Orthodox Church captured the progressive element of the Ukrainian population.[17] The more conservative element remained within the Catholic Church. In each group are to be found the good and the bad, for they do not all enjoy the same educational advantages and are not all equally patriotic.

This then is my account of the more outstanding events in the development of our church life in Canada. And now I shall tell of the political developments among us in our new fatherland.

Politics Perhaps nothing else held as much surprise for us immigrants in Canada as Canadian politics. At home in Galicia, elections to the regional diet and national parliament were held in an entirely different manner. Every peasant who paid any kind of tax was eligible to vote in the primary elections. These primary votes, held in each village, selected the "electors," the number depending on the population of the village. One was chosen for every 500 or so voters, and these electors went to the political center of the district with their ballots, and there voted for the candidates. Those few electors could easily be enticed or bribed. Although the peasants stood by their own candidate, they exercised no influence over the electors. And so it was that the winning candidate was very seldom the one chosen by the village. Usually, the winner was a big landowner or his stooge. If a peasant elector was illiterate, he marked his ballot with a cross beside the name that someone else pointed out to him, or else he did not vote at all.

Here in Canada, we found it altogether different. Here every citizen votes directly for the candidate of his choice. No one forces him; no one entices him. The candidates go to the people, present their platform, and appeal for the people's support. No candidate attacks his opponent. Here we saw true democracy.

Ukrainians in the Dauphin district voted in the Dominion elections for the first time in 1906. The Liberal candidate was Mr. Burrows, a man of great wealth who owned sawmills and lumberyards. The Conservative candidate was Glen Campbell, a farmer. He was a Scotsman, and his wife was a pure-blooded Indian. We all voted for the Liberal candidate. Some of us did so because we felt that the Conservative Party was made up of the rich; others because the program of the Liberal Party was somewhat similar to the program of the radical party in Galicia. But the main reason lay in the fact that it was the Liberal Party which opened the doors of Canada to us immigrants and granted us free lands.

Next came the Manitoba provincial election in 1908. In this election, we voted Conservative. The reason for our choice was that it was the Conservative government of Manitoba which had established bilingual schools and a teachers' college in Brandon for the training of Ukrainian teachers.[18] All these teachers and students campaigned among the Ukrainians for the Conservatives out of gratitude for their thoughtfulness with respect to the Ukrainians.

This then was the voting pattern among us for decades. During that long span of years neither party distinguished itself by its recognition of the exemplary farming done by the Ukrainians. Neither party could see its way clear to give at least one person of Ukrainian origin a government job or to offer him a government position. And both parties maneuvered politically so that we could never elect a Ukrainian candidate, even though we had people in our midst who were competent and suitable to represent us in the government. It was not until 1915 that the Ukrainians around Gimli ran a Ukrainian, T. D. Ferley of Winnipeg, and elected him. He was the first Ukrainian member of the provincial legislature in Manitoba.

Ukrainians found it to their disadvantage to be without their own representatives in the legislative bodies [and they could have had them because] . . . there were districts where Ukrainians were in the majority. That they didn't can be attributed partly to the low political consciousness of our settlers at the time, and partly to the influence of Ukrainian agents who solicited votes for the party that hired them. In due time, when the younger generation became eligible to vote, the situation changed. [In 1949, there were] . . . six Ukrainian members in the Manitoba legislature alone. In 1926, the Ukrainians in Alberta acquired a seat in the Dominion Parliament when they voted in Michael Luchkowich as member of Parliament. Later, that seat went to Anthony Hlynka. In 1945, the Dauphin district elected Fred Zaplitny to the federal Parliament. In 1949, voters in the Vegreville district elected a lawyer, John Dikur, as member of Parliament. The ridings of Ethelbert, Emerson, Fisher Branch, and Gimli have all sent Ukrainian members to the provincial legislature over a number of years. N. V. Bachynsky from Fisher Branch has served over twenty-five years and [for a decade was] . . . Speaker of the Manitoba legislature.[19]

All things must come to an end. We must finish our lives in Canada and lay down our bones here. But our children and grandchildren will enjoy a better life in this, their native country, a beautiful land of freedom.

Our cemetery at Kosiw is situated high on a bank of the Vermilion River. Beyond the cemetery, the hills are covered with forests that teem with wildlife and abound in majestic oaks and birches. Cedars and towering pines whisper in the breeze and lull our pioneers to their eternal rest in God, who has brought an end to the trials of their harsh life. Among them rests my father, Osyp Romanchych. Here in rows of graves rest my immigrant comrades, and their names inscribed on the stone crosses bear mute testimony to those first, hardy Ukrainian immigrants in our colony.

My house stands beside a well-beaten road that crosses the mountains from Dauphin to Brandon. My home provides shelter, refuge, and rest to every traveler who cares to drop in, be he working man, priest, teacher, tourist, or whatever. I am pleased to welcome each and everyone in my home, and I wish them all the best.

When there are no guests, I sit alone in the house—or, in summer, in the shade beside the house—and read or sing old Ukrainian songs. Sometimes I meditate or reminisce about the past and feel homesick for our native Carpathians which I left behind as a youth. I can almost see them and hear the gentle whisper of their pine trees, the burble of streams, the warble of the nightingale, and the trill of the lark.

8 A Ukrainian-English Dictionary

JOHN M ROMANIUK

Though the Ukrainian settlements made gradual progress in education, religion, and politics, some projects never achieved success. John M. Romaniuk's account of one such disappointment was published in the Ukrainian Voice *for 17 June 1942 as* "Ukraynisko-angliyskyi slowynk."

In 1905, a group of young fellows settled on farms near the present site of Myrnam, [Alberta,] remote from the railway, from other people, and from their own kith and kin. The most resourceful among them were my brother, Wasyl Romaniuk, and Pawlo Melnyk. Come an election or some conference, they were always in the forefront, going on speaking tours, serving as interpreters or advisers, and getting well paid for it all.

As more farmers settled in the area, they formed a statutory-labor district and elected my brother Wasyl as its secretary.[1] The difficulty he had to face was that his secretarial duties had to be conducted in accordance with the law, and though my brother knew English, he did not know it well enough. When it came to writing official letters, he had considerable trouble, mainly with spelling — which even an English person finds difficult. From time to time, he had to consult a dictionary to find the right word and how to spell it. The dictionary compiled by Mr. J. Krett was of little aid to him.[2] That gave him the notion of publishing an enlarged Ukrainian dictionary.

The two [Wasyl Romaniuk and Pawlo Melnyk] talked the matter over and wrote to Christie's Bookstore in Brandon for a couple of Webster's dictionaries. At that time, a Webster's cost seven dollars.

When the Webster's arrived, Pawlo opened one, and my brother exclaimed, "Oh, my goodness, what a big book! Thicker than the German Bible!"

As a matter of fact, the book weighed fourteen pounds; its pages were nine by eleven inches; it contained 1,956 pages of fine print from *A* to *Z*, an eighteen-page table of contents, 188 pages of appendices, maps of all parts of the world, and thousands of illustrations.

Reading the foreword, my brother learned that the dictionary had been published by Noah Webster, that it had taken thirty years to compile it, and 100 learned men, specialists with higher university education, to correct it. And here was my brother with Pawlo Melnyk attempting to translate it into the Ukrainian language. Neither of them had spent a single day in a university, although they had seen one from the outside. However, the sight of the English Webster's frightened neither my brother nor Melnyk from working on it. They bought up a quantity of scribblers, and my brother said to Pawlo, "I'm going to copy the letter *A*, and you get to work on letter *B*."

After some time, Pawlo and his wife paid a visit to my brother and found him hard at work. He was busy writing by the light of a lamp beside him on the table, and I, who am writing this reminiscence, was sliding a blotter down the list of words to point out the next one for my brother to copy. Pawlo looked at my brother's work and smiled as he remarked, "Oh, what a bunch of scribblers you have already filled!" And, indeed, on the table in front of my brother there lay a pile of scribblers, and yet he had hardly begun on the letter *A* in Webster's. A thought crossed my mind: should my brother succeed in translating Webster's, how would he be able to deliver his work to the printers — unless he used the "herlack" (hay rack)? He could deliver his translations to Melville in this way, and from there in a boxcar to the publishers.

"Pawlo," asked my brother, "how far did you get with the letter *B*?"

"I haven't even started yet," replied Pawlo. "Someone comes for his mail, then someone else comes, and my time is taken up. Then people drop in at night, and there is no way I can find time for writing."

"So what are you going to do about it?" inquired my brother.

"I have no idea," replied Pawlo.

Then my brother spoke. "It is no great matter to write, but who will print it?"

"The thing is to get it written, then something will turn up," replied Pawlo, and then added illogically, "Wouldn't it be better to find out first how much it would cost to have such a dictionary printed?"

Soon after spring work, my brother packed half a bagful of scribblers and, accompanied by Pawlo Melynk, set out for Rosthern. There they looked up a publisher. His typesetter, Victor Steshyn, was busy setting type for the newspaper *Novyi Krai*.[3]

My brother opened a suitcase full of scribblers and began to pile them in tens and twenties on the editor's desk.

"Well," responded the editor, "you have conceived a great idea, but it's a difficult proposition. It will take me a long time to print your dictionary, and it will cost you dearly. I have no linotype, and my one-and-only typesetter is barely able to meet the weekly deadline for the newspaper, besides having a few other things to do."

Steshyn, who listened to our conversation, heard the editor say "barely able to meet the deadline" and immediately resumed his typesetting with new vigor.

"For your dictionary I would have to find at least three more typesetters, and these days they are hard to come by in Canada," continued the editor.

"Well now," interjected my brother, "could you tell us, if you don't mind, how much it would cost to publish such a dictionary?"

The editor thumbed through the pages and found in one scribbler a number of English words which had been copied but not translated into Ukrainian.

"And what is the meaning of this?" he asked.

"That we don't know the meaning of those words in Ukrainian. We left them blank for the publisher to fill in their meanings."

"That means then that, in addition to typesetters, I would have to find an expert in the English and Ukrainian languages, some professor who knows several languages," the editor deduced.

My brother and Pawlo exchanged meaningful glances. And

The T. Shevchenko Ukrainian Educational Association, Transcona, Manitoba. The formation of such organizations reflected the desire of Ukrainian immigrants for learning.

Steshyn, to keep himself from laughing, pretended to cough.

The editor continued his questioning, "How many copies of the dictionary would you like to print?"

"At least 2,000 copies," my brother answered.

But Pawlo interrupted him, "What? Let's print 4,000 copies, since there's not a single copy in print yet either in Canada or United States. They'll move fast."

"It is true that there is no such dictionary in existence yet," declared the editor, "but to publish it one would have to have at least $40,000, and from $2,000 to $3,000 for proofreading. In order to get your money back and reap a small profit, you would have to price each copy at $45 to $50. And how many farmers would be willing to pay you that amount, when they are reluctant to pay for their newspapers?"

My brother and Pawlo remained silent, assessed the editor from head to toe, and then left, saying, "Not only the two of us but our entire district is not worth $40,000."

And so those $40,000 prevented us not only from publishing but also from compiling a Ukrainian-English dictionary.

9 PETER SVARICH
Organizing for Education

The next three narratives come from the pen of Peter Svarich. Mr. Svarich, who lived most of his life at Vegreville, Alberta, was a pioneer citizen widely known and highly esteemed among Ukrainian-Canadians. Arriving in this country as a youth, he passed through the hard school of pioneer life. In his pioneer days, he worked at a variety of jobs for a living but, in spite of his advanced education, he never looked upon manual work as degrading.

The image of the man which emerges from his memoirs is of one who faced life here with courage and with a sense of human dignity, who did not cringe before anyone, but put his skills to work in the new land and won respect for himself among strangers. Although his intelligence brought wealth within a relatively short time, he did not go the way of greedy materialists but used his resources for worthy causes. There was hardly a community enterprise to which he did not offer his efforts and money. And with his pen, he made numerous contributions to Ukrainian newspapers and almanacs.

In the 1950s, Svarich was asked to supply information on the educational development of Ukrainian communities in Alberta for inclusion in a university thesis. What follows is a translation of his response, which deals with a variety of interesting subjects besides education and reveals the author to be a very versatile and enterprising person who knew how to take advantage of the many opportunities open to him.

Because of my penchant for disseminating information and my interest in politics while a student in the gymnasium, I was about to be expelled from the school. I left of my own accord instead, studied privately, and took my matriculation examinations a year earlier than my classmates. I spent a year (1898-99) in the army cadet school at my own expense and achieved the rank of lieutenant in the Austrian army.

Due to political pressure on the part of the Polish-Austrian government, I saw no future for myself in Galicia and decided to emigrate to Canada.[1] I was also motivated by the fact that, in their early days in a foreign country, immigrant communities needed suitable leaders and patrons. I came to Canada with my parents and thirty other families from Sniatyn district in April 1900.

On the way, I experienced considerable difficulty with my "contingent," and it was even worse in our settlement in Alberta, located on the best land sixty-five miles east of Edmonton. Earlier immigrants numbering some 600 families had settled closer to town but in wooded and swampy areas.

In the first year, I invited a priest from the United States, the Reverend Ivan Zaklynsky, to minister to our settlers, and I used to tour the different colonies with him organizing church congregations and reading halls (to which I used to lend the books I had brought from the old country). I also went around collecting signatures for petitions to establish post offices at Wostok, Cracow (among Roman Catholic Ukrainians), Zawale, Sniatyn, Kolomea, Borschiw, Myrnam, and Slawa, as well as other post offices which were given English names — Whitfort, Soda Lake, Spring Creek, Wells Fort, and so on.

In 1901, I found a job in Edmonton, and soon afterwards I started a night school for Ukrainian boys and girls who worked in the city. In the late fall, I landed a job in a gold mine at Rossland, British Columbia, where a common laborer was paid 50 cents an hour, while wages for sectionmen were only 12½ to 15 cents an hour. During the winter I enlisted some sixty men to work in British Columbia mines, smelters, and sawmills.

The next year saw me prospecting for gold in the Klondike, near Dawson in the Yukon Territory. In a year and a half, I made $3,000 and returned home to the farm towards the end of 1904.

Now that I had the necessary financial resources, I took up farming, started a store, and opened a post office at Kolomea. At the same time, I organized a school district and a municipality and became secretary of both. I also became a building contractor: I built the first school in the area and secured a teacher for it in the person of Z. Bychynsky of Winnipeg. I formed a partnership with my neighbors, and we acquired the first steam threshing outfit in the area. As its engineer and machinist, I trained young boys to operate a steam engine and a threshing machine. In three years, twenty-six young fellows wrote and passed their examinations in steam-engine operation and received their certificates.

During the year 1905, when the province of Alberta was created and its government was established, I was able to obtain the following official positions: post master, registrar of vital statistics, game guardian, weed inspector, justice of the peace, and secretary of twelve school districts. The following year, I became a lecturer on farm operations—dairy, poultry, noxious weeds, grains, and livestock.

Vegreville, Alberta, 1904

In 1906, the CNR line was completed across our colony, and lots were surveyed for the townsite of Vegreville, seven miles from my homestead. I dismantled the log house that I had started building on my farm—a one-and-a-half-storey structure, thirty-two by forty feet—moved it to town, and within two months, I had a comfortable home in town, one-half of which I intended to convert into a store. But once I settled here, my plans took a different turn. Instead of a store, I opened up a real-estate office and became a notary public. I also started a night school at my home and lectured on the operation of steam engines.

In due course, I enlisted the assistance of John Bodrug, a Presbyterian minister in Manitoba, and we invited Dr. Broadfoot, who came from Toronto at the expense of the home-mission society and opened a little collegiate in my home. I was able to recruit some twenty students who had already received what was commonly called higher education in the old country and were employed here at various jobs in the towns and cities. After two years of studies, the more capable ones received their grade-eight standing. Some of them continued their education at the local high schools, completed grades nine and ten in one year, and proceeded to normal school. Upon completion of a six-month course at the normal school, they received a permit to teach in elementary schools in the province.

In 1909 and 1910, I traveled about organizing school districts on my own initiative and without official approval, with a view to becoming secretary of these districts during their initial years at least. In six of the districts, I was awarded a contract to build schools.

By that time, the Ukrainians had settled an area of some eighty by forty miles to the north of the CN line. . . . In the middle of this colony lay the town of Vegreville, and around this center, I organized the following school districts: Kolomea, Stanislawiw, Lviv, Brody, Zawale, Sniatyn, Podilia, Borschiw, Kyiw, Zaporozhe, Krasne, Pobida, Slawa, Myrnam, Myroslaw, Zhoda, Volia, and several others with Anglo-Saxon names. Besides myself, a self-proclaimed organizer of school districts, there was also an official government-appointed organizer, Robert Fletcher, who, with the assistance of an interpreter, T. Nemyrsky, acted in that capacity for five years. At the same time, he served as the official trustee and secretary of the schools he organized and hired teachers for these schools. He seemed to think that there was no one among the farmers competent to be a trustee or a secretary. There was a great deal of misunderstanding and trouble during his term of office.

Neither was I myself free of problems, as it was not always possible to find teachers for my schools, not even Anglo-Saxon teachers, let alone Ukrainian ones. In the years from 1909 to 1912, I persuaded ... [about a dozen] teachers from Manitoba and Saskatchewan to come to Alberta and secured permits for them. ... These teachers worked hard and conscientiously with their pupils and, during regulation school hours, used not only the English language for instruction but also Ukrainian. When school inspectors directed the attention of these teachers to the regulation that made English the only language permitted during school hours, while allowing Ukrainian only after the official school hours, many of them, unfamiliar with the Alberta Public Schools Act, failed to heed the inspectors' advice. They continued to teach as they were used to doing in Manitoba, where Ukrainian was permitted during school hours by the Conservative provincial government until the Liberals replaced the Conservatives and forbade it. Hence, there was quite a to-do about it in Alberta. Many of these teachers were dismissed by the government and went into business for themselves.

Teachers' salaries at that time were from forty-five to fifty dollars a month, and a few schools had teacherages built beside them. Each of the schools I built had a two-room living quarters for the teacher upstairs above the classroom.

In 1913, the third provincial election was held in Alberta. The Ukrainian settlers, upset by the Liberal government's refusal to permit the use of their language in schools during official school hours and by its failure to appoint either an official Ukrainian school-district organizer or a Ukrainian school inspector (there were qualified applicants for this position), nominated independent candidates in five electoral ridings. I was one of the candidates, but I lost by forty votes. Only one of them, Andrew Shandro, a Russophile, was elected.

*Andrew Shandro, 1886-1942,
the first Ukrainian MLA
in Canada, 1917*

Prosperous Ukrainian settlers

In this election, a lawyer, D. Boyle, was a winner in the Ukrainian district of Smoky Lake, and he was appointed minister of education. According to electoral law, he had to be reelected in his riding in order to remain a cabinet minister. The Conservatives mustered all their forces and funds to defeat Boyle, and he turned to me for help. Seeing how critical his situation was, I put forward certain requests and he was to give me a written pledge to fulfil them. If he were reelected and continued as minister of education, he would immediately publish a school act in the Ukrainian language and pay me $500 for its translation and for reading the printer's proofs. Also, he would open a teacher-training school where the young graduates of old-country gymnasiums could complete high-school and normal-school courses in three or four years and become qualified teachers. He agreed to honor these requests, and I went on a two-week campaign tour on his behalf, in my own car and at my own expense. In my appeal to the voters, I advised them to accept election money from the Conservatives but to vote for Boyle because he promised to give us a school act in the Ukrainian language and a school where we could train our own teachers for our children.

The election went off smoothly. Boyle won easily with a handsome majority, defeating the Conservative candidate Taylor, and thus became the minister of education. Soon afterwards, I received a contract to translate the school act into Ukrainian. I solicited the assistance of J. N. Kret, and together we completed the task in two weeks. Unfortunately, Shandro and his Liberal clique managed to convince Boyle that our translation was not accurate because it was not done in the literary language and style, and recommended that the Russophiles Ostrosky and Cherniak rewrite it. This they did, but in a Russian dialect using etymological orthography. When the school act was printed and sent out to the various school districts, it was returned by almost every school district with the complaint that the language was incomprehensible and, therefore, the book was of no use to them. Boyle, of course, realized that he had allowed himself to be deceived by the Russophiles and ordered the entire stock of the book to be burned. I got my $500, the Russophiles who were responsible for the mess got $1,000, and the printers got $2,000. And all of it gone down the drain!

As to the teachers' seminary, it was opened in September 1913, and I was commissioned to recruit suitable students, but they had to be residents of the province of Alberta. So, with the assistance of friends who had come from Manitoba and Saskatchewan, I advised prospective students who had completed the higher grades in the old-country gymnasiums to come to Alberta and apply for admission to this school. I undertook to supply them with all the necessary information. Within two weeks, some forty students had applied. Of these, I selected the thirty with the best qualifications, and they were accepted by the school, officially called the English School for Foreigners.

The course lasted three years and culminated in a third-class teaching certificate. The fee for room, board, and laundry was twenty-five dollars per month, paid in promissory notes (which actually were never collected). There was no tuition fee. During the three years (from 1913 to 1916) eight students dropped out. Having acquired a working knowledge of English, they decided to go into business. Of the twenty-two who completed the courses, only ten went into teaching. . . . The others found employment as clerks in the *Narodna Torhowla* [National Trading Company] which enjoyed phenomenal growth at this time, with branches in seven towns.[2]

The teachers' seminary was forced to close because the interruption of immigration during the war cut off the supply of suitable candidates with higher education. Another reason was that the local high schools were turning out large numbers of Ukrainian graduates who could go directly to normal school for their teacher training.

In 1916, when the P[eter] Mohyla Institute was opened in Saskatoon, the residents and farmers of Vegreville collected over $3,000 in contributions to this institution.[3] In 1917, it was decided to open similar boarding schools in Vegreville and Edmonton in order to enable the country students to attend high schools and the university. We collected some $2,000, and with this we established two boarding schools, the Taras Shevchenko *Bursa* at Vegreville and the Michael Hrushevsky Institute in Edmonton. In each of these boarding schools, there were approximately twenty students from the start. However, at Vegreville the enrollment of rural students in the public and high schools increased to the point where it was impossible to accommodate them all, and the school board had to refuse admission to students from out of town. It was then, in 1919, that we liquidated the Taras Shevchenko *Bursa* at Vegreville and merged it with the Hrushevsky Institute in Edmonton. . . .

The Michael Hrushevsky Institute existed from 1920 to 1950, and during those thirty years, it became the alma mater of hundreds of Ukrainian students. Today they are to be found in the various professions and in business, particularly in the latter. In 1950, the institute was sold for $30,000 and another building, a former Presbyterian college, closer to the university, was bought for $20,000. It was renovated and named Saint John's Institute. . . .

In addition to these facilities for Ukrainian students, the Presbyterian mission maintained the so-called Boys' and Girls' Home at Vegreville for twenty-four years. In it, some forty boys and girls each year received accommodation as well as high-school education; the mission maintained two paid teachers. The fee for board and lodging at this home was from five to fifteen dollars per month, and there was no charge for those who were unable to pay. For several years, I gave these students free private tuition in Ukrainian. When I quit, the tutoring was continued by Pastor R. M. Zalizniak. The Presbyterian mission hoped that eventually many of these students would become preachers, and thus the assimilation of Ukrainians would be hastened. But the venture proved disappointing to them for, having access to the students at the school, I was able to help them retain their cultural balance; out of some 200 students, only two became ninety-five percent assimilated. Although they understood Ukrainian, they did not speak the language. They married English girls and became members of the United Church, while all the others have retained their Ukrainian identity and remained in the Greek Orthodox faith.

Thanks to the educational institutions, our young people rushed to the city, filled up the boarding schools and the institute, and twice as many found lodging in private homes. They studied diligently and with enthusiasm and have won due recognition for themselves. . . . One can find many Ukrainian families with between three and five children who have graduated from universities and other institutions of higher learning and are now taking their places in Canadian society.

10 PETER SVARICH
Getting by

This excerpt from **Spomyny** *(Memoirs) by* **Peter Svarich** *originally appeared in the* **Ukrainian Voice** *on 11 December 1974. Here he recounts in more detail some of the experiences mentioned in the last chapter.*

When spring arrived [in 1901], I did not wait for the snow to melt and the water that inundated the roads to run off. Instead, I bade farewell to my family and took off for Edmonton to hunt for a job that would suit me, rather than waste my youth and my talent on a farm in the bush. My objective was to learn English well, to find a job in a store, and to earn enough money to set up my own country store some day, to open a post office, and to obtain an agency for the sale of farm equipment in my district.

In Edmonton, I applied for a job at every store, but none was available, since at that time there were only about ten stores on main street, two lumberyards, two hotels, three butcher shops, two restaurants, and a few boarding houses.

I landed my first job on the printing press of *The Bulletin,* owned by F[rank] Oliver, which was situated in a small frame building in the heart of the town. Here, my job was to operate the crank of the press that printed the paper and then to remove the type from the frames and wash it in gasoline. When that was done, I was to paper the walls inside the printing plant and plaster them with clay on the outside. For this work, I was paid six dollars a week, but half of my earnings went for board and room.

I found lodging with the John Kilar family, and soon after I moved in I agreed to build a house for him. He was to pay me forty dollars, but I had to cut the logs for the house by myself and float them on a raft as far as the bridge. This work took me a week, and I barely escaped drowning in the river.

In the meantime, a job paying thirty dollars a month turned up at Cushing's lumberyard. I sublet my contract to build Kilar's house to M. Rudyk, who paid me ten dollars for delivering the logs. At the lumberyard, I was kept busy doing a variety of tasks, such as unloading lumber from freight cars and piling it, as well as unloading shingles, bags of lime, and bricks. There were days when I made window frames and doors in the shop, and sometimes I worked as a carpenter building homes or as a painter painting them. I loved my work, though my pay was meager. However, I lived in hope of learning more about the business so I could become a sales clerk. The work would then be easier and the pay better. I felt sure of success in this firm, because the proprietor had taken a liking to me. Once in a while, he would give me an easy job in the office, such as designing detailed house plans, for I displayed a distinct talent for drafting.

But events took a different turn, and circumstances brought about a change in my plans. About the middle of June, the railway workers went on strike. It was unfortunate, for the railway was the chief source of employment for the first Ukrainian immigrants, who came here poor as church mice and had to have a job to keep their families alive. Some of them had left their wives behind in rented houses or in root cellars in the bush and had gone to work as section hands for the railway company. The pay for ten hours of hard work was seventy-five cents plus board and free transportation by rail.

Whatever the worker earned he immediately sent home to his wife to buy flour or a cow or clothing or footwear. If he earned eighty dollars during the whole summer, he felt a degree of satisfaction and pride when he returned home with the money in the fall.

The strike was called by the men in the railway workers' union, who were demanding higher pay. Our men were satisfied with the pay but were forced to quit their jobs because the strikers harassed them as scabs. They did not receive their pay for the first month and did not have a cent to their names. To make matters worse, the railway company would not provide them with free transportation from the section to town and would not feed them. Thus, these miserable souls, hungry and weary, had to foot it hundreds of miles from Medicine Hat to Calgary and from there to Edmonton, begging bread from farmers and ranchers along the way. In Edmonton, they had to wait several weeks before they got their meager pay cheques for a month's or six weeks' work. Hundreds of wretched, famished human beings milled around on the city streets without work and without food. Jobs in the city were just not available, and one could not go on begging for food forever.

I felt very sorry for those destitute fellows who roamed about the city—dirty, shabbily clothed, sunburned like gypsies, and totally helpless. I resolved to take it upon myself to help these people. I went to the land office and inquired if any help would be available for them. The officials responded sympathetically and took up a collection "for flour" which amounted to ten dollars. I told them that this aid would hardly be enough for one day.

Rally of unemployed Ukrainians, Winnipeg, in a vacant lot

It then occurred to one of the officials that there was a job available, and he fetched a map to show me. He revealed that plans were under way to clear an exhibition site on the riverbank beyond the bridge. Pointing to the map, he explained what actually had to be done and asked how much we would want for the job. I figured out that the area to be cleared covered about four acres, so I quoted eighty dollars as my estimate and asked him to let us keep the wood we cut. He agreed to my proposal. I took the news back to my men, and they were very pleased, as they could now earn enough to live on for at least a week. They asked me to round up enough axes for them and to show them where and how the wood was to be cut.

By now, I was convinced that these men were as helpless as children and that I would have to give up my job for a time and look after them. I procured axes and saws from the store, as well as some provisions, and as security, I put up our contract for eighty dollars. There were other men who were anxious to get a job with our group, but I had to make it clear that no one would be paid in cash for his work. The money would go towards provisions for all of them, regardless of whether they were employed or not. They would take turns at the job: ten men in the morning and ten in the afternoon, and new men each day.

The men were eager to work, and in a few days, we fulfilled the terms of our contract, received our pay, paid our debts, and still had enough cash left to live on for a few days.

In the city, there were several abandoned shacks, and we occupied them as our quarters for the night. A couple of them were [later] moved to the site of the present-day Macdonald Hotel, to serve as a market place on the riverbank. Here we made our headquarters and storehouse for flour and other provisions. We would stock several bags of flour at a time, half a pig (pork hocks and heads were given to us free by the butchers), as well as tea, sugar, and salt.

On the slope at the foot of the bank, we improvised kitchen ranges and heaters. We collected tin cans from bacon and conserves and used these as utensils for cooking, frying, and drinking. We baked flat cakes and biscuits, and cooked *pyrohy* and noodles which we greased with lard and greaves, [rendered pork fat chopped very fine]. We enjoyed our meals which we usually topped off with tea without milk and, at times, without sugar. If we managed to earn more than we needed for our provisions, we would divide sacks of flour in two and send a half bag to the wives and children of each of the unemployed, out in the country.

Since we had to have at least ten dollars a day to feed our crew, it was essential to be forever on the lookout for jobs. But jobs were hard to come by in the city, and work on the farm paid only five dollars a month. I went around knocking on doors in search of any kind of employment for these men. Usually, someone offered a chore around the house or store for a dollar or two. Needless to say, I came up with a variety of suggestions for jobs, such as cleaning toilets, moving outdoor toilets to new sites, building a new fence around a lot or mending an existing one, digging a well or cleaning the old one, cutting or trimming trees, grubbing out the stumps on a lot, plastering the stable or cowshed, repairing the roof, or bringing in a load or two of wood and sawing and splitting it. I went around and managed to pick up odd jobs here and there. As long as the townspeople took advantage of our low rates and hired us, we were not idle and did not go hungry.

For each kind of job, I had a brigade of workers equipped with the proper tools. I assigned the men to each job and explained how it was to be done. When the job was finished, my cashier and I collected the earnings. We had an elected committee and cashier, and if we had any cash on hand, we handed it over for safekeeping to Johnson Walker, the merchant from whom we bought everything we needed.

In this way, we managed to get by from day to day, hoping the railway strike would end soon. But we were disappointed, to say the least, as the strike dragged on throughout the entire summer and into the fall. In the meantime, my fellow workers each went his separate way, some to relatives in the country, others to the English and German farmers who paid ten to fifteen dollars a month at harvest time, and several to jobs in town—at the kiln, in the Humberson mines, or at Fraser's sawmills. And I returned to my former job at Cushing's lumberyard and helped to deliver bricks and lumber for the school that was being built on the site of the present freight offices by the station.

11 PETER SVARICH
Section Hand

A second installment of Mr. Svarich's recollections was published in the Almanac of the Ukrainian Voice *for 1953 as* "Urywok z spomyniw Petra Zwarycha" *(An Excerpt from the Memoirs of Peter Svarich).*

Fifty years have gone by since I worked for the CPR as a section hand. My work lasted only two weeks; it was in the year 1901 when railway workers began to organize into unions, and a strike was called in May.[1] Section men worked ten hours a day for $1.25, and from this amount, deductions were made for board, hospitalization, and so on.[2] The long-time workers, like the Italians and the Slovaks, were easily persuaded to strike for better wages, whereas our Ukrainian workers were, at first, happy with their pay. When the men quit working, the company stopped boarding them and delayed paying the wages they had coming. When the workers finally received their pay, some 200 of them quit and went their separate ways. Some headed for the ranches, some for the mines near Frank, and others set out on foot for Edmonton.

It was only after a long search that I finally landed a job — at digging ditches. When the strike ended and the company raised the wages from 12½ to 15 cents an hour, I signed up for work in the westernmost zone—then called Logan and now Lake Louise, the famous tourist resort—which lay on the border of Alberta.

On my arrival, the first thing I did was fumigate our living quarters, which were in a railway car, with sulphur fumes. Then I carried in enough pine boughs to make a bed. I furnished my residence with boxes and blocks of wood, and let other workers share it with me — two Slovaks and one "dago" (Italian).[3] We were all four of approximately the same age and temperament.

I was not conditioned to hard work, and the montonous tamping of ties all day long to the command of the boss — "Hurry up!" — squeezed the last breath out of me; my arms went numb, and I could scarcely drag my feet.

One day, over supper in a restaurant, I asked the roadmaster how long I would have to work on the section gang in order to

Boxcar dorms for railway construction workers

Railway construction on the Toronto to Sudbury line

become a foreman and then a rodmaster or even perhaps, a superintendent.

He asked me, "Are you a Galician or a German?"

"I am a German," I answered.[4]

"And what is your education?"

"College," I answered.

"If so, you can become a section foreman in a year or two, and a roadmaster in about ten years, and that's it."

"In that case, I am going to quit soon, as I cannot do physical work, only mental work, and for this I have the necessary qualifications—technical, mechanical, and other," I replied.

"Well, if that's the situation, you will work on locomotives in the roundhouse, cleaning, firing up, and so on, at 17½ cents an hour, as soon as there is a vacancy."

Back I went to tamp ties. I tamped until tears rolled down my cheeks and sweat dripped off my brows, but no matter how hard I pounded that gravel it would not stay underneath the tie. And the boss kept up his "Hurry up!" and swore at me every time I trailed behind the others. Finally, he grabbed the shovel away from me, handed me a scythe with a crooked, serpent-like handle which was even heavier than the shovel, and ordered me to mow along the track.

"Help me God," I said prayerfully, and down came the rustling willow shrubs, as my scythe swished through them. I had been a good mower even back in the old country, for I had learned the technique in the meadows. The next day I made myself a straight, Galician-type scythe—the handle from poplar wood—sharpened the blade, and, now working independently of the boss, continued to mow the shrubs and the thick wild grass in swaths along the railway track. I was dead tired, and I let the boss know that I would like another job or else to quit.

He replied, "Then you can burn the old ties in the ditches or clean up the yard."

"Good," I answered, "I will do both."

At this job, I took it easy for two weeks until I was assigned to shovel coal onto the coal chute.

At this time, news spread like wildfire that the heir to the British throne, the Prince of Wales (who ascended the throne as Edward VII following the death of Queen Victoria) was coming to Canada. While in Calgary, he heard of the beautiful lake up in the mountains near Logan whose placid surface reflected the blue sky and the magnificent panorama of snow-capped mountains. He wished to see this wonder of nature with his own eyes but, unfortunately, in those days there was no easy access to the lake. I had seen this lake quite often, both at close range and from a distance, as I liked to rove about the mountains on Sunday evenings and enjoy the lovely views. My superiors were aware of my jaunts to the lake since I used to talk about them at supper.

One day, the roadmaster called me to his office and inquired if I was familiar with the terrain between the station and the lake, and if I knew which was the easiest access to the lake. This I did know, and very well too, and to prove it I drew a map of the area one mile south of the station and marked on it the contour lines as well as the openings in the forest. As a result, he appointed me trail blazer to this lake which, incidentally, had not yet been named Lake Louise. He let me have four men and one day to clear a trail to the lake, wide enough for the cavalcade of the prince and his retinue. We took plenty of food with us, for we dared not return until our assignment was completed. In the meantime, the section foreman, with the help of three other men, cleaned and decorated the yard for the parade.

Being thoroughly familiar with the entire terrain, I joined my men in clearing a path a yard wide, broad enough for horses to pass through in a single file. When we had completed the trail all the way, we had ample time left to widen the path to four feet where we thought it was necessary. It took us sixteen hours to make the trail, which was almost a mile long. In addition, we erected a long pole with the Union Jack flying on top and piled rocks around it to hold it up.

The next day, the royal train arrived with the prince and his retinue. Sixteen Mounted Police, who, with their horses, had arrived earlier in an ordinary freight train, arranged themselves in two ranks to meet the heir to the throne. The prince, part of his retinue, and the Mounted Police proceeded along the path to the lake, while we workers, along with a couple of policemen, remained behind to guard the royal train. As we bantered with the policemen, one of us hinted that we should get some goodies from the royal table. Earlier on, we had greeted the prince with the yell: "Three cheers for the prince!"; now we yelled, "Three cheers for the royal cooks!" and "Three cheers for the butlers!"

Well, our cheering of the royal servants paid off, for they showered us with gifts from the prince's buffet—a variety of drinks, foods, and dainties as a pleasant memento of the visit by the prince to this spot in the Rocky Mountains near Field.

When the royal train departed for Vancouver and the Mounted Police returned to Calgary, we pioneers and trail blazers, together with section men and machinists, met in a restaurant and gave ourselves a royal banquet.

At this time, there were about thirty of us at this railway division point; today it is the largest summer resort in the national park, with magnificent hotels and tourist camps. An asphalt road leads to the semicircle of lake below the mountains. And to the right of this road is my path, serving the pedestrians to this very day.

12 JOHN M ROMANIUK
On the CPR

John M. Romaniuk of Myrnam, Alberta, contributed his reminiscences to the **Almanac of the Ukrainian Voice** *in 1942, under the title* **"Z Boha ne kepkui"** *(Scoff Not at God).*

It all took place after Easter in 1904. Neighbor joined neighbor, brother joined brother, son joined father as they packed their knapsacks and got ready to leave for work.

In Edmonton, the CPR was hiring men to work on the building of its railroads. First they were hired as laborers for the section gang, then for an extra gang or bridge gang, and finally, when the ground had thawed sufficiently, to operate the steam shovels. Although officially there was no fee for signing up for employment, that particular spring a fee of one dollar was charged to each worker.

All matters pertaining to employment were the responsibility of the superintendent in Calgary. When men were needed, he would send a telegram to the stationmaster at Strathcona who worked hand in hand with the agent. The agent signed up men for work and then escorted them by train to the different sections where workers were needed. There the men were dumped off. The married men, for the most part, schemed to get a job on a section close to home. In the summertime, the wife would send her husband a crock of cheese, some butter, a bag or two of potatoes, and this would mean an appreciable saving on his grocery bill.

Man proposes; God disposes. People plan one thing, but fate often has something else in store for them. Many a man who schemed to get a job closer to home ended up as far away as Medicine Hat or British Columbia. Wherever the snow happened to disappear first, that was where the men were dispatched first.

That year the winter was heavy, and all construction was delayed until late spring. The men in Edmonton were held up until the middle of May. There were so many looking for jobs that spring that the city streets were full of them. There were men from Galicia, Bukovina, Poland, and Wallachia. They were getting impatient with waiting for a call to work. But it was the married men who had

Laborers opening a new mine, Cobalt, Ontario

no relatives in the city who were the most anxious. There were some among them who had daughters working in Edmonton. They borrowed money from the girls and thus helped one another as best they could. No one suffered from hunger although some of the men arrived in Edmonton with only fifty cents or so in their pockets. Fortunately, people are not that hardhearted. One would lend a few cents, another would give a few cents, and thus the penniless fellow managed to survive from day to day.

In those days, there was still Christian love among our people. Squabbles over religion were unknown, and the people breathed the spirit which they had brought from Galicia—the spirit of religion and friendliness.

The situation was different in the case of young single fellows who had held jobs before. They could not be bothered to call at Strathcona every day to check when the next work crew would be departing. It was the married fellows and those who were trying for their first job who attended to that daily task. The single fellows got their information from them.

If the experienced workers preferred to go to the mines, to the camps in the bush, or to the sawmills, they knew they would have to pay train fare out of their own pocket. But they also knew how to get there without cost to themselves, since they had pulled the stunt before. Here is how: they signed up for work on the section or extra gang, and when they got free transportation to their destination, they took off for some other job, as men were needed everywhere in British Columbia.

"If I could only get to British Columbia, I'd wave good-bye to the CPR," one would say. "I'm not crazy about roasting in the sun tamping ties or carrying a lining bar for eighty-five cents a day.[1] Gone are the days when sweat flooded my eyes on the track. I can work in the shade of a roof at a sawmill, or in the bush. If I can't get a job in the mine at Frank, I can get one at Coleman or at Michel. Or at Fernie, for sure, because ever since they had an explosion there they are always short of men. Let the immigrant guys tamp ties, pump handcars, and eat what Paraska cooks and takes to them in her apron."[2]

The men who already had jobs could be distinguished from those trying for their first job by their white shirt collars, Sunday shoes, fresh shave every morning, and their daily strolls on the streets with their friends. And at night or in the morning, they liked to recount what they had seen in the theater.

The admission price to the theater was five cents between one and six o'clock in the afternoon and ten cents from seven to eleven at night, and for fifteen cents, one could see a vaudeville show where half-nude girls danced and performed silly acrobatics on the stage. Dances were rarely held because of the cost of hiring the hall and the orchestra. To add to the expense, collections were taken to buy beer. Besides, one seldom ever thought of dancing, for during those four or five weeks of waiting for a job, many a man's pocket became empty.

Every way of life has its compensations. One of the "old Canadians" was once overheard saying to another, "Come, let's go uptown, chum; we'll take in one more show, for tomorrow we might land in British Columbia."

And the other fellow answered, "I am not going. I have seen enough of those shows. I would rather have something to eat."

His "chum" pulled a quarter out of his pocket and said, "Let's go to the Chinaman and order some ham and eggs. You are not going to eat dry bread wrapped up in newspaper like that old fogey over there who lives on hard-boiled eggs and cheese brought from the farm. We don't belong to this kind; we should be living it up like city slickers. I borrowed five dollars from a woman yesterday, you know."

"Was it from the one that works at Namao?"

"I wouldn't bother with her! She is still a kid and a silly goose. I asked her how old she was, and the giddy thing says to me, 'Can't you tell by my teeth?' I borrowed from the one that works in the dining room of the Alberta Hotel. Mike swindled the gal that works at Queen's Laundry—got ten dollars out of her. And Pete, he gypped twenty dollars from some Bukovinian woman."

As they walked uptown, the first fellow continued, "Tomorrow let's go to church. Katie was telling me that the priest announced a series of services that he's going to conduct every evening for a month. Katie said she will let all the girls that work in the city know about it. There should be a lot of girls in church, and it will be worth our while to attend. Maybe your Dora will be there, too. I already told Mike and Pete about the church service. They said they'll come."

To help you understand what this is about, I should briefly explain about these evening services. When the construction of the Basilian church in Edmonton was nearing completion,[3] the young parish priest, Father Dydyk, announced May services in honor of Virgin Mary. Many were unfamiliar with this service since it had not been performed in rural churches. It began with evening prayers at four o'clock in the afternoon and ended with *acathistus* or with the celebration of the Eucharist.[4] The first service was attended by only three or four working girls. Most of the girls worked in hotels and restaurants and were too busy before supper to attend church. The nuns spoke briefly with the girls at the service and found out why there were so few of them in the church. There were at this time some 400 Ukrainian girls working in Edmonton and a large number at Strathcona. They were daughters of poor parents, and they took jobs in the city to earn at least enough to buy their own clothes. Having learned the reason why there were so few present at evening prayers, Father Dydyk changed the time of the prayers from four to seven o'clock in the evening, and the attendance improved.

When the cantor found it difficult to sing certain parts in this service, the nuns came to his rescue. There were two of them. One sang soprano and the other a melodious alto. Often when they sang a duet, the worshippers were spellbound by their harmonious voices, which seemed to rise heavenward until they melted into the unfinished dome of the church. Praise of their singing spread all over the city like wildfire, and each evening more people came to the church. And the more people there were, the longer the service got, as the priest now added a sermon and the anointment of the worshippers.

Here and there outside the church, single fellows stood in small groups waiting for the girls to come out. Then they escorted the girls, arm in arm, to their places of work. For some of the young fellows, these promenades had happy endings. Instead of paying back the money he borrowed from her, the young suitor would marry the girl when he returned from his work. In most cases, the newlyweds went back to the country and took up farming.

Finally, the long-awaited request for workers came. The agent in charge signed up enough men to fill two train coaches. Only a few of them were assigned to work on sections between Edmonton and Calgary. The others [of us] were all taken to Calgary. At Calgary, when I returned to the train after my supper in a downtown restaurant, I looked into two coaches and found them both nearly empty. All but a few of the men were gone with their luggage. Call them 'old fogeys' if you will,[5] but when the train stopped at the station and the men found out that they were to be assigned to dig ditches, they grabbed their bags, ran out the other door, and before their escort returned from his supper, there was no trace left of them. The only ones who remained were the few who were on the way to British Columbia.

"What's the matter? Where have they all gone?" asked the escort. He stood there for a while and walked away towards the nearby building which had painted on it in large, yellow letters the words "Superintendent's Office." After a while, he reappeared in the coach and announced, "If any of you men wish to buy anything uptown, please hurry as our train is due to leave shortly."

The men ran out to buy bread or sausage or tobacco, and in the meantime, the locomotive shunted another coach to the front of the station and left it there. When the men returned from town, they boarded this coach just before the train started to move. But did they ever get a surprise when they discovered that their coach had been shunted from the front of the station to a side track and was left spotted there! The windows in this coach could not be opened, and the doors at both ends were locked. The men locked up in this coach were assigned by the superintendent to jobs at points in British Columbia where runoff from snow melting in the mountains was washing away the railroad grade.

Toward evening, we arrived at Fort Macleod and were transferred to a passenger train en route from Medicine Hat to the mountains.

About eight o'clock in the morning, we were approaching the town of Frank. All of a sudden—Bang! Bang! like the sound of gun shots pierced the air. It came from torpedoes placed on the rails and now exploding under the wheels of the locomotive to warn of danger. The train immediately ground to a stop. On the track stood a guard with a red flag, and he warned the conductor of the danger ahead. The conductor attached a small apparatus to the telegraph wire, tapped it a few times with his finger, returned to the coach, and ordered the passengers to leave the train and take their luggage with them.

We learned that during the night the peak of [Turtle] . . . Mountain had come down in a landslide.[6] The CPR offered $150 to anyone who would climb up to the peak of this mountain and plant

Ukrainians employed in CPR construction,
Crowsnest Pass, about 1909

a red flag on top of it. As far as I know, there was no one brave enough to accept the offer.

The avalanche buried four square miles of the valley. By the time we had walked around the area and reached Blairmore (the first station past Frank), it was almost noon. Here another train was waiting to take us farther west. Our fear was indescribable as rocks thundered down the mountainside. The deafening roar resounded in the mountains and intensified the terror of our group, especially of the women who walked behind us men.[7] The river at the foot of [Turtle] . . . Mountain lay under the debris of the landslide, and the current was doing its work. One had to exert all his strength and skill to leap from one rock to another, over the water. This feat was out of the question for women, and we were compelled to look for an easier passage. Rock after rock kept hurling down, one coming straight at us. The women shrieked in fright, "Look, look! Coming our way!" and grabbed hold of the men, hanging on with both hands. Fortunately, the rock did not reach us. It hit the bottom and broke up into "small" pieces each the size of a large building.

Inside that mountain there was a coal mine. The miners who worked in it at the time were safe, for the entrance to the mine was not blocked by the landslide. However, the miners who worked day shift and slept at night were buried under the avalanche. It was

Men working in a mine shaft, King Edward Mine, Cobalt, Ontario

reported that seventy of them lost their lives. In the town of Frank, only one bank and one store escaped being buried.

Before we left Blairmore, several CPR gangs arrived at the scene of the tragedy. There was as much commotion and confusion as in a disturbed anthill. The Italians yelled, *"Alla svelta! Alla svelta!"*; the Swedes, "Yumpin' Yesus!"; others waved their arms frantically and shouted, "This way; this way!"

In the midst of this confusion, a few more men from our group disappeared. They were the same fellows who, back in Edmonton, had often wished, "If only we could get to Bill's."

Bill, whose Ukrainian name was Wasyl, worked in the mine at Frank and was making good money—$80 to $120 every two weeks. But he did not use his head. Now that he was a miner, he pursued the vices of a miner: boozing, poker, gambling, and so on. His earnings did not last from one payday to the next, and he was forced to borrow money from others. Some of the miners were expert card players, and Bill was no match for them. There were also those who traveled from mine to mine to play cards for high stakes. Picture Bill sitting at a card table with these sharks. A good hand, and Bill fairly leaps with joy. "Three Hudson Bay factories!" (that is, three kings); and one of the sharks responds as he lays his cards gently in front of Bill, "Three New York factories!" or "All blue!"[8]

In his three years as a miner, Bill's sense of religion deteriorated badly. He philosophized that there was no God, that God had been left behind in the old country. "Just to show you," he would say, "I worked on a holy day, and no harm came to me, although the shack where I used to live is now fifty feet under the avalanche. I am still here, alive and well! Holy days are an invention of the priests. Take that Slovak woman that used to board us. How pious she used to be! And yet she was buried by the landslide while her husband, who doesn't believe in God either, is also alive and well. Tomorrow is another holy day, but I'm going to work as usual, and nothing will happen to me. You will see! I've got to pay Slim the fifty dollars that I lost yesterday on a 'full house'."

Thus philosophized Bill, on the eve of the Feast of the Elevation of the Holy Cross, in disdain of those miners who were going to observe the feast by taking the day off.[9]

At nine o'clock in the morning of this holy day, Bill and his buddy were already in the mine. At noon, the miners picked up their lunch kits and began to eat, each in his own "room." On the way to his room, Bill began to poke fun at the religious fellows: "Yesterday they were so stubborn, insisting that it was wrong to work on a holy day. And yet, look! We have already finished half our shift, and nothing has happened to us. Come with me and I will show you how much coal I got with one blast. Half a roomful! And there will even be some left over for tomorrow."

The men to whom Bill was boasting were curious to see what he had done. They strolled over to Bill's room. Bill and his partner went inside, and the other two miners remained in the "pantry." From there they could see Bill's good luck. In the meantime, two other men appeared on the scene. They were the same fellows who the night before had had an argument with Bill about the existence of God. Bill spied them and hollered, "Take a good look, you fellows! See for yourselves that nothing has happened to me. Your arguments about today being a holy day were just so much rubbish. Take a good look—"

Those were his last words. A loud rumble, and Bill and his friend vanished. In a twinkling of an eye, the spot where they stood became a deep abyss, and they both landed 300 feet below.

Those who are familiar with the Frank mine know that the rooms in the mine were worked one above the other, since the coal seam ran vertically. The south side of the mine, though much older than the north side where Bill worked, did not collapse. Even the strong props on the north side did not help matters. Neither did Bill's boasting about his room being on the very top. It did not occur to him that his room was like the top rung of a ladder which

144

suddenly snapped and dropped him 300 feet below, under the ruins.

Was it ordained by Providence that the men with whom Bill argued over the existence of God were to witness the dreadful disaster? Their rooms in the mine were underneath Bill's, and now they were not able to get into them. But — much more important — they were alive and remained good Christians.

It took the miners a day and a half to dig out the bodies of Bill and his partner. Their bones were crushed into tiny splinters, and their bodies had turned as blue as if they had been painted with blue paint.

Funeral arrangements were in the care of the miners' union. The union bought oak coffins at $250 each and hired a Protestant minister to officiate, so that both bodies were given a Christian burial. The funeral was attended by all the miners. The two caskets were lowered into one grave. A few small stones were placed on it.

I shall never be able to forget those two men. On appropriate occasions, I like to relate the story of their tragic fate. I believe it has a lesson for all of us: never scoff at God.

13 NIKOLA WIRSTA
Endurance

Nikola Wirsta's narrative reads like a catalogue of the different jobs he tried in Canada, but it is interesting because it illustrates some of the problems immigrant workers had to face. It also reveals the strength and courage which made them such an asset in Canada's economic development. This account originally appeared under the title Moyi perezhyvanya w Kanadi *(My Experiences in Canada) in* W. A. Chumer's *book* Spomyny (Recollections), *published in Edmonton in 1942.*

There were nine of us in the family, five boys and four girls. The oldest brother died when he was seven, and eight of us remained. Our parents were poor. They began their husbandry with only a morg and a half of land, but they worked very hard, and before they reached old age, they had increased their holdings to a total of fourteen morgs. We children used to help them with their work.

As a small boy I went to school but learning did not come easy to children worn out with hard work at home. I had barely completed three grades when my parents appealed to the priest and the principal of the school to release me from classes on the grounds that my help was urgently needed at home. Thus my school days were cut short. Such was the custom in those days, for the older folk to show greater concern for their work than for the education of their children. At sixteen, I had to go to work with the mowers, swinging my scythe side by side with them in the landlord's grainfield like a full-grown man.

In 1907, I was called up by the army, and I served in the thirtieth regiment of the artillery, stationed at Pekulychi near Peremyshl in Galicia. At first, life in the army was quite a confusing experience, but when I got used to it, it wasn't all that bad. In 1909, I was transferred to Vienna for four months and then to Prague. I spent two months there. I learned a great deal in foreign countries, even to speak German. In 1910, I was assigned back to the regiment in Peremyshl. Shortly after that, I asked my major for a two-week leave to visit my parents at home. It was granted.

While I was in the army, four young men from our village had left for Canada. At that time, little was known about Canada in our country; it was always referred to as America. When I called on the families of the four young fellows, they showed me the letters they had received from the boys. All four of them said they were doing well, and each was earning fifteen crowns per day. They had even sent their parents some money.

I indicated to my parents that I, too, wanted to go to America. The sooner the better, so overwhelming was my desire to go. My father would not approve of it. He warned me, "Son, you are a soldier, and you can't desert the army or you will pay for it when you get caught."

My answer was that I had served the army for eight months without any remuneration, and there was not the least benefit from it to anyone. So I made up my mind then and there to quit the army. My brother agreed with me, and father stopped discouraging me. Instead, he asked, "And what are you going to do with your uniform and your sword?"

"I will send them back to the regiment."

That very same day, I wrote to the travel agents for information, and in a few days I received their answer. I appealed to the local magistrate, whom I knew well, to issue me a work book for employment in Germany, which he did.

I spent eight days of my leave at home. My father then took me to the railway station at Krehkovich. It was hard to say good-bye to dad. We showered each other with kisses and both broke down in tears. We both had the feeling that we would never see each other again. Dad implored me to watch my conduct in Canada, to respect others, to be thrifty, to remember my brothers and sisters at home, to never forget about God and never give up my faith.

Towards evening I arrived in Peremyshl and was strongly tempted to meet my acquaintances at the station. However, I dared not leave the coach for fear of being recognized in my civilian clothes. Through the window I spied a very close friend of mine, sergeant Orzyknowski, but I pretended that I did not know him. For a few tense moments, my heart was in my throat—what if someone should find out that I was a deserter?

At Myslowic, our passports were checked. I was accompanied by my cousin Petro Luklan, a young fellow who carried his work book with him; it was his pass to Germany. The agents immediately began to sort the passengers into groups according to their destination, and thus we fortunately got into Germany. I breathed a sigh of relief, for now I was certain that I would not be deported.

On 6 March, we were on our way to Antwerp in Belgium. While we waited for our ship, we went on a sight-seeing tour of the city and viewed the big buildings and beautiful churches.

On 9 March, we were at sea. Our ship was a freighter that

Some men left Ukraine to avoid military service.

transported cattle from Canada to Belgium. The bunks in the hull of the ship were of iron and were placed one above the other in a space jammed with over 200 men. Before our departure from Antwerp, the agents had lavishly praised the ship and its comforts, and made us believe it was an express ship with four funnels. Yet here we were in the same hull where cattle had been loaded for transport, now scrubbed and whitewashed to kill that bovine stench.

On 21 March, we reached Saint John and from there proceeded to Quebec. Here we had to submit to health inspection. On the ship, most of us were very ill, and the food was bad. We were served a lot of fish, but it only aggravated our illness. On inspection, each of us was required to show his money. It was rumored that if one did not have twenty-five dollars in cash with him, he would be sent back home. I was terrified since I only had fifteen dollars in my possession. However, an emergency can sometimes prompt one to think quickly: I folded my ten-dollar bill in two so that both top corners showed, and as we filed past the official, I showed him my "twenty-five dollars." When this ordeal was over, I was very happy to be safe and sound in Canada. Once on Canadian soil, I thought, all my trials and tribulations were behind me. In a few hours we boarded a train and were on our way, westward bound. . . .

At one small station before Winnipeg, we recognized a countryman of ours, Fedir Yatsuk, as he boarded the train. Unable to find a job, he was returning to Winnipeg. We were very happy to meet him, for we knew that he would be very helpful to us. We spent the first night with him, sleeping together on the same mattress on the floor, as he had no bed in his room. The next day, we went uptown to buy some food and to look for a job. However, there was no job to be found anywhere. On the third day while we were out again looking for a job, we came upon a group of men who were milling around in front of some office. We heard them speak Ukrainian so we approached them and asked them what they were waiting for. They replied that men signed up for employment at this place.

"What kind of employment?" we asked.

We learned from them that men were needed to plow and haul earth with mules and that the pay was thirty-five dollars a month plus board. That, I thought, was a pile of money. In the old country, one could not earn that much in half a year. We signed up for the job.

The next morning we left by train and towards evening arrived in a small town called Balcarres, in Saskatchewan. From the station, we had to walk about a couple of miles to a field full of all sorts of wagons, plows, scrapers, and other equipment as well as a herd of horses and mules. This field was part of a ranch belonging

Men on the move, about 1910

to D. J. MacArthur.[1] He was the chief road and railroad contractor.

The next morning, we got started on our jobs. We rolled up the tent, loaded everything on the dumping wagons, and set out westward like Tatars across the steppes. After driving about eighteen miles, we set up our tent on the banks of a beautiful little river. Unfortunately, its beauty was marred by a mass of snakes swimming in it; never in my entire life have I seen so many.

Our first job was to build a grade for a railroad. Some of us plowed; others hauled the earth with great big scrapers called "Fresnos." The men who worked with four mules or horses were paid forty dollars a month. Although the work was hard, the pay was good. The job lasted eight months, until freeze-up. From my earnings here, I was able to send sixty dollars to my parents and later, from Winnipeg, another forty.

In the winter, I signed up for bush work at Fort Frances at twenty dollars a month. I could hardly complete one month, for the winter was severe, the cold bitter, and the work hard. When I quit, I set out on foot for the railway station, a distance of eighteen miles. Fortunately there was a CN water tank alongside the track and, in it, a cheery fire in the heater. I warmed myself and continued on my way until I reached the station. In a few hours, the train arrived,

Immigrants worked at logging and other manual labor.

and I boarded it for Winnipeg. In those days, unemployed men carrying packs on their backs like beggars in the old country wandered from station to station. If a fellow did not have any money, he had no alternative but to hoof it hungry and cold, sometimes hundreds of miles. Sooner or later, however, all things good and bad must come to an end, and we wish to forget the bad.

After a few days in Winnipeg, I found a job on an "extra gang." The pay was $1.25 per day, but I had to board myself. The work was hard, but one had to work hard for a living in those days. I put in a whole month at this job.

I was toying with the idea of getting a job in a mine in British Columbia, but eventually I signed up for a job on road construction near Edson. That was in 1911. The pay was two dollars a day, but a dollar a day was deducted for board. From Winnipeg, we went on the CN to Edmonton and then to Edson. From Edson to Hinton, the train crawled at between five and ten miles per hour because the grade was flooded and littered with debris. It rocked like a ship, and we were scared stiff. It seemed as though at any moment it might tip over or roll off the tracks. From Hinton, we traveled on foot for two days to a place which was covered with tents and all sorts of equipment, ready for work. It was on the Grand Trunk Railway.

We took our mattocks, picks, spades, and axes with us, and felled trees and cleared brush for a wagon trail. The ground was still frozen. Our foreman was a Scotsman; he was hard to get along with and was forever swearing and cursing. After working two days under him, we fled. On the way back, we came upon another similar gang, and the foreman offered us a job. He was much more humane, and we worked under him until fall.

In the winter of 1912, we signed up in Edmonton for bush work west of Edson. We were employed there for two months but got nothing for our work because our contractor went bankrupt. Famished, we barely reached Edmonton. In Edmonton, we found a boarding house on Kinistino (Ninety-sixth Street) at twenty dollars a month, but neither of us had a cent to his name. For three days, we looked desperately for work in and around the city and finally found a job in a brickyard. We earned just barely enough to pay our landlady for board and room.

In the spring, we went back to Hinton again and found employment on a railroad track until fall. That winter, I signed up for a job in the bush again, this time at Prince Albert. I did not last long on the job because of illness and returned to Edmonton. In the summer of 1913, I worked at whatever odd jobs I found. In the winter of 1914, I moved to Brew Lake to square timbers for railroad ties. There I heard of a new coal mine that had just opened, and before long, I got a job in it. Our crew was assigned to dig a tunnel through to the coal bed. We blasted with dynamite day and night until we finally reached the coal. The tunnel was over 600 feet in length. The work was extremely dangerous, but man must work if man would live.

Even after the coal bed had been reached, the work was hard, for there was no fresh air until a shaft was dug for ventilation. But by that time, the miners had quit the job, and in the end, I had no choice but to return to Edmonton.

At this time, war broke out between Austria and Serbia, and all aliens were required to register. In Edmonton, Ivan Ivanitsky and I got a job at the Western Steel Company. After three months of employment we were laid off, presumably because we were aliens. We decided to go to Delph, Alberta, where our countrymen Mikhailo Tychkowsky and Wasyl Fedyniak lived. Here we landed jobs on a threshing outfit at fifty cents a day. We stayed through the winter. For something to do, I taught Ukrainian to children of Ukrainian parents at fifty cents per child per month.

In 1915, I returned to Brew Lake and found myself back in the mine. My boss was Mr. Blake and, later, Mr. Corrie. Both were very reasonable and fine gentlemen, and I got along very well at my job. I stayed with it for a year and a half and earned enough to go into partnership with two other fellows in a moving-picture business.

We rented a hall in the Rudy Block in Edmonton, but our business was short-lived because of high rent and the high cost of films. Charging five cents for admission, we could not make ends meet. In a month, our business folded up, and I left with Dmytro Halushko for the mines at Yellowhead near the Coalspur branch.[2]

A cave-in at a coal mine almost took my life. There was no point in staying here any longer, so I moved to Corbin, British Columbia, where I worked at odd jobs, and later to Blairmore and Rosedale. In 1918, I returned to the Coalspur and to another mine job, this time at Cadomin.

The war was over when, in 1919, I received a letter from the old country with news that conditions there were worse than they had been under Austrian rule; so I made up my mind to stay in Canada. I built myself a shack at Cadomin and resolved to get married. The girl who became my wife was the daughter of Wasyl Kutyr of Chipman, Alberta.

In 1920, there was a dreadful fire at Cadomin mine, and fifty of us miners labored for a month trying to extinguish it. We worked sixteen hours a day in that inferno with death at our backs every minute, but all our efforts were in vain. Most of the miners just quit and went their different ways, but a few of us who needed the money remained and succeeded in opening the tunnel from the other side of the hill. Once again, the mine was in operation.

In December of 1920, my wife became ill, and although the doctor at Cadomin tried his best for about a year to cure her, he was unsuccessful. I then took her to Dr. Allan in Edmonton who operated on her in Alexandra Hospital. On 1 January 1921, she died.

Because of all my woes, I lost interest in my work, as now there did not seem to be any purpose in anything. In July of 1921, I took a holiday in Toronto. There I met a few of my countrymen and a former neighbor from my home village, Mary, daughter of Mikhailo Melnyk and Anna, née Luklan. In December, she accompanied me to Edmonton, and we were married. My money ran low, so a few days later, she agreed to stay behind with some kind people in Edmonton while I went back to the mine again. But it so happened that the miners were out on strike, and there was no work until June 1922. I decided to bring my wife to live with me. While I crouched and crawled on all fours in the mine digging coal with other miners, she did our cooking and washing.

In 1925, I sustained serious injuries in a mining accident and was unable to stand up on my feet for two months. My legs have been weak ever since. That accident spelled the end of my mining career. We moved to Bellis where we bought a building that still bore the sign "Hotel" painted on it. It cost us a great deal of money and labor to remodel it into a hotel. In 1926, the government granted us a license to operate a beer parlor and provide accommodation for guests.

Two years later, I joined a company formed to operate a flour mill at Bellis. Business was good in the mill and in the hotel, but unfortunately both these business places were destroyed by fire and we sustained a loss of some $8,000. In time, however, we built another hotel.

I have lived through many harrowing experiences in Canada in the past thirty-two years, but it would take too long to relate them all. And I was not alone, for thousands of other Ukrainian immigrants like myself passed through similar, and in some cases even worse, experiences. What intrigues me now is how a human being can endure so much. All this notwithstanding, I derive a good deal of pleasure now from sitting back and reminiscing about those days. It is like a dream, and the incidents that actually happened in my life, like phantoms of a dream.

14 M HARASYMCHUK
In the Snows of a Foreign Land

This short story by M. Harasymchuk was first published as "U snihu na chuzhyni," in the January 1955 edition of the Ukrainian Pioneer. Though it is probably fiction, it has the ring of truth.

Day after day, Stulko wandered about in the big city of Montreal. Although he did not actually squander his money, he was nevertheless not able to hang on to every dollar. It was now nearly a month since he had come here to have his fling, and though he had nothing to show for his money, he had already blown forty dollars. And forty dollars in 1913 meant a lot of money, much more than today.

Since his arrival in Canada eight months before, he had managed to earn eighty dollars. To spend forty dollars in just one month was more than he could afford. That wasn't the way he had planned it, but what could he do? Work on construction of the new railroad was completed, and he had to have a place to stay.

Quite often, Stulko visited the private employment bureau of Mr. Kirier. Although many men sought employment through this office, most of them could not afford the fee that Mr. Kirier charged. He made it very clear to them that if they did not have at least a dollar to pay him for his services, they had better not bother him. But still they kept pestering him and hanging around his office as if expecting a miracle.

Hundreds of people without a dollar! Was this really the Canada that Stulko had dreamed of since his childhood? Shivers ran up his spine. A job! He must get a job! He could not see himself living a solitary life in a foreign land without a dollar.

In the midst of the confusion that arose when the proprietor tried to chase out the "penniless," Stulko managed to edge closer to Mr. Kirier's desk.

"What do you want? Do you have a dollar?" demanded Kirier angrily, and his eyes shot daggers at Stulko.

"What do I want? I want a job, that's what. Your office is here to give people jobs."

Immigrants at an employment office, about 1910

"Have you got a dollar?"

"I have."

Mr. Kirier looked Stulko over from head to foot and, as if suddenly reminding himself of something, asked, "Where do you want to work, here in the city or some other place?"

"I'll work wherever there's work for me. If there's work in the city, well and good. If not, I don't mind going somewhere else. What's the difference? All of Canada is mine."

"Good! Come early tomorrow morning, and I'll have a job for you. Before nine in the morning!"

"Good, I'll be here," replied Stulko, obviously pleased. But what kind of job and where? He forgot to ask.

The following morning, Stulko returned to the employment bureau. Here Mr. Kirier and three other men were waiting for him.

"Very well, now that you are all here, and before anyone else comes, I want to talk to you," began the manager. "The job I promised you is not just any ordinary kind of job. It is in a gold refinery, you know—where they purify gold. They don't accept just anybody at all for this job. They need honest people who can be trusted. It took me three days to pick the four of you, and I'm a pretty good judge of human nature. There are many who are willing to pay me fifty dollars and more to recommend them for this job, but I can't do it; I am responsible for the men I select. Take you, for instance; I have confidence in you. I take one glance at a man, and I see right through him. But, gentlemen, to get this job the fee is not one dollar, but five."

The "gentlemen" glanced at one another and made wry faces.

"I don't have five dollars," pleaded the Bukovinian, Semen Sirak. "I had that much yesterday, but not today. I paid for my room and now I'm left with only three."

"Maybe one of your friends can lend it to you," suggested the manager. "With your earnings, it won't take long to pay back the loan. Gentlemen, help one another!"

Sirak's fellow countryman, a neighbor from the same village, gave a nod of approval.

"There you are! That's the way to do it," commended Kirier.

The men dug their fingers into their purses and, pronto, on the desk in front of Kirier lay three five-dollar bills.

"And what about you, boy?" The manager turned to Stulko.

"You didn't even tell us the whereabouts of this job, how much they are paying, and what the working conditions are like. Since you haven't mentioned anything about it, I don't know . . ."

"The job is at Marmora, Ontario. You will be getting two dollars a day plus your board and lodging. You can't get a better deal anywhere."

Stulko reflected: his job on railroad construction had paid him two dollars a day, and he was docked sixty cents for board. Now he could be getting two dollrs a day clear. "All right," he said, and a fourth five-dollar bill landed on the manager's desk.

Mr. Kirier seemed pleased. He picked up the five-dollar bills, thrust them into his pocket, and began to write the "contracts." The three older men signed their papers with an X, and Stulko signed his full name. His handwriting was no better than Mr. Kirier's Ukrainian.

"I want you to be at the railway station tonight, at exactly nine o'clock. I will be there, too, to buy tickets for you. You will pay for them from your earnings, and everything will be fine," announced Mr. Kirier.

At the station, he handed the men their tickets and put them aboard the train. A whistle, a rumble, and they were off.

During the night, there was nothing to do in the train but sleep. And the men did just that. At Trenton, early in the morning, they were transferred to another train which sped away to the north.

It was the end of February. The weather was cold — as cold as Siberian weather — when they arrived at Marmora. What was the place like? Two or three buildings and some old shops covered with dust. Some men were waiting at the station to meet the passengers and escort them to the workers' camp. The next morning, they were to be assigned their jobs.

McKinley Darragh mine near Cobalt, Ontario, 1908

At supper time, the laborers returned from their work and washed the dust off their faces. Stulko was appalled to see those faces covered with pimples or with scabs. Speaking with the men, he learned that there were Ukrainians among them. "Our people" were "conquering" Canada!

An elderly man, old enough to be Stulko's grandfather, asked him, "What made you come here, son?"

"What do you mean? I came here to work, of course. You have to work somewhere for a living," explained Stulko.

"You won't be able to work here, son. You'd do better to slip away from this camp and skip out. See those scabs on our faces? That's from the work we do here. We grind rock which is supposed to contain gold, but I don't know — I've never seen any of it yet. All we see is rocks and dust. The dust is very bad for your health. No one has been able to work here any longer than a couple of months. Many would quit their jobs at the end of the first day if they could—if they didn't owe the company anything."

"I owe for the train fare from Montreal."

"That's the way they trap you here! The men that they bring in must work for them to pay back the price of the train ticket. It will cost you two weeks' wages. By that time, you'll be covered with scabs. Even your own mother won't be able to recognize you. But that's not all there is to it," continued the old man. "Some parts of our bodies become swollen and so painful that we can hardly move. Watch us walk with our legs spread out. I'm giving you a piece of sound advice: flee this place; it's not for you."

There was no doubt in Stulko's mind about the sincerity of the old man's words and the wisdom of his advice. But—where to flee? How? He was confused.

"There's another fellow here who is prepared to escape tonight," continued the old man. "If you want me to, I can introduce you to him, and then—Godspeed."

The supper bell rang, and the old man escorted Stulko to the kitchen. Stulko sat beside the old man, but he was in no mood to enjoy his meal.

"Don't feel downhearted, my boy, but help yourself to a big meal and stuff your pockets with food," encouraged the old man. "Your mother isn't here to look after you. You've got to do it yourself and take things in your stride."

Stulko took the old man's advice. He downed a big supper and stuffed his pockets with bread and cakes. After supper, the old man introduced him to Andrushko, a "Russian" from the district of Kaminetz-Podilsky.[1] Together they laid plans for their escape. Andrushko was all set, so Stulko went to his bunk, put on all his best clothes, and gave the rest to the old man in appreciation of his advice. For a long time, he debated with himself about whether he should wear his hat or his cap. The hat had cost him $1.25 and the cap $.50. He chose the hat. Economy!

"Unnoticed"—although everybody knew what was going on, as such scenes took place here almost every night — Stulko sneaked out and joined Andrushko who was already waiting for him. All set!

Had they chosen to follow the railroad track, they would have had to head straight south toward Trenton, and from there, they would have had to go east. But at the railway station, there was always the danger of encountering a search party in pursuit of them; hence they decided to take a shortcut to the southeast. They would thus elude pursuers and, at the same time, save themselves ten or fifteen miles by cutting an elbow off the longer route....

Stulko was young and inexperienced, and his companion was an elderly man. It later became evident that neither one of them was very wise.

They set out in high spirits, tramping over ditches, knolls, and rocks. They clambered over uprooted trees, occasionally falling into holes and pulling each other out, but doggedly forging ahead, more often on all fours than on their two feet. All around them, everything was covered with a heavy layer of snow. But it was not ordinary soft snow. On a mild day, the surface of the snow had softened, and now the frost had turned it into a crust of ice. It was too thin to support a person walking on it, but too thick to be pushed aside with a foot. When either Stulko or Andrushko tried to walk on the crust, he would crunch through into knee-deep snow. And each step meant they were only a few inches farther ahead. Such progress was not very encouraging, but they were now too far from the camp to turn back. On the other hand, moving at a pace of a tortoise, they were not making much headway.

Necessity is the mother of invention. Stulko picked up a stick of deadfall and began to break up the crust with it. Tediously, he pushed forward with Andrushko close behind him. After a while, Andrushko took Stulko's place: he picked up a dry limb and began to break up the crust while Stulko "rested" by walking behind. Thus taking turns, they crawled forward, painfully slowly, but ever forward.

All around them was the forest; under their feet, crusty snow; overhead, bright stars twinkling; and all of this seemed to be welded together by a severe frost. Not even the sound of a dog barking, a rooster crowing, a wolf howling. Any sound would have been welcome now to assure them that somewhere life still existed. But no, only the sound of two human beings struggling with snow!

Was there a better way to do it? They sought each other's advice. And always the same answer—"Forward!"

Exhausted though they were, rest was out of the question. It could mean "rest in peace forever" in the snows of a foreign land. They found a long stick and took turns with it all night, thrashing the snow ahead of them. Finally, a ray of hope—daybreak! Now they would be able to see better, to avoid rocks and deep ditches—at least, most of them.

Low over the horizon ahead a glow appeared. That must be east, where the sun rose! Their spirits buoyed up. Now they were certain that they were headed in the right direction. According to plan. Only the thrashing of the snow was not "according to plan." But it had to be done, so they kept doing it.

About noon, they heard the whistle of a locomotive. It seemed quite close, and it was music to their ears. Like dear mother's own voice! Hope gave them strength, and in a couple of hours, they were tramping down a railway track towards a small station. The sooner they could reach it, the better. How they longed to sit down and rest! A few extra spurts of energy, and they were inside the station. They sat down—no, dropped down—on the bench.

The warm air in the building made them drowsy. In a short while, Andrushko was fast asleep. Stulko would have been, too, but he was in trouble. His ears began to feel as hot as fire, and he felt something dripping on his shoulders. He touched his ears. He was horror-stricken.

An elderly woman, sitting on a bench close by, watched him.

She strolled over to him to tell him that he had frozen his ears; now they were thawing and dripping discharge on his shoulders. Stulko was helpless; he did not know what to do. The woman felt sorry for him in his plight. She took some pieces of cloth out of her bag, and with these she tried to bandage his ears. In the process, she spoke to him so sympathetically, so gently, that she reminded him of his mother, who had died of poverty back at home in Galicia. She asked him who he was, where he was from, where he was going, and other similar questions. Stulko did not wish to lie to this kind lady, so he pretended he did not understand her — which was close to the truth since he was not at all proficient in English.

Aside from the pain in his ears, Stulko felt the pangs of hunger. He had had supper yesterday, and now it was supper time again. To occupy himself and to take his mind off his ears, he took a piece of bread out of his pocket and sank his teeth into it with such gusto that one would have thought he had never tasted bread before.

Using words and sign language, this kindhearted woman insisted on finding out where Stulko wanted to go. He did not know himself, but something prompted him to say "Ottawa." On second thought, maybe that's where he should go. And the more he thought about it, the more he wanted to go to Ottawa. He had been there nine months ago when he first arrived in Canada. He knew some of his own people there, people from his home village. Maybe they would keep him from perishing. Ottawa it shall be then!

The kindly old lady said she, too, was going to Ottawa; the train would be leaving in half an hour. Not being quite sure that he understood her, she showed him her ticket stamped "Ottawa." Stulko nodded to signify that he, too, wanted to go there. The woman then bought another ticket to Ottawa and handed it to him. He got his purse out to pay her, but surmising that the poor frostbitten creature had very little or no money, she declined to accept payment from him. However, Stulko showed her his money and insisted that she accept the price of the ticket, which she finally did.

In the distance, a locomotive whistle could be heard. The woman adjusted the pieces of cloth on Stulko's ears, and they got ready to leave. Stulko felt ill at ease about this strange woman's concern for him, but at the same time, he was grateful for her help in need.

Aboard the train, the woman took a seat next to the wall and pointed Stulko to the space beside her. He could not refuse her. "What shall I do?" thought he. "It seems I can't shake her off."

Rocked by the train, Stulko felt drowsiness come upon him. How he longed for some sleep, but—beside this woman? Before he could figure out what he should do, he was fast asleep.

On awakening, Stulko felt very embarrassed. For—his head was resting on his benefactress's breast. Bewildered, he sheepishly looked around him. Now he understood his predicament and began to apologize profusely to her.

"Oh, that's nothing; don't worry about it," she assured him. "When you fell asleep, your head was hanging over the armrest. It must have been very uncomfortable. I moved your head." A tear glistened in her eye. Stulko noticed it and felt more at ease. He even began to talk to her.

"I once had a son who resembled you so much. He died." The woman spoke with tears in her eyes.

"I once had a mother as loving and kind as you. She died," responded the youth.

Both tried to suppress their tears. Stulko excused himself and went into the washroom. He looked into the mirror. "Oh, horrors! Who is this?" he exclaimed. The pieces of cloth stuck to his ears and hung down to his shoulders. They were filthy, soiled by the discharge that oozed from his ears. The sight in the mirror reminded him of a pup with long ears — a poor, helpless, little pup with ugly ears.

He washed up, soaked the pieces of cloth, gently removed them from his ears, and looked at himself in the mirror once again. Where his ears used to be hung long pieces of flesh which reminded him of marinated herrings.[2] The sight was repulsive. He stood there, his gaze fixed on the creature in the mirror, but he could not recognize himself. "So you wanted Canada, Stulko! Now you have your Canada. Delight in it!" sneered Stulko to that other Stulko in the mirror.

When he returned to his seat, his benefactress bombarded him with questions. Did he know anyone in Ottawa? What was he going to do there? Where was he going to live? More and more questions.

Stulko now talked much more freely to her. He assured her that he had acquaintances there, and they would not let him perish.

At the station in Ottawa, they parted.

"Good-bye, son."

"Good-bye, mother."

15 THOMAS KOBZEY
Out of Work

Born of peasant parents in the district of Sniatyn in Western Ukraine, Thomas Kobzey attended the village school where his radical views were shaped by his teacher. At the age of thirteen, young Thomas was compelled to leave his studies in order to help his father with work on the land.

When he came to Canada, he faced the same hardships and problems as most other Ukrainian pioneers. He took an active part in Ukrainian labor organizations and, later, in the Ukrainian branch of the Communist movement in Canada. However, like so many others, he became disillusioned with the movement when he recognized the true nature of Communism and its goals, and he defected from it.

His personal experiences as a laborer and in the Communist organization are described in volume one of his memoirs, Na ternystykh ta khreshchatykh dorohakh: spomyny z piwstoricha w Kanadi *(On the Thorny Way and Crossroads: Memoirs of Fifty Years in Canada), published by* Narodna Volya, *Scranton, Pennsylvania in 1972. What follows are excerpts drawn from that book.*

My first job in Canada. On [4 July 1911], the second day after my arrival at my brother-in-law's place [in Calgary], I went to look for a job. I learned from different people that jobs were available at digging ditches for water mains. I went to inquire and announced through an interpreter that I was seeking employment.

"No, you can't get a job," answered the foreman through the interpreter.

"Why not?" I asked.

"Because you're too small and too young and too weak — unless we hire you as a water boy, but we don't need a water boy at this time." He ended the dialogue with a grin.

This, my first failure in job hunting, depressed me terribly. For almost a week, I was restless. I continued to hunt for a job, but all my efforts were in vain. Then one day, I met a countryman who was in Canada for the second time around and could speak some English. I told him about my failure in my first attempt to find a job. He listened to me and said, "We'll have to do something to

*Laborers at the Winnipeg railway station, on their
way to the western grain harvest*

make you look a little heavier. Tomorrow morning, you'll put on a
couple of sweaters or jackets to make you look bigger than you look
now—like some poor little wretch. Then you'll go across to the
other side of the Bow River. There you will see workers pick up
spades, picks, and pickaxes from tool chests. You, too, will grab a
spade and a pickax and start digging alongside the men. When the
timekeeper comes to you at ten o'clock and speaks to you, you will
answer, 'No savvy. Nick.' "

The next morning, I did as my fellow countryman had advised
me. I hauled out a spade and a pickax and started to work alongside
the other men. I dug and shoveled out the earth until my whole
body was soaked with perspiration, from head to toes. I found the
work hard, and the summer heat was torture.

It wasn't long before the foreman appeared. He stopped to talk
briefly to each man and then said something to me. I answered with
the three words that my countryman had taught me, and the
foreman walked away from me. As I kept on digging, one thought
kept bothering me: What if he should come back to me? If not
today, then maybe tomorrow? What should I tell him then?

Shortly after this, I could see the foreman coming, accompanied
by my countryman, Nick. As they chatted, they kept glancing in my
direction and then walked away.

I continued to work in fear and suspense until evening. After work, later in the evening, I got word from Nick that I was hired for the job. But what was the good of it when the palms of my hands were covered with blisters? All night I sat up soaking them in cold water, and in the morning, I went back to work again. As the blisters broke open and discharged their oily, fluid contents, perspiration seeped in, causing unbearable pain. Every day, I went through this torture until calluses formed on my palms. But without hope of another job, I continued to dig ditches in order to stave off death by starvation.

One day, I met a traveling buyer, a Jew from Ukraine.[1] In the course of our conversation, I asked him where he came from, and he asked me the same question. I then told him the story of my hardships. He listened sympathetically and offered me this advice: "If you wish to make your life easier, go to night school. There you can learn not only the English language but, if you have any desire for knowledge, many other useful things, too."

It was sound advice, but I did not heed it. And to this very day I have borne the consequences of my mistake. The happy-go-lucky attitude of my youth had obscured my vision of the future.

Living conditions of workers. I would like to say a word about the living conditions of our immigrant workers and about their contribution to the development of Canada's trade, commerce, agriculture, and civilization in general. Our earliest immigrants comprised two distinct groups: agriculturalists who settled on land, and workers who found employment in factories, mines, bush camps, and road crews.

The conditions of work for workers on farms, in factories, and elsewhere were harsh. The length of the working day was from ten to twelve hours. The pay was from ten to fifteen cents an hour. There was no social security of any kind. The labor unions, though active in Canada since the 1820s, were still too weak to protect the legitimate interests of the workers. Nor could the central body, the Trades and Labor Council, which had been in existence since 1873, do much, as there was still no class consciousness among the workers.[2] Many workers still believed that they could earn more on their own.

The living conditions of the workers varied with the type of work. Those who worked in the bush, in quarries, on railroads, or at blasting tunnels lived in camps. Filth, fleas, lice, and infectious diseases were the workers' common lot. Feeding the workers presented no problem. It was quite simple, if not primitive: bread, cabbage, cucumbers, potatoes, cheap meat, cornmeal, and black coffee.

To get a job was a much more difficult matter. I found that out as soon as I arrived in Canada, as well as on later occasions. It was necessary to have some pull—acquaintance with the foreman or someone at the labor office—or to bribe an agent and thus pay your way into the labor force.

At such work as mining, railroad building, blasting tunnels, and felling trees, the men performed the various operations with primitive tools — spade, pickax, pick, ax, wheelbarrow, and such. Safety measures were unknown. Injury or even a fatal accident was no concern of the employers, and they offered no aid. The workers were thrown upon their own resources and the good graces of their colleagues, who helped them as much as they could in the event of some tragic accident.

As for the level of our national consciousness and political, cultural, and religious life in Canada, generally speaking it did not measure up to that of the villages in the old country; nevertheless, it did flourish here. . . .[3]

It's an ill wind that blows no one any good. Soon after I got married, in 1913, an economic depression set in. There was widespread unemployment which had an adverse material and moral effect on workers. Even worse was the depression of 1914. Hundreds of thousands of workers found themselves without jobs. Once a worker lost his job, he had no choice but to fend for himself the best he knew how or perish.

Before the depression, I rented a home and sublet some rooms. I had as many as fifteen tenants at one time, most of them my countrymen. They were not earning much; hence they could not pay me much. During the depression, the situation got worse. My tenants had lost their jobs and could not pay their rent. Yet I had to pay rent to my landlord, though I could not afford it. I had no money to pay for fuel, light, or water. The city cut off my water. The hydro cut off my electricity. When winter came, I found myself in the predicament of the proverbial cricket that had made no provisions for the winter.[4] Fortunately, my landlord was an understanding person and did not evict us from the house.

Hunger stared all of us in the face, for none of us in the house had any money saved up to tide us over the depression. Our meager savings were soon spent, and all of us faced the stark reality: what was ahead of us, and how were we going to survive?

Of all my tenants, only my cousin still had some money—fifteen dollars—left from his savings. Every day, he took us all to a Chinese restaurant where you could eat all you wanted for fifteen cents. When we had all had our fill, there were usually enough leftovers to take home for supper. Some would go to a hotel where, for five cents, you could get a pint of beer and all the biscuits you wanted for a snack.

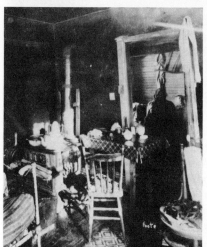

Living conditions in an immigrant neighborhood, Winnipeg

To heat their homes, people used to fill their bags with coal from along the railway track where coal cars were spotted for unloading. For kindling wood, they used to yank out wooden supports and split them into small chips. For light and water, people had an ingenious way of plugging their lines into the main lines at night; in the morning they would disconnect them for the day. There were those who created employment for themselves. For example, one of my countrymen would rise early in the morning, take a walk to the residential section of the rich, pick up the bottles full with milk, and take them home. When spring arrived, my countrymen dispersed in different directions to parts unknown.

The First World War. In 1914, I landed a job at Ogden, where water mains were manufactured. But I did not hold the job very long. As soon as the war broke out, I was dismissed because I was not as yet a Canadian citizen. In order to forestall a long period of unemployment and starvation, I left for the coal mines at Hosmer, British Columbia. There was a large number of Ukrainians working there, and among them several from my native village, including my cousin John Kyryliuk.

To get a job in the mine at that time was not an easy matter. One had to bribe the boss or, as they used to say, "grease the palm of the boss's hand." The price paid to get a job was quite high considering the times — from $25 to $150 — depending on the kind of job one got. For the most arduous kind of work, it was $25; for the easier jobs, it was more. To operate a machine, one had to pay $150. But the pay for this type of work ranged from $15 to $25 for an eight-hour day.

In the mine, I worked as an assistant to the digger, who happened to have been a neighbor of mine in our village. Despite our close acquaintance, he was so bossy that he scared the wits out of me. One might have thought that I was earning big money, but it was only three dollars a day.

The work in the mine was hard and dangerous. Every miner left for work in the morning prepared for any eventuality, including death, which could have been caused either by the collapse of the supports or by an explosion of gases. I recall the day when I almost caused a catastrophe myself. It was my first day in the mine. Having finished my lunch, I automatically, by force of habit, rolled a cigarette and was about to strike a match to light it when, fortunately, I realized that the mine was full of gases and that smoking was prohibited. Not only that, but workers were prohibited from taking tobacco and matches with them into the mine; I, however, had forgotten all about it. I immediately buried the matches and the tobacco deep in the ground and trampled it down. From then on, I never again took any tobacco or matches with me into the mine.

My problems were compounded by my cousin John. As I mentioned before, he had been working in the mine long before me. When I got the job, he approached me with a request to pay him twenty-five dollars which, he said, he would transmit to the boss.

He warned me that if I did not come across with the money I need not show up for work.

"But I don't have a cent to my name yet, as I only started working a week ago. I have a wife, and I need a few dollars for living," I explained.

"Then pay me at the end of two weeks," he answered.

"Very well," I agreed, and we parted.

When the two weeks were up, he came to me with the same story. "Tom, give me twenty-five dollars or don't show up for work."

"I'm not giving you anything," I snapped back angrily. "I've only earned forty dollars, and I must spend half of it to pay my debts."

"In that case, there's no point in your coming to work tomorrow," announced John and walked out.

The morning after this confrontation with John, I went to work anyway. But the place where I worked was now barricaded. There was no one to talk to, as my partner would not answer me. That was the end of my job as miner.

Before me loomed a grim future. What to do next? Where to look for a job? What kind of a job? Besides, it was not safe to walk the streets job-hunting, for with the outbreak of war, feelings among the populace ran high.

In the cities, soldiers were carrying out a virtual pogrom, ransacking and demolishing restaurants where young Ukrainian or German men and women worked. Hatred was vented against aliens, particularly against Austrians and Germans. A drive was launched also against those Ukrainians who called themselves Austrians. All Ukrainians who came from Western Ukraine, that is, Galicia, had to report to the police every month. Many people were sent to concentration camps where they were forced to work for next to nothing. At first, I could not understand what was going on and why the aliens were persecuted, especially the former citizens of the Austro-Hungarian Empire.

The attack on the Ukrainians during the First World War began as a result of an appeal issued by the Austrian consulate to all former citizens of the Austro-Hungarian monarchy to respond to its call to arms.[5] The Canadian government, headed by Robert Borden, seized on this opportunity to proclaim all who came from Austro-Hungary "enemy aliens." Since there were many Ukrainians in Canada who came from Galicia, Bukovina, and the Carpathian region—territories which were then under Austro-Hungarian occupation—they, too, were classified as "enemy aliens."

In addition to the actions of the government, the Ukrainian workers who had been duped by Austrophilism from the old country compounded the problems. I recall how every day groups of Ukrainian workers would stand in front of the newspaper buildings reading the war news on the bulletin boards. At that time, the Russians were storming Peremyshl, and when news came that the Russians were being destroyed by tens of thousands or taken as prisoners of war, these workers would roar "Hurrah! Hurrah!"[6] Such conduct led the authorities to intensify their harassment of those Ukrainians, though they were completely innocent.

In those days the newspaper *Novyny* (News), published in Edmonton, strengthened this Austrophile element by its editorials on the progress of the war. Although there were other Ukrainian papers published in those days, such as the *Kanadyiskyi Farmer* (Canadian Farmer), *Ukrainskyi Holos* (Ukrainian Voice), *Kanadyiskyi Rusyn* (Canadian Ruthenian), and a socialist paper *Robochyi Narod* (The Working People), none of them interpreted the course of events for the benefit of the Ukrainian workers and farmers from the standpoint of an independent Ukrainian politics. There were not many Ukrainians in Canada who belonged to the intelligentsia, and the ones who did quarreled among themselves, and each followed the political philosophy best suited to himself.

The hostile attitude towards Ukrainians can also be attributed to the influence of a strong Russophile movement which was very active in Canada at the time and which even had a number of supporters among the Ukrainians themselves.[7] Many of our people were arrested and sent to concentration camps where they were confined until the end of the war. Some of them died there.

As a result of the war, all connections were severed between Ukrainians in Canada and their kith and kin in Western Ukraine. Only a few were able to receive news from their loved ones and then only in a circuitous way....

I had no news from home. It was only from newspapers and letters written to others that I learned what was taking place in the district of Sniatyn. People were wary about writing home from Canada to their native villages and towns for fear of harm to themselves or their relatives. Besides, it was commonly believed that during the war letters could not get across the front line.

Looking for a job. The day after I lost my job in the mine, I left Hosmer and returned to Calgary. I had some money with me, but after paying for a few purchases, I was left almost penniless again.

Unable to find work in Calgary and having run out of money for the necessities of life, I was compelled to leave the city in search of a job. But where and how? I decided to go to Edson, some hundred miles from Edmonton, in Alberta, as there was a lot of talk about prospects of a good job on railroad construction. But since I only had a few dollars in my pocket, I decided to travel free. I was advised that the best way to do it was to "ride the rails." It was possible to hide between the freight cars so well that one could not be detected.

I thought about it; I decided; I acted. I said good-bye to my wife and set out. In Edmonton, I met another fellow who, like myself, was looking for work. The two of us boarded a boxcar at night and were on our way to Edson. This mode of travel served its purpose. We arrived at Edson about midnight.

Now we had to look for accommodation for the night—a cheap hotel or a private home. All I had in my pocket was seventy-five cents, and my partner swore up and down that he did not have a cent to his name. We found a place to sleep at a Chinaman's for twenty-five cents for the two of us.

When I woke up in the morning, my partner was gone. "What happened?" I asked myself. "Where did he disappear to? He probably decided to go outside for a walk."

I lay there for another half hour, but my partner did not show up. The meaning of it became clear to me: the fellow had pulled one over me. He probably had some money on him and was leery about traveling with me, so he had quietly slipped out early in the morning, leaving me behind.

I had my breakfast, paid a dime for it, and walked out to check how often the trains were running. My idea was to find out which train to catch in case I could not find a job here. At the railway station, I called in at the workshop and inquired about prospects for a job.

"No," said the boss, "there is no work to be had now. If anything does turn up, it will take a few days."

"Then, do you promise me a job in a few days?"

"I'm not promising; I'm only humoring you. What else can I tell you when there are hundreds of others like you who come here every day?" answered the man with a chuckle.

"Thanks for the consolation," I replied and walked out. In my heart, I felt anguish and bitterness which made the whole world seem loathsome. I looked about — at the sun, at the town and the people, then at the mountains surrounding Edson—but the bitterness would not go away. I felt it welling up in my throat, dissolving in my saliva, filling my mouth, and permeating my entire body. My thoughts turned to the words of a *kolomyika*,[8] and I repeated them over and over:

O, my world, my world,
My bitter world;
Why are you so sweet to some
And so bitter to me?

I could not bear my anguish any longer and burst into tears — tears over my harsh fate.

"What shall I do now?" I asked myself. Strange town, strange people, and only forty cents in my pocket.

I wandered about town until noon. Instead of going for lunch, I turned into a side street and there I saw a group of section men sitting having their lunch. I walked up to them, greeted them, shook hands with them, and asked where they hailed from. They were all older men, and most of them were from the district of Borschiw.

"And who is your supervisor, or as the English say, 'foreman'?" I asked.

The workers pointed out the foreman for me. He was English-speaking. I approached him with tears in my eyes and asked him if he would give me a job. He pondered awhile, looked me up and down several times, and said, "Very well, grab a spade and start working this afternoon."

I was so pleased with his decision that I completely forgot about lunch and went to work unfed.

It was not an easy job for me for two reasons. First, I had never done that kind of work before, and second, no one showed me how to do the job. Instead of being helpful to me, the men who worked next to me laughed and reproached me for working too slowly, because they had to do my share of the work, they claimed.

I survived on the job until evening, though not without physical and mental anguish. At supper time, the men all went home, but I had no home to go to. Neither did I have any money to rent even a cheap room for, say, a week. The forty cents in my pocket I guarded like some great treasure, for ahead of me there loomed only a gloomy unknown.

I noticed that my fellow workers regularly went in and out of a rather small structure which they called the boxcar. At first, I was under the impression that that was where they kept their spades and other tools. But one of them told me that was where they lived.

"Would you mind letting me stay with you?" I asked the men.

At first, no one answered, but after exchanging meaningful glances among themselves, they all spoke out almost in unison, "Well, then move in with us."

I did. But what was I to do after that? They began to cook their meals; I sat there unhappily.

Then one elderly fellow felt sorry for me and said, "Don't worry. We won't let you starve among us. Come with me to the store. I will vouch for you, and the storekeeper will sell you groceries on credit until you get paid."

I could not thank the man enough. Here, I thought, was a fortune that cannot be found lying on the road.

I purchased a few groceries at this store and returned home. By that time, my colleagues had finished their cooking, and one of them loaned me his frying pan with lard in it so I could fry myself some supper. I can't remember anything more delicious than the omelette with sausage that I had made for myself.

Although I had worked for only half a day, I was so exhausted that after supper I went to lie down on the grass. In spite of myself, my thoughts flitted to my wife, and even farther—to my native village. "My dear relations have no idea about the work I do, about my living quarters, about how I eat. Is this kind of life really fit for a human being?"

I was awakened from my reverie by two young men. They appeared to be ill or exhausted or perhaps famished. As our conversation progressed, they told me all about themselves. They were looking for work, like I was, and they begged for a piece of bread, as they had not had a morsel of food for two days.

Knowing from my own personal experience what it meant to be jobless and hungry, I gave each of them a piece of bread and some sausage. They could not find words to thank me for it. I felt that since people were kind to me I should pass on the kindness to others.

When I got back into our shack, my colleagues all but lynched me for giving away my food to strangers. "After all," they argued, "we vouched for you in the grocery store, and now you're giving away food to strangers, or to 'bums' as they call them here."

"But they were hungry," I defended myself. "You should have seen how miserable they looked."

But my explanation did not convince any of them. They were all of one mind: guys who don't work should not be given any aid at all.

"There you are," I thought to myself. "That's what some people think of others who are no different from themselves, except for worse circumstances."

After supper, all the men who worked with me went to the restaurant and invited the foreman with them. When they got back, one of them lectured me, "Listen, boy, you can't shy away from us like that. You must join us every night and take the foreman out for a drink."

"It is fine for you to say that I must go out with you every night and buy the foreman a drink, but tell me, how can I do all that when I have no money?"

"I'll lend you a dollar," answered one of the men.

"I don't need your loan just to spend it on drinks with the foreman," I answered.

"If you don't need it—well, that's your business," retorted my "friend," and our conversation ended abruptly. I could see that here, too, as was the case in the coal mine, you had to buy the good graces of your supervisors with drinks.

Following this episode, I worked another half day. At noon, the foreman said to me, "Your job is finished. Here's your cheque, and get out of here."

I looked at the cheque. It was only for $7.50. "How can I afford to live here?" I wondered.

My thoughts were interrupted by my guarantor at the grocery store. He came running to me and shouting, "Hey, come on to the store with me, boy, and pay up your debt there. I'm not going to pay your bill for you. I've seen guys like you before. They work for a day or two and then skip out. And those who vouch for them have to pay for them."

"Have no fear, uncle;[9] I'm not one of those who run away," I assured him. "Come with me; I'll pay my debt right away."

After paying the bill in the store, all I had left was six dollars. Now the question before me was "What shall I do now? Where shall I go?" I had only half a day to find the answer.[10] With this burden on my mind, I took a walk uptown.

Job-hunting once again. I roamed about town until evening but failed to find a job anywhere. I then decided to ride the rods to Edmonton. A neighbor of mine from my village, Dmytro Ferbey, lived there. He owned a bookstore, but unfortunately I did not know his address. "It doesn't matter much," I thought. "A man who runs a bookstore should be well known by our people." Thus consoling myself, I sneaked into an empty boxcar on a freight train that took me to Edmonton.

It was Sunday morning. There were hardly any people to be seen on the streets. The only thing to do was to wait. I wandered around for an hour or so, and as more people appeared on the streets, I asked a few if they knew Dmytro Ferbey. Unfortunately, none of them did. Then I went to the railway station to check out the time the freight train was leaving for Calgary. I decided to try my luck there once again. It was due at half past ten that night, so I settled down for a long wait at the station, and after that — God help me.

At about ten o'clock, two big husky fellows, each appearing to be as strong as an ox, approached me. One was white and one was black. They sat down beside me and struck up a conversation.

"Which way are you going?"

"To Calgary," I answered. "I'm going to look for a job there."

The two exchanged glances, and the white fellow said to me, "I know a contractor in Calgary who builds hotels. I can recommend you to him, and you can get a job on his crew."

Woman with children, Winnipeg, around 1910

"Thank you very kindly," I answered. "I know they are building a hotel in Calgary because I tried for a job there more than once but had no luck."

"Well, this time you'll be able to get one," remarked the black fellow and grinned.

I was so happy I couldn't sit still. "This is the second time that fortune has smiled upon me," I comforted myself.

Then the two fellows got up and invited me for a walk with them. Entertaining the hope that I could easily get a job in Calgary, and not sensing anything wrong, I agreed.

As we walked out of the station, my companions flanked me, and after a while, I noticed that we were headed toward a dark alley. A feeling of foreboding prompted me to slow my pace. The black fellow spoke: "We came here from Calgary to work in the freight shed loading grapes for shipment. But today being Sunday, we cannot find a place to cash our cheques. You give us your money, and tomorrow we'll pay you back."

Now I realized that I had definitely fallen into a trap, and I began to fear for my life. Without much thought, I pulled my wallet out of my pocket and handed it over. "There's my money—five dollars. That's all I have."

The black fellow snatched the wallet, rifled it, helped himself to the five dollars, and left the change for me. Then he proposed, "Wait for us at the station. At midnight, we'll join you, and we'll travel to Calgary together."

"Very well," I uttered in a barely audible voice and just stood there dazed. My two "friends" left me and disappeared in the field ahead where they were swallowed up by the darkness and were lost to my sight.

Bewildered, I dragged myself back to the station. The clock showed a few minutes before eleven. My freight train was gone. I had no choice now but spend the night at the station.

In the morning, I met an elderly Ukrainian and related to him my experience of the night before. And this is what he had to tell me: "You're lucky, young man. Lucky to be alive, for several have met a different fate here. They are all in the great beyond now. You're lucky that your robbers did not take you for a walk to the bridge. There, they might have taken not only your five dollars but also your life. They could have drowned you."

I thanked the good man for his warning and went uptown to look for a job. But jobs were very hard to come by. I returned to the station and at night hopped the freight train to Calgary.

At home was my wife, famished and frightened. She feared that something terrible had happened to me. When I told my story to her, she wept bitterly and resolved then and there never to let me go away again and leave her behind alone. "If I could survive on the few cents you left me, you too could have survived on the money you took with you, and you would not have had to go through those horrible experiences."

I had no answer. I knew that she was right. She had bought half a pound of tea, half a pound of sugar, and half a bag of dry bread at the bakery, and this fare had sustained her during the two weeks that I was away.

Still looking for a job. We did not stay long in Calgary. There was nothing to keep us there. Lack of steady occupation kept me away from home. On one of my job-hunting trips, I happened to land in a small town called Hanna. Here I was fortunate to find work not only for myself but also for my wife. Although I had never been a cook, I got myself hired as one at a restaurant. And my wife got the job of keeping house for the proprietor of the restaurant.

After three months at this job, we noticed that the restaurant was in financial difficulties. Rumors were circulating that it was going bankrupt and that it might be sold by auction, which actually happened later. Besides, there were rumors that our people were being harassed again as "Austrians." The wife and I deemed it prudent to quit our jobs and move elsewhere. We notified our employer to that effect and left for Saskatoon.

In Saskatoon, I found a job with the city parks department, and my wife, in a restaurant. Here we began to establish ourselves.

16 PHILLIP YASNOWSKYJ Internment

In his book Pid ridnym i chuzhym nebom *(Under Native and Alien Skies) Philip Yasnowskyj describes his experiences in an internment camp for aliens during World War I. The author was working in a mine at Schumacher, Ontario when the war broke out, and though an Austrian only by citizenship and not by nationality, he and thousands of others like him were defined as enemy aliens by the Canadian government and, as such, were rounded up and confined in forced-labor camps.*

The outbreak of the World War did not cause much of a stir in Canada. The war was a safe distance away and did not affect Canada directly. But among the workers, there were men from Austria and from Russia. Before the outbreak of the war, there was no political strife among them. However, as the flames of war spread and the Russian troops entered Galicia, the Russian workers here became obnoxious.

At our boarding house, the Russians plagued us with their taunts: "Did you hear, you Austrians, that the Russians have occupied Lviv?" Or "Hey, you *khakols*,[1] the Russians are already in the Carpathians!"

Our people avoided arguments, but eventually we were compelled to return these taunts with our own until the Russians calmed down. At the beginning of 1915, the Russians here became even more insolent. When news came that the Russians occupied Peremyshl, there was no end to the crowing by the local Russians. We retaliated by reminding them of Makiwka where, in one night, 40,000 Russian troops covered the battlefield with their dead bodies.[2]

The Russian immigrants felt quite secure in Canada since England fought on the side of the Entente as a partner of Russia. And Canada was an English dominion.[3]

The winter gradually began to spend its force, and little by little the rocks started to appear from underneath the layers of snow. As time went on, a chokecherry bush began to turn green here and there. It was already the month of May.

I had been without work for two weeks. Rumors were circulating that the inspectors were coming to ascertain if there were any sizable deposits of gold here [in northern Ontario]. But exactly when they were coming and when we would start working, I had no idea.

One day, I received a letter from my wife. I had waited a whole year to hear from her. I looked at the envelope. On its postmark was the tsar's eagle. The address, Schumacher, Ontario, Canada in English script, was crossed out and rewritten in Russian lettering. I was anxious to hear the news about the way our village was run by the new rulers. As I read the letter I could almost see my wife writing:

> There is a war on here; you probably know about it. All our men are in the army. Even the crippled were conscripted to operate a carting service with horses and wagons. Only the old men, women, and children remained in the village. There is no equipment to work with in our fields, not even to haul out the little bit of manure from our yards. The women mow grass for hay, and when their scythes need sharpening, they take them to the old men. This hay they carry home in bundles on their backs for their cattle.

> For money, we do not use crowns here any more, only kopecks.[4] Women carry their milk and vegetables on foot to the markets in Lviv as they did in the past, but they do not want to be paid in kopecks, for they do not know their value and they are not paid enough. When Felix's wife Annie refused to accept kopecks from the soldiers, she was thrown into jail for a day and given fifteen lashes on her bare bottom.

> The village is full of Russian troops billeted in our homes and their horses in our stables. They get along well with the people, but the villagers complain that every night their hay has been disappearing. Some of the soldiers speak our language; they are Ukrainians from Russia.

> The soldiers cook their meals in a large caldron on the village common. Most often they cook borscht with cabbage, and buckwheat gruel. If any food is left over, they call the children to eat it up.

> In town, the turnpike is no more.[5] The town is full of Russian soldiers, every single one of them as robust as an oak.

> At the Krakiwskyi and Striletskyi,[6] there is no shortage of bacon, grits, and sugar. The horses of the Russians are large with long tails, and instead of collars, they wear hoops on their necks. They say that the tsar is supposed to come to Lviv to take up residence here, but whether it is true or not, I don't know. What the future holds for us, only God knows.

The letter had taken a long time to reach me. It bore unmistakable marks of its long journey. Evidently it was read by the censor, as parts of it were blotted out with a pencil.

After reading the letter, I began to reflect: "They conscripted everybody to fight the war, even the crippled. What about me? Should I be glad or sorry to be here? Maybe it is really better that I save my neck here rather than face certain death from a Russian bullet on some Serbian or Italian front, or perhaps even in the Carpathians. Over there, they probably consider me a deserter, though, in fact, I had never deserted any army.

"This poses problems for me. At present it is out of the question for me to think about returning home. Should Austria win the war, what sort of welcome would await me at home? Perhaps I would not officially be accused of deserting, because I left home long before the war broke out. But I can imagine how the people in the village would feel towards me. No doubt they would treat me with contempt and derision. The braggards would start boasting about their heroism—how they cut up the Russians and so on—and they would pester me with jeers that I was hiding under a woman's skirt.

"Under the circumstances, one really does not know what to do. My Czech colleague thinks that we should sit out the war here. My Polish colleague claims it would be better for us to leave this place and move elsewhere, perhaps to the United States, as we could be faced with a lot of criticism here.

"For some reason, there are those among the local Ukrainians who believe in the victory of Austria and Germany. Other national groups do not have the slightest doubt that the Central Powers will suffer defeat. No wonder the Russian immigrants here got to be so cocky. Here, in Canada, immigrants from Austria and Germany are looked on with contempt."

The situation got to be so bad that it was even hard to find a job in Canada. My Polish friend and I decided to move to the United States because that country was not at war. It would be better to stay in a neutral country.

In May 1916, I set out on my journey. The documents I had with me were beyond recognition, ruined by moisture during the time that I roamed around the country between Calgary and Winnipeg. I chucked them out and took with me only the letter from my wife. At seven in the morning, I boarded the train.

I went to North Bay, on to Toronto, and then to Saint Catherines. At Saint Catherines, I could not buy a ticket to go farther. I had no pass and could not get one. Without a pass, it was a foregone conclusion that I would be turned back. I decided to watch for a night freight train; I would hop it and thus cross the border into the United States.

After my long trip, hunger was getting the best of me, so I sought out a restaurant. No sooner had I passed through the doorway than a policeman followed me in. "This bodes ill," I thought to myself. "I am sunk." I tried to make myself as inconspicuous as possible, but my heart pounded with fear and my thoughts kept turning around my predicament. "I am in hot water now if I ever was. I am a citizen of a foreign country, and I will be dealt with as an enemy alien here." I was as lost as a pup at a bazaar.

Without wasting any time, the policeman approached me and demanded to know where I came from and what I was doing here. I tried to remain calm as I answered that I was from Porcupine and that I had come here to look for a job.

The policeman raised his eyebrows. "From Porcupine to Saint Catherines for a job? Your pass?"

That was my undoing. To make the best of a bad situation, I showed him the letter from my wife. Perhaps it would make him believe I was a Russian, as the stamp and the postmark were Russian. The policeman looked at the letter, then at me, and turned to the proprietor of the restaurant. "Give him something to eat."

As a matter of fact, I had lost my hunger all of a sudden, but I ordered chicken anyway. The policeman sat at the next table and ordered a sandwich for himself.

As I chewed on the cold chicken, I kept asking myself, "What's going to happen to me next?" All my thoughts were gloomy, and despair cast a shadow over all my plans. There was a thundering noise in my head, and my heart pounded like a hammer. What rotten luck!

I paid for the meal and proceeded to walk out of the restaurant. Bah! the policeman was right behind me. He grabbed my hand and spoke. "Come with me."

He escorted me to a large building and led me downstairs into a room in the basement. There he locked me up. My choice was made for me. I wanted America; I landed in the clink.

I had company in jail—four other inmates. But they were ordinary bums who had been roaming about the country jobless and penniless. Now, surely, the policeman could not mistake me for one of them, since I was not without money in my pocket. My case was much more serious; I was a citizen of an enemy country roving about without a passport or personal identification.

About ten o'clock the next morning, a detective came to see me. I could not believe my ears — he spoke in Ukrainian and very fluently at that. "I see," I thought to myself. "Our countrymen have infiltrated even this racket." He was a lively young fellow of twenty-five, smart in appearance and intelligent looking. He took my money away from me (over $200), as well as the letter from my wife, and conducted me to the barracks. There he handed me a questionnaire to fill out.

"Since I am a Ukrainian," I thought, "I will answer in Ukrainian. I will defend myself by claiming that I came from Russia." The scheme I devised was to combine the name of my birthplace with the name of another place; to be more precise, I put down that I was born in Lutsk in Volhynia and that made me a citizen of Russia. Who could prove me wrong?[7]

When I finished filling out the questionnaire, the agent took it away from me and ushered me into a hall in which there were ten others like myself. They sat still and occasionally cast furtive glances at one another. Like me, they had been apprehended by the police in different places and brought here. They were immigrants from Austria-Hungary. In about half an hour, the detective summoned me to his office and began to interrogate me.

"Was that letter from your wife?"

"Yes."

"Why did you state in the questionnaire that your citizenship was Russian?"

To answer his question, I invented a fantastic story about my ethnic origin. "My father was a Pole who lived in Russia. There were no Catholic churches there, and since my father was very religious, he moved to Galicia. According to the laws of Austria, one must have resided in the country for thirty years in order to acquire Austrian citizenship. I never served in the Austrian army and never will. Please release me."

Of course my story was pure fabrication, but I could not think of anything more plausible. As I related it, I watched the detective closely and wondered if he was convinced by it. But I could not tell from his facial expression.

He examined the letter from my wife once more and scrutinized the envelope closely without saying a word. He just ushered me back into the hall.

In the confines of the hall, I began to contemplate my fate. "That letter from my Yuzunia will be my downfall.[8] I will be taken to the Austrian consul, then put aboard a ship, and straightway despatched to the battlefront. What a future to look forward to!"

On the third day [of my imprisonment in the hall], I knocked on the door. No one answered. After a while, I knocked again but more forcefully. A detective answered my knock and asked me what I wanted. I pleaded with him to have me released as I was not an Austrian; I was from Russia. He smiled at me gently and put this question to me: "Listen, my dear fellow, if I gave you $1,000 where would you go from here? To Russia or to your wife? I am sure you would choose to go to your wife. Don't try to pull my leg, and don't give me that yarn about Russia. Better keep calm and don't start creating any fuss or we shall have to send you to jail. That will teach you order and discipline."

That was it! The end of my freedom. I resigned myself to it, waved the detective away, and began to pace the floor.

Life in the internment camp. I remained under this arrest for two weeks. Every day until noon, we were confined to the hall. In the afternoon, we were let out into the courtyard for an hour. There we were subjected to military drills even though we were not soldiers. I would have no part of military training in Austria; it caught up to me in Canada.

Our meals were very plain, with plenty of water to wash the food down. We slept on the bare floor. I could not help but reflect on my lot. "This is a fine mess. How long is it going to last? What crime have I commited against Canada? What if they decide to charge me with espionage or some other offense? Why did I have to leave Schumacher in the first place? I could have stayed there a little longer, and maybe I could have landed a job. Instead, I landed here in these confounded barracks!"

After two weeks, armed guards transferred us to Stanley Barracks in Toronto. We were not alone here. Interned in these barracks were also a number of our countrymen from Galicia, together with a few Germans.

The barracks were located near a lake. From a distance, the view was impressive, but we were not moved by it. As internees, we were treated in the same manner as prisoners of war. Here, too, we had to sleep on the bare floor, but by now we were used to it. I do not remember whether we were served breakfast and supper, but I do remember that all we got for lunch was two slices of bread, a

Internment camp, Vernon, British Columbia, 1916

piece of meat, a leaf of raw cabbage, and tea with sugar. Before lunch was over an officer would appear in the doorway and holler, "Any complaints?"

Everybody answered, "No."

I did, too, but actually I felt there were a lot of things to complain about. "Wait," I said to myself, "we shall find out what kind of justice they practise here."

A few days later, after lunch, instead of shouting back the usual answer, "No," I hollered, "Yes."

The fellows sitting beside me whispered in dismay, "Shut up."

The officer looked around. Everyone was seated; I was the only one who stood up. He stalked up to me and demanded to know why I was complaining.

I spoke out. "I want more food."

The officer muttered to himself and walked out.

The German inmates immediately got after me to keep quiet and not make any demands for fear that even the little that we were getting would be cut off and we would end up fasting.

It so happened that protest was ignored, and I dared not complain again.

Every day, we were allowed time for a walk in the courtyard. It was enclosed by barbed wire and guarded by two soldiers with bayonets fixed to their rifles.

Among the internees was a Turk, about fifty years of age, who did not care to go walking. He would squat on the ground and talk to himself, often repeating the word *Dardanelli* and waving his hand at the same time. No one ever spoke to him, and the guards left him alone.

We were confined to the barracks for six weeks. Cut off from the rest of the world, we led an animal-like existence, completely ignorant of what went on in the world outside.

One afternoon, a guard assembled us in the courtyard, all of us except the German inmates. No one had any idea what it was about, and everybody was confused by all sorts of conjectures. We were arranged in columns of four, surrounded by guards with bayonets, and marched off to the railway station. That could only mean we were going to be transported to some unknown destination.

We were packed into the train; the doors of the coaches were locked; a guard was placed at the entrance to every car; and each of us was issued his rations, which consisted of a couple of sandwiches.

Our journey lasted several hours, and we whiled away our time in conversation. It was not until we were given orders to get off that we learned the name of our destination. We had arrived at Kapuskasing, the site of special camps for aliens.

Austrian prisoners of war, Morrisey, British Columbia, 1918

Here we were assigned to the different barracks. Mine was barrack number three. As soon as I went in, I was surrounded by a number of inmates. They were for the most part Ukrainians from Galicia. They bombarded me with questions: "Where did you come from? Where were you captured? How is the war progressing? Is it true that the Russians were driven out of Galicia?" and so on. They vied with one another in firing question after question at me, but unfortunately I was unable to answer most of them.

Towards evening, the barrack swarmed with men returning from their work. Then came the call for supper. The meal consisted of a spoonful of sauerkraut and a potato served on a tin plate, and tea served in a tin cup. There was plenty of bread and half a gallon of jam to go with it. We newcomers, famished while awaiting supper, cleaned up every last morsel of our food.

After supper, the barrack hummed with conversation until nine o'clock. Then came the curfew, and everybody was off to bed.

We rose at seven in the morning. Our breakfast was skimpy and not as tasty as the supper. After breakfast, the guard flung the door wide open, and we all rose to our feet in two files. The guard called out a number, and the inmate bearing that number answered "Yes." A few who had belonged to the reserve army in Austria answered "Here" and stood at attention, though the camp regulations did not call for it. That kind of response comes only from the veins of a soldier or, perhaps, from the veins of a slave.

Within an hour, we were all outside doing something. Mostly, it was some work in the woods or at road construction. Those of us who were new arrivals were told to wait a couple of days for our work assignment.

That assignment came three days later. Each one of us was supplied with a long-handled shovel, and we were conducted at bayonet point to a large building across the railway tracks. It was built of massive timbers, and guards were stationed around it. That was the camp jail. Nearby, some of the internees worked on road construction. They dug ditches on each side of a strip cleared for the road and pitched the earth onto the middle of the strip. Such was the exploitation of manpower in a forced-labor camp!

I worked steadily until lunch which, by the way, was about as tasty as pepper is to a dog. After lunch, my whole being revolted. Had I come to Canada to do state-imposed labor? Had I murdered someone or stolen from someone? Just because the country in which I was born was at war with the Allies and thus with England, was I to be held responsible for it? Why should I work at the point of a bayonet for a spoonful of plum jam? I just stood there on one spot and kept twirling the handle of the shovel like the dasher in a churn.

There were more than fifty men working at this job under a civilian boss. He strode up to me and angrily inquired why I was just standing there and not working.

"Big shot," I thought to myself, "what right have you got to threaten me?" I answered calmly, "Go to hell, you." Those were among the first English words I had learned.

The boss's face turned red with anger, and he ordered the soldier to throw me into jail. The soldier shoved me in front of himself and barked at me to get going. I had no choice but to obey the command, for-what else could one do in the face of brute force?

We hadn't covered more than twenty steps when I heard men shouting behind us, "Hey, let us go, too." Turning around I saw the men all drop their spades and shovels and follow me. What a wonderful feeling it was to see that they, too, understood what freedom meant! It was not a long walk. The soldier put me in jail, and then men all headed for the barracks.

The problem of camp routine. Prison is prison, no matter where. When you are alone, all sorts of thoughts cross your mind. My thoughts were disturbing: "What a sad commentary on a system that uses jails to drive fear into the hearts of innocent people and subject them to forced labor! What good will it do me to rebel? It is wartime, I have no rights here, and as an alien, I could be severely punished. A great many other people are already being punished; why wouldn't I be? Instead of protesting, would it not be better to resort to subterfuge and deceit?"

187

The next morning, at about ten o'clock, a guard showed up, unbolted the door, and propelled me to the courtroom with his bayonet. Behind the table sat the entire tribunal. In the middle was the major; he was flanked by lower-ranking officers. On my left was an interpreter and, on my right, a soldier clenching a rifle.

In addition to the regular questions pertaining to my identification, the major asked me why I had refused to work the day before. I put on a bold front and answered in an aggressive tone, "From childhood until yesterday, I had never held a shovel in my hands, and I do not know how to work with one."

As the interpreter translated my answer into English, the major raised his brows. "What kind of work did you do?"

I then put on an even more imposing front. "My father had a large plantation of roses at Zamarstinov and a large florist shop on Karl Ludwig Street in Lviv. I was in charge of the potted plants."

"What made you come to Canada"?"

"I came to Canada in search of seeds of exotic flowering plants, and then I was to have gone to Australia to familiarize myself with its indigenous flowers." I assumed a pose of innocence. Who could tell that I was lying?

I noticed that from time to time the major glanced at me in a kindly way, as though he believed me. He exchanged a few remarks with the officer on his right, who kept nodding his head as if to signify his agreement, and finally said something to the interpreter. All I could understand was the word "papers."

The interpreter rose to his feet and explained to me the decision of the court. Instead of my going to Australia to pick flowers, from now on I was to pick papers and litter around the barracks. That was to be my new job.

When I walked out of the courtroom, I could hardly keep from laughing. It's a wonder I was not commissioned to grow flowers in the camp! I know as much about flowers as the man in the moon. The only kind of plants that my father had anything to do with were the weeds in his rye field.

As far as I was concerned, I was the winner. My trickery had worked. It helped me to get out of the tasks that the other internees were required to perform — and at little cost at that. My rebellion stood me in good stead. From then on, as long as I stayed in the camp, I never again had to touch a shovel or an ax. And what were my duties? Where was I supposed to look for litter when, before long, everything was covered with snow nine-feet deep?

For the winter, the internees were issued good army boots, flannel shirts, warm underwear, warm pants, and waterproof mackinaws. Those who worked in the bush felling trees were also supplied with warm mitts. The army garb served to drive home our state of captivity.

At the end of the month, everyone received a book of thirty coupons, each worth ten cents. These coupons could be exchanged in the canteen for tobacco or oranges.

The snow continued to fall without a letup. In a few days, it was knee-deep. Every day, it got deeper and deeper. The temperature dropped to thirty and forty degrees below zero. Notwithstanding the deep snow and the bitter cold, the men, guarded by soldiers armed with rifles, continued to cut brush in the woods.

One redeeming feature of the winter was its short days. Before it got dark, all the men quit their work and returned to the barracks. After a skimpy supper, they livened up the barracks with chatter and amusements.

In all, there were over 1,300 men in the camp. The majority of them were young men, between twenty and thirty years of age; the rest were from thirty to fifty years old. One-third of them were Ukrainians from Galicia, and the others were Croats, Poles, and Hungarians. There were also a few hundred Turks, but they were lodged in separate barracks.

In the evenings, it was very easy to tell the Ukrainians from the others. When the day's work was done and they had free time, they would get together for a singsong. There seemed to be no end to the number of songs they knew. I joined in, too, to take my mind off our imprisonment, at least for the time being. In the other barracks, the Ukrainians made music on different instruments and danced the *kolomyika* and the *hopak*.[9] In one barrack, the young fellows were learning their parts for a theatrical performance. They were rehearsing *Swatania na Honcharivtsi*.[10] One could not help admiring their perseverance in such an undertaking under such adverse conditions. When the play was staged, I went to see it. It went off well even though the fellow who played the role of the young lady could not, for the life of him, change his voice to sound like a young woman's, and neither the skirt he wore nor his wig of braided hair were of any help.

In one barrack, the Croats played their mandolins and sang the same melody over and over again, "*Hai, hai, hai, sikiru mi dai....*"

The men sought entertainment and whatever else would take their mind off their sorry lot, but this was next to impossible under barrack conditions. And yet, not all of them were interested in gaiety. In one barrack, I saw a man sitting on his bunk reading prayers from his prayer book and not paying any attention to the merrymaking that went on all around him.

Or take the forty-year-old Ukrainian from Zalischyky whom I shall never forget. With only a couple of small pocketknives, he produced a variety of exquisite carvings of very high artistic quality. Among them were not only picture frames but also a violin

Christmas in an internment camp, 1916

made from 365 pieces of wood glued together. To look at this man, one would get the impression that he was just a useless slouch. But he possessed a most remarkable talent for carving pictures and figurines. His carved figure of Hetman Khmelnytsky mounted on a horse with a mace in his hand reminded one of the statue of Khmelnytsky in Kiev.[12] This man was a true master of his art, by the grace of God.

We had only one newspaper, the Polish *Dziennik Ludowy*.[13] But we could not learn much that was of interest from this paper. We were permitted to write letters, even to the old country, but no one ever received an answer. We complained to the major about not receiving letters from our families though we had been writing to them frequently. The major replied, "We see to it that your letters are sent overseas, but it is not our fault that the Germans sink the boats."

Maybe our letters had been sent out, but we did not ask him how many boats had been sunk. There must have been quite a number of them, since not one of us had ever received a single answer to his letters.

Slowly but surely, the winter was drawing to an end. In the clear spaces where trees had been cut, one could see stumps three to four feet tall, and a mass of felled trees resting on these stumps. It was a dreary spectacle. Only an occasional raven winged his way over this desolate scene. The sky remained overcast, but one could detect a breath of warmth in the air. In the camp, there was anticipation of Easter.

Finally Easter Sunday came, gray and dull. And it went by like any other Sunday with one significant exception—there was no work for us that day. To hold a service of worship was out of the question as there was no priest. The men sat the day out in the barracks, silent, depressed, and wrapped up in their somber thoughts. Only now and then someone would softly strike up "*Khristos Voskres.*"[14] Each one was weighed down by his own misery. The thought that gnawed most fiercely at all of us was "How long is our punishment going to go on? When are we going to be out of here, free once again?"

There was no observance whatever of either Easter Monday or Easter Tuesday.[15] We were all forced to work on those days as on any other day.

The resistance that brought us freedom. There was no more snow on the ground, and once again I went back to my job of picking up litter. There wasn't much litter around, and I spent more time just going through the motions of working than actually working. But no matter what I did, I could not shake off the sense of captivity which depressed me.

One day, barrack number four was ordered to vacate. Its inmates were assigned to other barracks. We were told that number four was to get 100 new occupants.

And, indeed, one afternoon a couple of days later, a train arrived with a transport of new internees. As soon as they got off, they were taken by the guards to the vacant barrack number four.

We were appalled by the appearance of these men. Their faces were yellowed and emaciated, and they all looked haggard—old and young, without exception. It was a frightful sight. We tried to find out from them where they had been rounded up. Their speech was hard to understand, for they all spoke with difficulty—some through tears. They complained that they had not yet had a morsel of food in their mouth that day.

We got busy and collected several coupons to buy food for them. Each one of us donated as many as he could, and we exchanged them for a couple of oranges and a chocolate bar for each of the new arrivals. That was all that was available in the canteen.

For supper, they were served the same kind of meal as we were, but some of them had lost their appetites completely and did not eat at all.

After supper, we listened to their stories about their hard lot. They had been interned in the camp near Petawawa. There were 600 of them in all. All were forced to do hard labor. When the Feast of Annunciation rolled around, the internees at the camp asked for a day off from work to observe the holy day.[16] But it was not to be. No one paid any attention to their request. The commander of the camp responded with "To hell with your holy day," and the internees were all ordered to go to work that day.

The next day, no one turned up for work. All of them, to the last man, stayed in the barracks. The camp officials summoned them one by one to the office and demanded an explanation of why they refused to go to work. The one most important question, which was asked of each internee, was "Why don't you want to work?"

They all had a ready answer. One replied, "You did not capture me on the battlefield. I came to Canada not to fight a war but to earn a living and to enrich this country with my labors." Another argued, "I am already forty years old. I always observed that holy day in the same way as did my grandparents and my great-grandparents. My ancestors shed their blood for the privilege of observing this and other holy days, and here you are forcing me to commit sacrilege by going to work on a holy day. I would rather be put to death on this day than trample upon my faith."

A third one had this explanation: "Before I came to this country I heard that there was freedom of religion and speech here, that everyone had the right to abstain from work on his holy day. But you would not let us observe our holy day, and you mock us, besides. Not one of us whom you have locked up here is responsible for the war in any way. But you have desecrated a holy day, and for that you will answer before God."

Others fell back on the Third Commandment for their defense and declared that God's commandments take precedence over orders from camp administration and that no one is a slave forced to work on a holy day. And all the men vowed that they would rather suffer persecution than work on a holy day.

In the end, one of them declared in the name of the entire group, "Because you are forcing us to work on a holy day, we are not going back to work ever."

At eight o'clock in the evening, an officer visited barrack number four and gave the newcomers a short talk. He told them that other men at the barracks had worked faithfully over the past two years and obediently discharged their duties. They received good meals, clothes, and pay, and they were satisfied. When he finished praising the former inmates of the barrack, he reminded the men that there was a war on and one must obey wartime regulations passed by the government. Then he asked, "Will you go to work tomorrow?"

From all around came the resounding answer, "No! No! No!"

The officer stalked out of the barrack.

We were perturbed by their story. We asked our new comrades in captivity whether it was worth their while to lay themselves open to further persecution.

They replied, "Calm yourselves; we are not afraid of persecution." And they recounted the instances of persecution they had experienced every time that they refused to work. "Our food rations were immediately reduced by one-half, the straw from our bunks was removed, and our warm clothing was taken away from us. We were forced to run, fall to the ground, and rise to our feet again repeatedly while we were being flogged. We were forced to carry fifty-pound bags of sand a distance of thirty miles. Our daily food ration continued to be progressively reduced until we had only bread and water. One hundred of us were transferred to this camp. What is going to happen to the ones left behind we do not know. But we are not going to work here either."

Deep down within us, we admired their decision and their determination to stand up for their rights. Their spirit was praiseworthy. They put us to shame for our submissiveness and slavish acquiescence to servility. In our hearts, a new spark of indignation was kindled, but we remained silent.

The next day, the guard unbolted the door of barrack number four and ordered the men to work. Not a soul stirred. In the brief moment of silence which ensued, one could have heard a pin drop.

Around ten o'clock, all the occupants of barrack number four were chased out and summoned one by one to the major's office. Each one individually was asked why he did not want to go to work. Some pleaded sickness. They were sent back to the barrack. Others replied that since they were not captured on the battlefront, they did not consider themselves prisoners of war, and no one had the right to force them to work.

Out of a 100 men, only the nine who pleaded illness were allowed to return to the barrack. The rest of them were punched and pushed and shoved forcibly out of the office by the soldiers. They were assembled in one spot where they were arranged in files of four. Soon, more soldiers arrived from the barracks and surrounded the captives on all sides. The major, the captain, and the lieutenant emerged from the office and ordered the men to proceed towards the barrack.

This unique parade moved slowly forward as some 300 of us watched on. As the procession approached us, a young voice suddenly called out from among the spectators, "Hey, fellows, these men are being marched to their torture. They are our brothers; let's protect them!"

In fact, that was exactly how every single one of us felt, but none had dared to make the first move. Now that call, like a marching order, prompted an immediate response from us. We all rushed to block the advance of the procession. It ground to a halt. One Polish fellow from our group strode up to within a step of the major. The major pulled out his revolver and fired a shot into the air. He then used it to hit the Pole on his bald head and knock him to the ground.

The men raised an uproar, yelling, shouting, and whistling. In the midst of the clamor, one could hear their calls of "Shame! Beat him up! Stone him!"

There was confusion among the troops. The major gave the signal to sound the trumpet, and the soldiers rushed at us with fixed bayonets. We scurried away and headed for the barracks.

The incident was not without its toll. Several of us were wounded, and before we managed to reach the barracks, the pursuing troops had left their mark upon each one of us. A bayonet grazed my right arm, and for several days, I felt the pain, though the wound was not serious. Those with minor wounds treated themselves in the barracks. Nine men were seriously wounded and had to be hospitalized.

This incident was a turning point for us. We all resolved to ignore every order to go to work. Needless to say, I never again showed up for my job of gathering litter. We were ready to suffer the same fate as our comrades from barrack number four. Our food rations were reduced by half, but we did not worry about that. Persuasion did not move us, and threats did not scare us.

A few days later, a special commission arrived to investigate the incident. At the inquest, we all stressed the point that we were not prisoners of war and therefore would not submit to forced labor. In defense of our stand, we were ready to shed our blood again.

News of the incident spread far and wide. News items and editorials appeared in Canadian and American newspapers, with reverberations in all parts of the world. Ukrainian readers can find the story in detail in the yellowing pages of *Svoboda* published during those memorable days of the years 1916 and 1917.[17]

Shortly after the investigation, we were all set free. This convinced us that freedom can be won if we are ready to shed blood for it. We should never take freedom for granted.

At first no one wanted to leave the camp. Some said they would not move from the place until they were paid for two years of their lost time. Others demanded assurance that they would be returned to the jobs from which they were torn away.

The administration of the camp was helpless; for a long time, the inmates refused to abandon the camp. Eventually, however, the camp began to break up, and the inmates left one by one, each going his own way. Memories of the camp gradually began to fade away. But one could never really forget it completely.

Notes

CHAPTER 1

How We Came to Canada

1. If the bridegroom did not have a home of his own, he customarily went to live with his wife's parents or in a home she received as a dowry from her parents.

2. The *starostvo* was the office of the head of a county.

3. Stryi and Peremyshl are major towns in Western Ukraine, then under Austria.

4. A *rynsky* was the Austrian gilder or florin. A gentleman in Fort Frances, Ontario recalls that when he left for Canada, before World War I, a *rynsky* was worth about forty cents.

5. Whenever Pylypiw uses the terms "our language" or "our people," he means the Ukrainian language and the Ukrainian people.

6. Free tickets were probably only available for trips made on the recommendation of a government agent. If you went on your own or on the advice of someone else, you apparently had to pay your own fare.

7. Pylypiw lists the names of Yusko Paish, Antin Paish, Mikhailo Romaniuk, Mykola Tychkowskyi, Stefan Chichak, Yurko Panischak, Ivan Panischak, Wasyl Fedyniak, Wasyl Pitsyk, Dmytro Wyzynowych, Wasyl Seniuk, and Mykhailo Eleniak.

8. What became of Mrs. Eleniak, whom Pylypiw had agreed to bring back with him, is not clear.

CHAPTER 2

"Canadian Ruthenia," a Traveler's Memoirs

1. Kyrylo Genyk was born at Bereziw, Galicia, in 1857. After graduating from the secondary school in Lviv, he taught public school at Bereziw, where a school had been established through his efforts in 1880. He passed the examinations necessary to qualify as a postal clerk but was refused appointment because of his socialist leanings. He gave up

teaching and established a general store in the neighboring town of Yabloniw.

His interest in emigration led him to collaborate with Dr. Oleskiw in promoting Ukrainian settlement in Canada. In 1896, Genyk himself emigrated with his wife and four children, as leader of the second party assembled by Dr. Oleskiw. The group arrived in Winnipeg on 25 July 1896 and settled on homesteads in the vicinity of Stuartburn in southern Manitoba.

Because of Genyk's good command of Ukrainian, Polish, and German, as well as his working knowledge of English, Dr. Oleskiw recommended him to the minister of the interior for employment as an immigration officer. Genyk received the appointment and moved to Winnipeg with his family. He was the first Ukrainian in the Canadian civil service.

From the time of his appointment until his resignation in 1911, Genyk was a friend to the thousands of Ukrainian immigrants whom he helped to settle on land. He was not only their official interpreter but also their adviser and guide. He died in Winnipeg on 12 February 1925.

2. The Liberals, under Wilfrid Laurier, were elected in 1896. The reorganization of the Department of the Interior by the new minister, Clifford Sifton, was one of a number of factors which stimulated massive immigration to Canada around the turn of the century.

3. In the early years of Ukrainian settlement in Canada, there were no Greek Catholic priests in the country. Roman Catholic priests from Poland tried to bring the Ukrainian Catholics into their fold, using the argument that both Greek and Roman Catholics share the same religious beliefs and follow the same Pope. Besides, the Ukrainians would have had no difficulty in understanding services in Polish because most of them had come from Galicia, where Polish was in common use. The trouble was that Ukrainians who joined the Polish (Roman Catholic) Church became alienated from their Ukrainian countrymen. They now fraternized with the Poles; in fact, many of them regarded themselves as Poles.

The Russian Orthodox Church sent missionaries to Canada specifically to work among the Ukrainians. As it turned out, the Russian missionaries were also performing "missionary work" for "Holy Mother Russia," trying to Russify the Ukrainians in Canada. For the Ukrainians, it was a question of retaining their national and religious identity in the face of pressure to assimilate with the Russians or with French or Polish Roman Catholics.

4. In the following paragraph, which has been omitted here, Dmytriw lists the principal Ukrainian colonies with which he is familiar: "in Manitoba, Winnipeg and district (for example, Gonor and Beau-

sejour), Lake Dauphin, Stuartburn; in Alberta, Edmonton, Edna; and in Assiniboia, Pheasant Forks." At that time, Assiniboia was the name given to a band of land spanning all of what is now southern Saskatchewan as well as the southeastern corner of present-day Alberta.

5. Missler was a steamship agent in Bremen, Germany.

6. *Muzhik* is Russian for "ordinary fellow." Ukrainians who lived under Russian rule or in close proximity to the Russians applied the term to their own, the peasants. Dmytriw is here describing a rite observed by adherants of the Eastern Church during Lent. Every time one makes the sign of the cross during prayer, one bows to the ground in adoration of God. Obviously, the author has used exaggeration for dramatic effect.

7. Vestments, cross, chalice, and so on used by the priest for celebrating the Mass.

8. In 1848, the Emperor of the Austro-Hungarian Empire promulgated a constitution which granted many new liberties to his subjects, including the Ukrainians. The most important reform was the abolition of serfdom.

9. See chapter two, note three.

10. See chapter two, note six.

CHAPTER 4

Beginnings in Canada

1. According to a Ukrainian idiom, anyone who behaves with reckless abandon acts "as if the sea were knee-deep."

2. This poem and the one later in the chapter were written by Maria Adamowska. The "myrtle" mentioned in line six is a low, trailing evergreen plant with a rich symbolic significance in Ukrainian culture. The "falcon" (line thirteen) is thought of as a bird that knows what goes on in the world since it travels far and wide and is able to see everything from "way up there." It also functions as a bearer of news in Ukrainian folklore. In addition, it suggests the idea of freedom — "free as a falcon high above the cares of the world."

3. See chapter two, note one.

4. This was not an oven in the kitchen stove like the ones we know today. It was an indoor oven built of clay, and it served more than one purpose. At night, when the fire was out and the bottom of the oven had cooled sufficiently, someone could sleep in it. There were spaces in and on the oven for pots, pans, and tools: the one in the story had a special cubbyhole for the ax.

There were outdoor ovens also, used only for baking bread.

5. An oven rake was a tool like a rake or hoe which was used to clean coals and ashes out of the oven.

6. It was a Ukrainian custom to address an elderly woman as "auntie" even if she was not a relative. Similarly, the expression "uncle" was used for an elderly man, and "girl" or "boy" for a young person.

7. This poem is by Maria Adamowska.

8. Cornmeal was cheaper and could be purchased in smaller bags.

9. The family had another source of cash in the senega roots which were dug by the mother and children. It was an eight- or ten-mile walk to where they grew and a twenty-eight-mile trek to Yorkton to sell them. One bag of roots bought half a bag of flour.

10. Ivan Franko was a Ukrainian writer regarded as second only to Shevchenko. "Abou Kazem's shoes" is a humorous poem based on an Arabian tale. It tells of a rich merchant in Baghdad who was so stingy that he kept mending his old shoes, adding pieces of leather and patch upon patch until they were so big and clumsy that everyone made fun of them.

    When his footwear lead him into a series of embarrassing incidents, the old miser tried various methods of getting rid of it, but the shoes always came back to him in some mysterious way. Trouble piled upon trouble, eventually culminating in an uprising against Abou and his imprisonment.

    In prison, Abou had time to reflect upon his miserly life, and he repented of his stinginess. Thereafter he lived the life of a respectable citizen, and when he died, he was proclaimed a saint.

11. After the grain was harvested, it was allowed to dry and then was spread out on a hard, level surface where it could be beaten with the flail until the grain was separated from the chaff. The straw was then removed, and the grain was winnowed from the chaff by means of a sieve.

12. A sickle is a curved blade attached to a handle which was used to cut grain at harvesttime. A scythe had a much longer blade and a much longer handle. It was used for mowing hay. While the sickle could be worked with one hand, the scythe took two.

13. John Danylchuk was born on a farm near Canora, Saskatchewan in 1901. He completed his education in Saskatoon and became a school teacher. He taught in country schools in Ukrainian districts and was active in cultural affairs.

    He began to write poems as a student and had them published in a student paper, *Kameniari,* and in the *Ukrainian Voice* and the *Canadian Farmer.* In 1929 he published a collection of his poems under the title *Svitaye Den' (The Day is Dawning).*

In 1923 Danylchuk and A. Novak were instrumental in forming the Association of Writers and Journalists of Canada. Eventually, Danylchuk left teaching to devote all his time to literary pursuits. He became editor-in chief of an English-language magazine, *Ukrainian Canadian Review,* in 1941. He died suddenly after editing only ten issues of the magazine.

14. The Doukhobors spoke Russian.

15. It was not common to grow hemp in Canada, but those pioneer settlers who knew how to extract the fibers and make ropes did produce it for their own use.

16. From the earliest days of Ukrainian settlement in Canada, Jewish merchants ran general stores in Ukrainian communities. As a rule, these storekeepers taught themselves to speak Ukrainian.

17. The *Serafymtsi* were named after the priest Serafym who, in 1903, established the Independent Greek Church for Ukrainians in Canada. This church was also known as the Ruthenian Independent Church, the Independent Orthodox Church, and, more simply, as Serafym's Church.

18. *Paska* is Ukrainian Easter bread.

19. *Pysanky* are Ukrainian Easter eggs.

20. Osyp Cherniawsky, a priest at Goodeve, Saskatchewan, was murdered as a result of religious differences.

21. A box twice the usual height was used for hauling grain.

CHAPTER 5

Encounters with the Indians

1. Pasichny was apparently an old-country friend of the Yureichuks.

2. A Ukrainian peasant from the Carpathian region was called a *hutsul.*

CHAPTER 6

Homestead Girlhood

1. See chapter four, note six.

2. People who had lived in the same areas of the Austro-Hungarian Empire probably had at least one language in common.

3. The gristmill, being the largest building in the hamlet, was probably the only place that could accommodate a meeting of Serafym's followers. It is not inconceivable that ordination of deacons could be held in such a place on a Sunday, when the mill was not in operation.

CHAPTER 7

The Dauphin District

1. *Landsdragoons* is a corrupt form of the German *landsdragoner*. They were mounted soldiers in the Austro-Hungarian imperial army.

   Throughout the eighteenth century, when Ukraine was under Polish rule, there were many insurrections against Polish nobles who attempted to impose serfdom. Much of the resistance came from bands of bandits who were seen by themselves and by the Ukrainian people as avengers and defenders of the common folk. Their attacks were directed against merchants and nobles who were identified as oppressors.

   The leader of one such robber band was Oleksa Dowbush, the son of a poor laborer from the village of Pechenizhyn. Oleksa was widely known around the Pruth and Cheremosh rivers for his raids on wealthy Poles in that area between 1738 and 1745. He was killed in an ambush near Kosmach in 1745. Many allude to him as a Ukrainian Robin Hood.

2. These words come from a poem by Shevchenko in which he calls upon Ukrainians to discover and retain their true national identity. Born a serf in 1814 and free for only nine years of his short life, Shevchenko is credited with initiating modern Ukrainian literature and with sparking the revival of Ukraine as a distinct national identity.

3. Dr. Osyp Oleskiw (1860-1903) was a Ukrainian intellectual whose organizational and promotional work were instrumental in encouraging the emigration of Ukrainians to Canada. He wrote two pamphlets, *About Free Lands* and *About Immigration,* which were widely read and very influential in Galicia. In 1895 he visited Canada to assess conditions for himself, and a few years later he became an official agent of the Canadian government in Galicia. Although he held this position for only two years, his efforts to facilitate emigration to Canada spanned a much longer period.

4. At this point, Romanchych deals at some length with his voyage to Canada.

5. Romanchych and Genyk were natives of the same Ukrainian village. See chapter two, note one.

6. Romanchych lists those who first selected homesteads near Ethelbert as follows: Danylo Syrotiuk with two sons and a son-in-law, W. Wetsal, Gapko, Hawrylo Symchych, Ivan Malkowych, Nykola Sula-tytsky, Semen Negrych, and Wasyl Milowsky. He identifies the last five as natives of Bereziw.

   He names Ivan Negrych and his brother Wasyl, Yakiw Genyk, Nykola Pidlasecky and a large family of Hryhorchuks as being among those to settle near the Drifting River, north of Ethelbert.

7. Romanchych goes on to list others who settled in the area: "Yakiw Herman, Kost' Boyko, Yurko Iwasiuk, the brothers Prokip and Panko Hrushowy, and Petro Iwanchyshyn. From Zalischyky came Fedir Merenchuk, Lev Shimansky, and Ivan Zajac. From the district of Peremyshyl came Pawlo Potocki..., Kachur, Ferentz, Koschak, Zarucky, Nakonechny, Garlinsky, Kowalyk, Dowhun, Braschak, Litowych, and a few others. All of them settled in the Sifton area."

8. The men from Bereziw who settled in townships twenty-three and twenty-four, range twenty and twenty-one, near the Riding Mountains, are listed by Romanchych as "Antin Genyk, Ivan Genyk, Nykola Genyk, Stefan Urbanowych, Wasyl Symchych, Theodore Sklepowich, Osyp Romanchych, Dmytro Romanchych, Antin Milowsky, Semen Ficych, Ivan Slyzuk, Mykhailo Ilnicki, Dmytro Malkowich, and Wasyl Shmilsky." In May 1898, a group arrived from Hleschova in the Terebowla district. It included "Petro Pidodworny, Wasyl Pidodworny, Mykhailo Leskiw, Mattey Kumka, Petro Matlashewsky, Mykhailo Koshowsky, Mykhailo Chorny, Semen Magelas, Tomko Tabaka, Ivan Bosiak, Fedko Shkwarok, Adam Urbansky, Pukhalsky, Trach, and a few others."

9. *Prosvita* is a Ukrainian word meaning "enlightenment."

10. A "People's Home" is a Ukrainian community hall.

11. A "Russian German" was a person of German extraction who lived in Russia.

12. See chapter two, note three.

13. The official name was the Independent Greek Church. See chapter four, note seventeen.

14. *Ranok* means "morning." It is still being published, now under the title *Evangelical Morning*.

15. The Presbyterians donated the proceeds of book sales to the priests.

16. They had to sell them to meet legal expenses or to pay fines.

17. The "Ukrainian Orthodox Church" is a shortened version of the "Ukrainian Greek Orthodox Autocephalous Church."

18. Teachers in the bilingual schools used the English and Ukrainian languages.

19. Mr. Bachynsky became Speaker of the Manitoba legislature in 1949 and served in that capacity until 1958.

CHAPTER 8

A Ukrainian-English Dictionary

1. In an area in which there is no organized municipality, a group of residents may apply to the government to have a "statutory-labor

district" created. Under such an arrangement, residents are required by law to perform such tasks as road building and maintenance, ditch digging, and so on. Statutory-labor districts were common in pioneer days before municipalities were organized.

2. J. N. Krett's dictionary, *The Ruthenian-English and English-Ruthenian Dictionary,* was published by the Ruthenian Book Store, Winnipeg, in 1912.

3. *Novyi Krai* (The New Country) was the official organ of the Association of Canadian Ruthenian Farmers, which was founded at Rosthern, Saskatchewan in March 1910. Ukrainians from every part of Saskatchewan sent delegates to the meeting, which was called by members of Ukrainian cultural organizations.

    The assembly dealt with a number of issues, such as how to prevent the exploitation of Ukrainian farmers by farm-implement companies, what position Ukrainian farmers should take during provincial and federal elections, how to get better railroad and postal service in Ukrainian communities, and how to arrange for better insurance coverage. They also discussed their need to have provincial government documents translated into Ukrainian and the importance of establishing and maintaining Ukrainian cultural organizations and a Ukrainian press.

    The basic appeal was for unity: the Ukrainian farm population, which numbered about 40,000 and wielded considerable economic clout, could exert a greater influence if people acted together. The organization's political ambition was to run several Ukrainian candidates in provincial and federal elections. Their overall objective was the improvement of living conditions among Ukrainian farmers and the elevation of educational and political standards. The association helped to consolidate Ukrainian-Canadians in Saskatchewan and led to the formation of national organizations.

CHAPTER 9

Organizing for Education

1. A number of ethnic groups lived within the Austro-Hungarian Empire. In order to prevent any effective opposition to the empire from developing, the government adopted the stratagem of "divide and rule." The nationalist feelings or each group were encouraged, and the administrative units were so arranged that the Poles, Ukrainians, Slovaks, and other minorities were arrayed against one another. To make matters worse, the Ukrainian peasants were still being oppressed by Polish landlords. The electoral system favored the land owners, with the result that the Ukrainians did not hold a majority in any self-governing body. The heads of the county councils were usually Polish landlords, and the Galician diet, which was

controlled by the land-owning classes, passed laws that favored the Poles.

2. The company was formed in Vegreville in 1910, with $20,000 in capital raised by selling 1,000 shares at $20 each. The vast majority of shareholders were Ukrainians. Within ten years the company had branch stores in Edmonton, Radway, Chipman, Innisfree, Lamont, Andrew, and Smoky Lake in the Ukrainian districts in Alberta, and its own wholesale in Edmonton, "Independent Wholesales Limited." As more and more general stores were established by individual Ukrainians, the branch stores were sold one by one to private businessmen.

3. The idea of establishing a *bursa,* or educational hostel, originated with a small group of Ukrainian teachers and university students. They called a convention in August 1916 which was attended by nearly 500 Ukrainians, mostly from Saskatchewan. The convention resolved to establish a *bursa* and to name it after Petro Mohyla, a Metropolitan of the Ukrainian Orthodox Church who, in the seventeenth century, had organized an academy in Kiev and brought many prominent scholars to teach in it. In 1917, the *bursa* was incorporated as the Petro Mohyla Ukrainian Institute. At various times since then, temporary branches have been established in Winnipeg and Canora.

The institute in Saskatoon is today and always has been more than a boarding home for university students. It offers classes in Ukrainian language, history, literature, crafts, and folk dance.

CHAPTER 11

Section Hand

1. It is not clear how this stint as a section hand fits into Svarich's other activities in 1901, as he describes them in chapters nine and ten.

2. Judging from Svarich's earlier remark that section hands made seventy-five cents a day, it is probable that the deductions totalled fifty cents.

3. "Dago" is Svarich's term.

4. Since he came from Austria and spoke German, he was able to increase his chances of getting work by posing as a German. There was considerable prejudice against the Ukrainians, who were known interchangeably as "Galicians," "Bukovinians," and "bohunks."

CHAPTER 12

On the CPR

1. A lining bar was used when laying track to make sure that the rails were always the same distance apart.

2. "Paraska" is a Ukrainian women's Christian name. It is also applied to any talkative, easy-going, happy-go-lucky woman.

3. A "Basilian church" is one served by the Basilian Order of Greek Catholic priests.

4. *Acathistus* is a prayer of praise to Christ, the Virgin Mary, and the saints.

5. "Old fogeys" may have been the name which the newcomers applied to those who had been working in Canada for some time.

6. Romaniuk calls it "Frank" Mountain. The slide occurred on 29 April 1903. The red flag mentioned in the next sentence may have been intended as a warning of the continuing danger of landslides.

7. Romaniuk does not explain what the women were doing there. They might have been accompanying their husbands or going to jobs of their own.

8. Romaniuk does not explain these terms.

9. This feast is celebrated by churches of the Eastern rite on 14 September according to the Julian calendar.

CHAPTER 13

Endurance

1. The spelling is uncertain; it could be Macarthur or McArthur.

2. Coalspur is on a branch off the main railway line running west from Edmonton to the foothills. It is located almost directly west of Edmonton, near the McLeod River.

CHAPTER 14

In the Snows of a Foreign Land

1. Andrushko may have been masquerading as a Russian. Or perhaps he was a "Russophile," as the Russophile movement was quite strong among Ukrainians in Canada at that time.

2. This description is difficult to credit.

CHAPTER 15

Out of Work

1. He probably was a cattle buyer.

2. Kobzey is mistaken about the history of the Trades and Labor Council. It was the Canadian Labor Union which appeared in 1873; Trades and Labor Councils were not organized in Canada until the 1880s.

3. In succeeding paragraphs, which are omitted here, Kobzey lists the organizations to which he belonged and summarizes their activities.

4. He is referring to a Ukrainian proverb.

5. In another passage, Kobzey also mentions a pastoral letter from Bishop Budka, the head of the Greek Catholic Church in Canada, urging Ukrainians to "rally to the defense of the threatened Motherland. ... Later Bishop Budka issued another pastoral letter explaining what he actually meant in his first letter when he spoke of going 'to the defense of the threatened Motherland.' " Bishop Budka's letters also disturbed the Canadian government.

6. In the initial stages of the battle, the Russians lost heavily, but when they brought in reinforcements and surrounded Peremyshl, the Austrians blew up the fortress and retreated. The Russians then occupied Peremyshl, but a few weeks later they were forced back.

7. Missionaries of the Russian Orthodox Church encouraged the Russification of Ukrainian adherants. During World War I, many Ukrainians preferred to call themselves Russians rather than face the prospect of concentration camps. By posing as citizens of one of Britain's allies, they escaped harassment and repressive measures.

8. A *kolomyika* is a Ukrainian folk dance.

9. See chapter four, note six.

10. Apparently the next freight train was due in half a day's time.

CHAPTER 16

Internment

1. *Khakol* was a term of contempt used by the Russians in addressing Ukrainians; it is equivalent to "low-down cur."

2. Peremyshl: see chapter fifteen, note six.
   The battle at Makiwka was another of the numerous battles fought between the Russians and the Austrian and German armies on Ukrainian territory.

3. Yasnowskyj confuses the terms "England" and "English" with the terms "Britain" and "British."

4. As the Russian army occupied the area, they required the populace to exchange their Austrian crowns for Russian kopecks.

5. The Russians did away with the turnpike as an "evil" of the Austrian regime.

6. These were open markets on Krakiwska and Striletska Streets in Lviv.

7. Yasnowskyj was actually born on 29 October 1881 in the village of Dublane, north of Lviv, Galicia, then under Austrian domination.

8. "Yuzunia" is a diminutive of Yosefa (Jessie).

9. Both are Ukrainian folk dances.

10. Freely translated, the title means *The Wooing at Honcharivtsi.*

11. "Hey, pass me that ax." The Croatians have a folk dance in which they wield an ax.

12. Bohdan Khmelnytsky was Hetman, or leader, of Ukraine from 1648 to 1657. He led a successful uprising against Polish rule which resulted a great national movement and the establishment of the Ukrainian Hetman state. The statue in Kiev was carved by Mikhailo Mykeshyn.

13. *The People's Daily.*

14. "Christ is Risen," a stirring, traditional Ukrainian Easter hymn.

15. Ukrainians of the Greek Catholic and Greek Orthodox faith observe Easter Monday and Easter Tuesday as holy days.

16. The feast is celebrated on the fortieth day after Easter.

17. *Svoboda,* the oldest Ukrainian daily in North America, was founded in Jersey City, New Jersey in 1893.

Bibliography

BOOKS IN UKRAINIAN

Biletsky, L. *Ukrayinski pionery w Kanadi, 1891-1951* (Ukrainian Pioneers in Canada, 1891-1951). Winnipeg: Canadian Ukrainian Committee, 1951. An outline of the early Ukrainian settlements in Canada with emphasis on the development of Ukrainian cultural life.

Bozyk, P. *Tserkow ukrayintsiw w Kanadi* (Church of the Ukrainians in Canada). Winnipeg: The Canadian Ukrainian, 1927. Materials relating to the history of churches among the Ukrainians in Canada from 1890 to 1927.

Chorneyko, Michael. *Shchob ne zabuty* (Not to Forget). Saskatoon, 1964. Reminiscences of a Ukrainian teacher in the districts of Dauphin-Ethelbert, Manitoba and Arran, Saskatchewan. Includes episodes from the life of Ukrainians in these areas and a collection of ninety-eight poems dealing with the realities of life of the early Ukrainian settlers in Canada.

Chumer, W. A. *Spomyny* (Recollections). Edmonton, 1942. A collection of episodes from the life of Ukrainian pioneer settlers and workers (for example Nikola Wirsta's story, *"Moyi perezhyvanya w Kanadi,"* "My Experiences in Canada"), as well as glimpses into the beginnings of their religious and secular organizations.

Demkovich-Dobriansky, Mykhailo. *Ukrayinsko-polski stosunky u XIX storichi* (Ukrainian-Polish Relations in the XIXth Century). Munich: Ukrainian Free University, 1969. The work traces the conflicts between the Poles and Ukrainians in Western Ukraine in the political, social, and economic areas, conflicts which prompted many Ukrainians to emigrate.

Doroshenko, D., ed. *Propamyatna knyha Ukrayinskoho Narodnoho Domu u Wynnypegu* (The Memorial Book of the Ukrainian National Home in Winnipeg.). Winnipeg: Ukrainian National Home Association, 1949. The richly illustrated chapters of this volume contain "... collections of authentic documents, records and interviews gathered during a period of years, all aiming to portray as fully as possible ... the life of Ukrainian

Canadians, their development, their work and success in social, educational and cultural activities for the past half century." Among these is the story of Dmytro Romanchych, "Ukrayinski koloniyi w okruzi Dawfyn" (Ukrainian Colonies in the Dauphin District).

Ewanchuk, Michael. *Do istoriyi ukrayinskykh poselentsiw w okolytsi Gimli* (On the History of Ukrainian Settlers in the District of Gimli). Winnipeg, 1975. A scholarly, well documented history of the Ukrainian settlers, their schools and organizations in the Gimli district in Manitoba by a former school superintendent, a native of the district.

Hawrysh, Wasyl. *Moya Kanada i ya* (My Canada and I). Edmonton, 1974. Memoirs and stories of Ukrainian pioneers including the author himself.

Humeniuk, Ivan. *Moyi spomyny* (My Recollections). Toronto, 1957. The author deals with the cultural and social development of Ukrainians in Eastern Canada. A few pages are devoted to the period before the First World War.

Humenna, Dokia. *Vichni vohni Alberty* (Eternal Flames of Alberta). Edmonton, 1959. Stories of pioneering experiences of Ukrainian women in Alberta, among them Mrs. M. Kotyk's "My First Encounter with the Indians" and Maria Yureichuk's "How We Traveled on a Raft from Edmonton to Our Homestead."

Kobzey, Thomas. *Na ternystykh ta khreshchatykh dorohakh: spomyny z piwstoricha w Kanadi* (On the Thorny Way and Crossroads: Memoirs of Fifty Years in Canada). Scranton, Pennsylvania: *Narodna Volya,* 1972. Kobzey's memoirs of fifty years in Canada.

Kohuska N., *Novymy dorohamy* (New Roadways of Life). Winnipeg, 1972. A biographical sketch of William J. Perepeluk. The volume is a record of his pathway during the seventy years of his life, from extreme pioneering hardships to incredible success as a businessman, attained by his own efforts and initiative though he lacked formal education.

Marunchak, M. H. *W zustrich ukrayinskym pioneram Alberty* (Among Ukrainian Pioneers of Alberta). Winnipeg: General Library "UKT", 1964. A richly illustrated volume of stories and facts on the Ukrainian group settlements in Alberta.

Piniuta, Harry. *Sotsiyalno-ekonomichnyi rozvytok ukrayintsiw Kanady* (The Socio-economic Development of Ukrainian Canadians). Ph.D. dissertation, Ukrainian Free University, 1971. A comprehensive historical survey, replete with statistical data and case studies, of the beginnings and development by Ukrainian-Canadians of trade, commerce, industry, fraternal societies, and various types of co-operative enterprises, from the first individual enterprises to multi-million-dollar businesses.

Propamyatna knyha z nahody yuvileyu poselenya ukrayinskoho narodu w Kanadi (Memorial Book on the Occasion of the Golden Jubilee of the Settlement of Ukrainian People in Canada). Yorkton: The Redeemer's Voice, 1941. This profusely illustrated volume, compiled by the Ukrainian Catholic clergy across Canada, contains the history of every Ukrainian Catholic parish, separate school, newspaper, and organization in Canada over a period of fifty years, 1891 to 1941.

Rudnyc'kyj, J. B. *Kanadiyski mistsevi nazvy ukrayinskoho pokhodzhenya* (Canadian Place Names of Ukrainian Origin). Winnipeg: Ukrainian Free Academy of Sciences, 1951. A collection of 180 such names, with a note for each on its origin.

_____. *Materiyaly do ukrayinsko-kanadiyskoyi folklorystyky i diyalektologiyi* (Ukrainian-Canadian Folklore and Dialectological Texts). Winnipeg: Ukrainian Free Academy of Sciences, vol. 1, 1956; vol. 2, 1958. A collection of folklore materials (stories, songs, legends, proverbs) from Ukrainian settlers in western Canada, many of which reflect the harsh realities of their pioneer life.

Tesla, I. and Yusyk, P. *Ukrayintsi w Kanadi—yich rozwytok i dosyahnenya (Ukrainians in Canada — Their Development and Achievements)*. Munich: Ukrainian Technical-Economic Institute, 1968. Important authoritative information in concise form about Ukrainian-Canadians. Contains illustrations and statistical tables.

Yasnowskyj, Philip. *Pid ridnym i chuzhym nebom* (Under Native and Alien Skies). Buenos Aires: Julian Serediak, 1961. The author tells of his harrowing experiences as an immigrant worker before the First World War. He was fired several times during the war years as each new employer discovered his "alien" national origin. Because of bureaucratic bungling and anti-alien wartime hysteria he landed in a forced labor camp for enemy aliens. He relates his experiences in the camp until the time of his release.

BOOKS IN ENGLISH

Anderson, J. T. M. *The Education of the New-Canadian*. London and Toronto: J. M. Dent and Sons, 1918. A treatise, by an inspector of schools in Saskatchewan, on the problem of providing proper training in intelligent citizenship for children of Ukrainians and other "New Canadians."

Baran, A., Gerus, O. W., Rozumnyj, J. *The Jubilee Collection of the Ukrainian Free Academy of Sciences. Winnipeg:* Ukrainian

Free Academy of Sciences (UVAN), 1976. Among the articles contributed by scholars and researchers to this volume, we find one by an ex-superintendent of schools in Manitoba, Michael Ewanchuk, entitled "Development of Education Among the Early Ukrainian Settlers in Manitoba: 1896-1924," a valuable source of information which was used in preparing the introduction for this book.

Chamberlin, William Henry. *The Ukraine: A Submerged Nation.* New York: Macmillan, 1944. The book contains information on the history, culture, and political prospects of Ukraine.

Darcovich, William. *Ukrainians in Canada: The Struggle to Retain Their Identity.* Ottawa: Ukrainian Self-Reliance Association, 1967. The title correctly identifies the contents of the book. It includes numerous statistical tables.

England, Robert. *The Central European Immigrant in Canada.* Toronto: Macmillan, 1929. An outline of the history of immigration into Canada of the peoples from central Europe (Ukrainians included), the problems associated with immigration and settlement, as well as an expression of concern about their status as future citizens.

Gray, James H. *The Winter Years.* Toronto: Macmillan, 1966. Contains a section dealing with the problems faced by those with Polish and Ukrainian names in finding jobs, even as late as the Great Depression.

Hardy, W. G. *From Sea unto Sea.* Garden City, New York: Doubleday, 1961. In one of the chapters the author gives credit to Ukrainians who were once sneered at for their illiteracy, strange customs, but who by hard work became first-rate citizens, active in politics, professions, industry, etc.

Hrushevsky, Michael. *A History of Ukraine.* New Haven: Yale University Press, 1941. A survey of the history of the Ukrainian people and their lands from the dawn of civilization to the reunion of their lands under the Soviets during World War II.

Humeniuk, Peter. *Hardships and Progress of Ukrainian Pioneers.* Steinbach, Manitoba, 1975. Memoirs of a pioneer Ukrainian teacher. Deals with Stuartburn and the other Ukrainian districts where he taught school and includes a history of the Stuartburn district and of his student days.

Hunter, A. J. *A Friendly Adventure.* Toronto: The Committee on Literature, General Publicity and Missionary Education of the United Church of Canada, 1929. A story of the United Church mission among the New Canadians at Teulon, Manitoba with special reference to the Ukrainians. Contains an informative section on education.

Kaye, V. J. *Early Ukrainian Settlements in Canada, 1895-1900.* Toronto: University of Toronto Press, 1964. A documentary history of the beginnings of Ukrainian settlement in Canada.

Lazarenko, Joseph M., ed. *Ukrainian Pioneers in Alberta.* Edmonton: Ukrainian Pioneers Association in Edmonton, 1970. A systematic collection of the biographies of Ukrainian pioneer families in Alberta.

Lysenko, Vera. *Men in Sheepskin Coats.* Toronto: Ryerson, 1974. Subtitled "A Study in Assimilation," this is a social history of Ukrainians in Canada, dealing with the beginnings of their settlement and their social adjustment in the process of Canadianization.

MacGregor, J. G. *Vilni Zemli — Free Lands.* Toronto: McClelland and Stewart, 1969. A chronicle of Ukrainian immigration to Canada from 1891 to the 1920s with special reference to the impact of their settlements on western Canada.

Mackintosh, W. A. *Prairie Settlement: The Geographical Setting.* vol. 1. Toronto: Macmillan, 1934. Contains information about the political and economic conditions of the Canadian West that made it ready for settlers from continental Europe.

Mandryka, M. I. *History of Ukrainian Literature in Canada.* Winnipeg: Ukrainian Free Academy of Sciences (UVAN), 1968. The author shows how the highest human ideals brought to Canada by Ukrainian pioneers corresponded with the ideals of Canadian democracy. The work includes biographical sketches of Ukrainian-Canadian authors, among them Maria Adamowska whose reminiscences are included in this volume.

Manning, C. A. *The Story of Ukraine.* New York: Philosophical Library, 1947. A history by a noted scholar of the centuries-long struggle of Ukrainian people to maintain their national independence and freedom.

Marunchak, M. H. *The Ukrainian Canadians, A History.* Winnipeg and Ottawa: Ukrainian Free Academy of Sciences (UVAN), 1970. This work has an encyclopedic character. It has been described as the fullest and most complete source of information about the Ukrainians in Canada.

Mirchuk, Ivan, ed. *Ukraine and Its People.* Munich: Ukrainian Free University, 1949. A handbook of Ukrainian history with maps, statistical tables, and diagrams by Ukrainian scholars.

Paximadis, Mary. *Look Who's Coming: The Wachna Story.* Oshawa, Ontario, 1976. The fascinating story of a pioneer homesteader, Theodosy Wachna, and his family. Because of his higher education and knowledge of the English language, the "patriarch" of the Ukrainian pioneer settlement at Stuartburn, Manitoba, helped over 1,000 Ukrainian immi-

grants to settle and to solve their pioneering problems —
building of roads, bridges, schools, a church. In the process he
became the secretary-treasurer of the municipality, notary
public, storekeeper and secretary-treasurer of twelve newly
organized schools. All of his fifteen children, most of them
university graduates, are in business or the professions. The
book is illustrated by William Kurelek.

Piniuta, Harry. *The Organizational Life of Ukrainian Canadians.*
M.A. thesis, University of Ottawa, 1952. The introduction
includes an outline of the history of the Ukrainians in Canada
from 1891 to 1951, with a review of their progress in the
cultural, social, economic, and political life of Canada. The
body of the thesis gives an account of the beginnings and
development of their religious and secular organizations, their
aims and objectives.

Romaniuk, Gus. *Taking Root in Canada.* Winnipeg: Columbia
Press, 1954. An autobiography which tells of a variety of
interesting pioneering experiences in northern Manitoba. The
author worked as logger, harvest hand, driller, fireman,
fisherman, barber, merchant, cattleman, fur trader, innkeeper,
and councilor.

Rudnyc'kyj, J. B. *Ukrainian Canadian Folklore.* vol. 3. Winnipeg:
Ukrainian Free Academy of Sciences (UVAN), 1960. Contains
texts in English translation of volumes one and two, which are
in Ukrainian.

Simpson, G. W. *The Names "Rus", "Russia" and "Ukraine" and
Their Historical Background.* Slavistica no. 10. Winnipeg:
Ukrainian Free Academy of Sciences (UVAN), 1951.

_____. *Ukraine: An Atlas of Its History and Geography.* Toronto:
Oxford University Press, 1941. Both of these books by
Professor Simpson contain information on the European
background of the Ukrainians.

Skwarok, J. *The Ukrainian Settlers in Canada and Their Schools,
1891-1921.* Edmonton: Basilian Press, 1958. The author deals
"with that difficult period between 1891 and the end of the
First World War when the Ukrainians were confronted with
the problem of settling down, opening new lands, and
educating their children."

Ukrainians in Alberta. Edmonton: Ukrainian Pioneers' Association
of Alberta, 1975. A wide range of historical and current
information about Ukrainians in Alberta, together with
biographies of Ukrainian pioneer families.

Woycenko, Ol'ha. *The Ukrainians in Canada.* Ottawa and Winnipeg, 1967. A portrayal and a critical analysis of the process of
integration of Ukrainians into the mainstream of Canadian life
and their endeavors to preserve their ethnic identity.

Young, Charles H. *The Ukrainian Canadians.* Toronto: Thomas Nelson and Sons, 1931. The first historical synthesis by a researcher of Anglo-Saxon extraction of the life of Ukrainians in Canada.

Yuzyk, Paul. *The Ukrainians in Manitoba, A Social History.* Toronto: University of Toronto Press, 1953. An authoritative, informative history of the Ukrainians in Manitoba dealing with the beginnings of their settlements, the development of their social and cultural institutions, and their integration into the social and political life of the province.

————. *Ukrainian Canadians.* Toronto: Ukrainian Canadian Business and Professional Federation, 1967. Written on the occasion of Canada's Centennial Year, to provide all the important, authoritative information in concise treatise form about Ukrainian-Canadians.

ARTICLES IN ALMANACS

Adamowska, Maria. *"Pochatky w Kanadi"* (Beginnings in Canada). *Almanac of the Ukrainian Voice,* 1937, pp. 93-102.

————. *"Pionirski harazdy w Kanadi"* (The Lot of Pioneers in Canada). *Almanac of the Ukrainian Voice,* 1939, pp. 95-105.

Bobersky, I. *"Yak pershykh dwokh ukrayintsiw zayikhalo do Kanady"* (How the First Two Ukrainians Came to Canada). *Almanac of the Canadian Farmer,* 1937.

Farion, Anna. *"Moyi spomyny"* (My Recollections). *Almanac of the Ukrainian Voice,* 1942, pp. 87-97.

Kazymyra, Bohdan. *"Osyp Oleskiw i poselenya ukrayintsiw u Kanadi"* (Osyp Oleskiw and the Settlement of Ukrainians in Canada). *Almanac of the Ukrainian News,* 1964, pp. 76-80.

Kossar, W. *"Shistdesyat rokiw u Kanadi"* (Sixty Years in Canada). *Almanac of the New Pathway,* 1951, pp. 127-153.

Romaniuk, John M. *"Z Boha ne kepkui"* (Scoff Not at God). *Almanac of the Ukrainian Voice,* 1942, pp. 114-119.

Rudnyc'kyj, J. B. *"Do pochatkiw ukrayinskoho poselenya w Kanadi"* (On the Beginnings of Ukrainian Settlement in Canada). *Jubilee Calendar-Almanac of Canadian Farmer,* 1963, pp. 137-138.

Svarich, Peter. *"Urywok z spomyniw Petra Zwarycha"* (An Excerpt from the Memoirs of Peter Svarich). *Almanac of the Ukrainian Voice,* 1953, pp. 82-86.

ARTICLES IN NEWSPAPERS AND PERIODICALS

Dmytriw, Nestor. *"Kanadiyska Rus'"* (Canadian Ruthenia). *Svoboda,* 1897. (His series of articles ran in different issues during the course of the year.)

Harasymchuk, M. *"U snihu na chuzhyni"* (In the Snows of a Foreign Land). *Ukrainian Pioneer,* January 1955, pp. 7-10.

Hobart, Charles W. "Adjustment of Ukrainians in Alberta: Alienation and Integration." *Slavs in Canada* 1 (1966): 69-85.

Kalbach, Warren E. "Some Demographic Aspects of Ukrainian Population in Canada." *Slavs in Canada* 1 (1966): 54-68.

Romaniuk, John M. *"Ukrayinsko-angliyskyi slownyk"* (Ukrainian-English Dictionary.) *Ukrainian Voice,* 17 June 1942, p. 3.

Royick, Alexander. "Ukrainians in Canada in the War of 1812." *Forum Ukrainian Review* 1 (1967): 29.

Stechishin, Julian. *Ukrayintsi w Kanadi pered 1891-ym rokom?* (Ukrainians in Canada before the Year 1891?), *Ukrainian Voice,* 26 August 1970, p. 4.

Svarich, Peter. *Spomyny* (Memoirs), *Ukrainian Voice,* 11 December 1974, p. 7.

Wagenheim, E. D. "Problems of Research on Ukrainians in Eastern Canada," *Slavs in Canada* 1 (1966): 44-53.

Photographic credits

Mrs. Mary Drabiniasty, Winnipeg; p. 56

Glenbow-Alberta Institute, Calgary: pp. 38 bottom, 46, 50 top, 90, 125 top, 142

Manitoba Archives, Winnipeg: pp. 60, 63, 80, 87, 94 top, 107, 110, 119, 151, 158

Provincial Archives of Alberta, Edmonton: pp. 83 bottom *E. Brown Collection B. 5584,* 98 *E. Brown Collection* B. 705, 123 *E. Brown Collection B. 2640*

Public Archives of Canada, Ottawa: pp. 29 bottom *PA 10401,* 50 bottom *PA 88459,* 74 *PA 88504,* 77 *C 6607,* 103 *PA 88497,* 104 *PA 88422,* 184 *C 17583,* 186 *C 21066,* 190 *C 14105*

RCMP Museum, Regina: p. 43

Saskatchewan Archives, Regina: pp. 29 top, 44, 66, 125 bottom

Ukrainian Museum of Canada, Saskatoon: p. 149 *Turetski Collection*

United Church Archives, Victoria University, Toronto: cover, pp. 34, 38 top, 94 bottom, 131, 134, 138, 143, 152, 160, 166, 169, 177

Western Development Museum, Saskatoon: p. 83 top

Index

Index

Index

Index

Gray — Grandmother from Guelph
mc Farlane street &
C. P. R —
1,000.000 people from U. S. a —